SCHOOLING FOR WOMEN'S WORK

£ 3

gc

18/49

By the same author

Women and Schooling

Schooling for women's work

Edited by Rosemary Deem

Routledge & Kegan Paul
London, Boston and Henley

First Published in 1980
by Routledge & Kegan Paul Ltd
39 Store Street,
London WC1E 7DD,
9 Park Street,
Boston, Mass. 02108, USA and
Broadway House,
Newton Road,
Henley-on-Thames,
Oxon RG9 1EN
Printed in Great Britain by
M & A Thomson Litho Ltd
East Kilbride,
Scotland.

British Library Cataloguing in Publication Data

Schooling for women's work.
1. Education of women - Great Britain -
History - 20th century
2. Women - Employment - Great Britain -
History - 20th century
I. Deem, Rosemary
376'.941   LC2042   80-40407

ISBN 0 7100 0576 8

Contents

Figures and tables

Notes on contributors

ROSEMARY DEEM is a Lecturer in Sociology in the Faculty of Educational Studies, the Open University.

MADELEINE MACDONALD is a Lecturer in Sociology in the Faculty of Educational Studies, the Open University.

KATHERINE CLARRICOATES is a research student in the Department of Sociology and Social Anthropology, University of Hull.

MANDY LLEWELLYN is a research student at Leicester University School of Education.

MARY FULLER is a Lecturer in Sociology at Bulmershe College of Higher Education, and was formerly with the SSRC Ethnic Relations Research Unit, Bristol.

JENNIFER SHAW is a Lecturer in Sociology at the University of Sussex.

GABY WEINER is a former researcher with the National Foundation for Educational Research, and now works for Project Full Employ in Lambeth.

JAN HARDING researches in the Centre for Science Education at Chelsea College.

TERESA KEIL is a Senior Lecturer in Sociology at Loughborough University.

PEGGY NEWTON works in the Department of Behavioural Sciences, Huddersfield Polytechnic.

DAVID ASHTON is a Lecturer in Sociology, University of Leicester, and director of the 'Youth in the Labour Market' project there.

M. MAGUIRE is a researcher on the 'Youth in the Labour Market' project at the University of Leicester.

MOIRA GRIFFITHS is a Research Assistant in the Survey Research Department of the Open University.

MARGHERITA RENDEL is a Lecturer in Human Rights and Education at the London University Institute of Education.

LYNNE CHISHOLM is a PhD student of Tübingen University, West Germany, and was formerly a Lecturer at the New University of Ulster.

DIANA WOODWARD is a Senior Lecturer in the Department of Applied Social Studies, Sheffield City Polytechnic.

Acknowledgments

I should like to thank John Eggleston and David Godwin for suggesting the possibility of a reader on women's education and for their help and encouragement whilst it was being put together. Without the assistance and contacts provided by the Sexual Divisions Study Group and the Education Study Group of the British Sociological Association, many of the contributions to this volume would not have existed. In addition, four of the chapters in the collection (Llewellyn, Harding, Griffiths and Chisholm/Woodward) were originally given as papers at a weekend Seminar on 'Women, Education and Research', organized by the British Educational Research Association at the University of Loughborough in April 1978, although they have subsequently been revised for publication. Two of the organizers of that seminar, Gaby Weiner and Gill Kirkup, have given a great deal of helpful advice towards the production of this book.

Women, work and schooling
The relevance of gender

Rosemary Deem

It seems not unfair to say of the British system of schooling that differences between the education of females and the education of males have long been recognized as existing, but that it has not been realized until comparatively recently that such differences in the educational experiences of women and men may be seen as problematic because they may give rise to contrasting educational achievements between the sexes and prepare each sex for a quite different style of life. The relationship between gender, education and work in capitalist societies is, of course, as Wolpe has pointed out, much more complex than this, involving many factors whose analysis lies outside the scope of this volume. But what the collection of views presented here attempts to do is to show how, in a variety of educational settings and establishments but also in the context of entry to the labour market, the category of gender, which may be defined as, 'the psychological and cultural definitions of the dimensions "masculine" and "feminine"',(1) is made relevant in the education of women, is influential in structuring their actions, beliefs, values and life-chances and provides them with a set of contradictions about their role in society.

What the research evidence documented here demonstrates only too clearly is that despite the passage in 1975 of a Sex Discrimination Act prohibiting discrimination on grounds of sex in many areas of education and public life, and not withstanding the many changes which have occurred in the openness of access to education, and in the position and status of women, girls and women in education are still seriously disadvantaged and discriminated against in relation to boys and men.(2) This is not to say that men may not also be disadvantaged in schooling, particularly if they are of working-class origin: however, the educational experiences of the majority of men are likely to be superior, both while at school and in terms of the consequences of those experiences, to those of most women.

Because most of the accounts presented in this collection are based on research about women in education, it seems worth while at this juncture to raise what is one of the most hotly debated issues in contemporary feminist circles: the nature of the relationship between research, theorizing, and feminist practice intended to bring about changes in the position of women. There are a number

1

of different perspectives which may be brought to bear on this issue,
but there are three in particular which merit further attention.
The first is the argument that although research and theorizing may
have a part to play, what really counts is the development of policy
statements and strategies for change, and that unless the latter
stage is accomplished by the same individuals who undertake the
research and theorizing, then the exercise of finding out and developing theories about the situation of women is a waste of time.
Such a view is clearly held by Byrne, who argues in a review of
'Women and Schooling' that:(3)

> The book is strongest in its analysis of sociological interpreta-
> tions of the implications of different socialisation processes
> of boys and girls .... Factually sound, a good introductory out-
> line to those new to the field ... does not, however, appear to
> lead to new ideas for replacement or counter-strategies.... The
> book seems in fact aimed predominantly at the student.

But the claim that knowledge and explanation of an existing situation is of no importance unless accompanied by policy suggestions
is equivalent to arguing that only a limited number of people are
capable of deriving ideas from information about a particular state
of affairs, whereas it is actually much more likely that the reverse
of this is true. That is, if the dissemination of research findings
is as wide as possible, the likelihood of the emergence of a large
number of ideas and strategies is greatly enhanced.

A second view on the relationship between research, theory and
feminist practice is the postulation that it is essential for all
research to be theoretically informed. A strong case for this
position is constructed by Kuhn and Wolpe.(4) And certainly it
cannot be denied that presentation of research findings in an un-
structured manner, without reference to theories and explanations
which transcend the limitations of a small-scale project or analysis, is tantamount to providing a set of tools without specifying
the task for which they are to be utilized. However, the question
of theoretical coherence in feminist work also raises problems
about the extent to which highly theoretical analysis is accessible
to a wide audience, or whether it is only intended for a small
number of individuals who already possess the expertise and conceptual apparatus required to untangle complex threads of arguments.
Theoretical sophistication may be desirable either politically, in
terms of developing a 'party line', or from the standpoint of an
academic discipline concerned with maintaining its cognitive boundaries. But equally it may be perceived as undesirable because it
can serve to mystify and obscure issues rather than clarify them,
and hence limit severely the degree of accessibility which a piece
of work possesses.

What this volume tries to achieve is some kind of middle way
between these two extremes; that is, to present research findings
in a way which does not deny access to those who are not trained in
a particular academic discipline nor versed in certain politically
theoretical doctrines, but to do so in such a way that there is an
attempt to achieve some kind of theoretical coherence and linkage
between the different chapters.(5) There is also an endeavour in
a number of the chapters to suggest strategies for change, although
the nature of some of the analysis, especially the ethnographic

ones, does not allow this to be present uniformly throughout the
volume.

In addition, the separate accounts themselves need to be judged
in terms of whether they represent feminist research. It is important to recognize that research is not automatically feminist
because it is about women. Indeed, the use of certain kinds of
research techniques and methodologies may actually conceal or
prevent the observation of vital data.(6) And because one of the
major aims of feminist research must be, as Maynard has noted, to
make women 'visible', not only the methodology but also the interpretation of research data must be sensitive to this objective.(7)
Further, as Spender contends (1978, p.11), 'It is not just "visib-
ility" that is required for females within the feminist perspective; it is new models of the female and of the male - and new and
more appropriate ways for formulating these models and theories.'
The research presented in this volume has not all necessarily been
conducted from a feminist perspective in the first place, although
much of it undoubtedly has been; but all the chapters sensitize us
to certain kinds of issues and problems which are particularly
important in considering the relevance of gender to the schooling
and labour-market entry of women, and strive to make women 'visible'
in a way that much previous educational research has failed to do.

In so doing, the accounts lay themselves open to claims that
they are too subjectivist, a charge which has been levelled by
Wolpe at a number of existing analyses examining the position and
experiences of women in education.(8) Wolpe argues that where
the focus of attention is the individual in the educational system,
rather than the complex of structures which give rise to the experiences of individuals, although such research is descriptively
useful, it lacks explanatory power. That is, she contends, subjectivist research concentrates mainly on achieving a redistribution of males and females within a system which remains fundamentally unequal, and fails to account for the existence of
inequality or the conditions which give rise to inequalities.
Furthermore, Wolpe suggests that subjectivist analyses give no
conception of how the orientations of women may be transformed,
because they base themselves on a circular explanation which
imputes women's orientations to their role in the social structure,
whilst at the same time explaining those roles in terms of their
distinct orientation. In many ways Wolpe's criticism is an important one, particularly in view of the number of pieces of work
which attribute gender inequalities in education to the rather
simplistic notion of 'underachievement' by women. For instance
Byrne has argued (1978, p.15) that 'My deepest concern is with
girls whose alternative to staying at home for 40 years is not the
professions ... it is low pay ... the typewriter, the unskilled
labour market, short-term employment. The cause: a different,
often inferior education', without recognizing that the inferior
education received by many girls is only one aspect of their
subordination to men, a subordination based on the dominance of
patriarchal relations, the capitalist mode of production, the
labour process, the social and sexual division of labour, and the
family, as well as on schooling. However, if by subjectivism Wolpe
is also referring to work which focuses on particular individuals

and their experiences within the educational system, which looks at
processes of interaction between girls and their teachers, which
examines the progress of individual women through the labour market,
in other words if her criticisms can be extended to any work which
does not as an integral part of that work offer any kind of structural analysis, then a defence of such subjectivism is necessary.
Subjectivist research not only achieves the objective of making
women 'visible', but is also able to convey something of the qualitative experiences and contradictory demands which women are likely
to meet, whether these stem from the curriculum, the 'hidden' curriculum, gender categorizations, ideologies, the process of knowledge
transmission, or from any other source. Although research of this
kind does not necessarily make explicit connections between what
happens, for example, in schools, and what occurs in the labour
market, nevertheless it prepares the way for perceiving how and
where there are disjunctures between what the school prepares girls
for and what they actually find in the real world of the labour
market, the family and marriage, and an unevenly developing economy.
It does not, of course, allow us to see the importance of political
struggles both inside and outside the educational system about what
is legitimate in schooling and what counts as valid knowledge, or
about the rationale underlying the education of girls; neither does
it prevent us from going on to analyse such struggles, because it
has been made clear that girls and women do not in any sense under-
go uniform experiences during their schooling or their entry to
the labour market.

In addition, subjectivist research alerts us to the all-
pervasive nature of patriarchy and patriarchal relations, because
it is able to show how these two phenomena work. For whilst it is
important to argue that the economies of capitalist societies,
their productive forces and their labour processes are very relevant to an understanding of the ways in which women are schooled
for their work (whether paid or unwaged) it is also necessary to
see these processes in the context of patriarchy.(9) Otherwise
there is the danger that the subordination of women will be attributed solely to capitalism, whilst the evidence suggests that in
pre-industrial societies, whilst women possessed some power, they
derived that power from membership of family or kinship groups
rather than as individuals in their own right,(10) and that in
socialist societies the subordination of women has remained largely
intact, despite the supposed abolition of class relationships and
private ownership of the means of production.(11) Subjectivist
research does not usually help us to understand patriarchy in a
theoretical way, of course, but that need not minimize the importance of research of this nature. As Frankenberg has argued 'If I
seem to be suggesting an essentially subjective approach - I will
accept the charge providing I am allowed to assert that objectivity
comes from living through and then transcending the subjective.'(12)
Thus, if we take as a starting point McDonough and Harrison's
definition of patriarchy as 'first, the control of women's fertil-
ity and sexuality in monogamous marriage and, second, the economic
subordination of women through the sexual division of labour (and
property)'(13), then subjective research can help us to see and
feel how patriarchy is perpetuated, even if that research alone

does not help us to analyze the exact mechanisms whereby patriarchy is reproduced and maintained.

MacDonald's chapter does indeed endeavour to put into a coherent theoretical framework the more empirical chapters which follow hers. She argues that many of the existing theories of schooling fail to realize the importance of the sexual division of labour within education, and miss or underplay the impact of that division of labour in shaping the relationships which exist between the family, schooling and labour processes. Concentrating on theories of social and cultural reproduction, MacDonald is able, by examining the work of Althusser, Bowles and Gintis, and Bernstein, both to show the shortcomings of these theories in terms of their peripheral treatment of patriarchal relations and gender categorization, and also to demonstrate how those theories may be adapted to take patriarchy and gender more fully into account, using the empirical material presented in subsequent papers. She stresses the importance of, and points the way towards developing, a theory of education which not only tries to account for the form of schooling by examining the mode by which the work force is reproduced, but which also recognizes patriarchal relationships as a central organizing principle in both the process of reproduction and within the labour process itself.

Clarricoates, in her study of four primary schools in northern England, offers evidence which suggests that the ways in which the gender code is transmitted and patriarchal relationships reproduced vary from one establishment to another. Hence the process of constructing definitions of femininity and masculinity must be understood as a very complex one, drawing on the sexual division of labour which exists in the community around a given school, as well as on the beliefs and ideologies held by parents, children and teachers. For example, in Dockside, where a strong male culture emphasizing the importance of manual labour exists (even though, alongside this, there is a high degree of employment of married women outside the home), segregation between the sexes during primary schooling and separation of gender stereotypes is much stronger than in Applegate, a predominantly middle-class area where few married women are employed outside the home but where mental labour is of far more importance than manual labour. In the latter area, however, despite less sex segregation and gender stereotyping, academic achievement by boys is something to which a high priority is attached, whilst girls (and this is true also of Dockside) are merely expected to be well-behaved. In the rural area of Linton Bray, the importance of a rigid sexual division of labour, based on the heavy manual work required of agricultural workers, is apparent in the schooling of both boys and girls, even though the girls themselves are frequently expected to 'help out' with agricultural work. Clarricoates's study is also important because it takes us beyond the usual confines of sexism in reading schemes and segregation of the sexes in play or sport which comprise most existing research on primary schooling, towards a much greater understanding of the actual mechanism by which boys and girls are taught gender-appropriate behaviour.

Llewellyn's examination of two single-sex girls' schools is able to perform a similar function for the second school. Her work not

only provides us with a detailed ethnography of two schools, but is
also able to relate what happens to the groups of girls she studied
in school to the female sub-cultures which envelope them whilst out
of school. Just as MacDonald points out that theories of cultural
and social reproduction have often ignored or glossed over gender,
so Llewellyn notes that much ethnographic research on schools has
either concentrated only on boys or else assumed that gender was
only of minor importance in shaping processes of interaction. Even
though Llewellyn's work focuses on single-sex schools (which, Shaw
argues in Chapter 5, may provide an education for girls which places
less emphasis on gender-stereotyping than does mixed schooling), she
shows how, because of the influence of their lives and experiences
outside school 'Crucially, girls' and women's experiences are structured in response to male definitions'. Llewellyn shows how different groups of girls operate with different stereotypes of feminity
and a variety of notions of gender-appropriate behaviour, yet all
of these demonstrate the critical relevance of the category of
gender to the experiences of girls both inside and outside school.
Teachers, instead of resisting or trying to change the monotonous
futures faced by most of their pupils both on entry to the labour
market and in marriage, accept the legitimacy of the sexual
division of labour, and expect not academic success but only some
minimal level of skill acquisition and 'decent' behaviour from most
of their pupils, although aware that many might not even achieve
this much.

The parallels between these expectations and those of the primary
school teachers in Clarricoates's study are clear. Female pupils,
on the other hand, could use their gender identity as a means of
escape from the need to be academically successful, by retreating
into what they see as the greater fulfilment provided by marriage
and domesticity, a very different form of 'resistance' from that
found amongst working-class male youths.(14) This is so despite the
fact that many adolescent girls, through contact with older sisters
or by constant observation of the lives of their own mothers, are
aware that domestic labour and marriage are not as Utopian as the
magazines that they read tend to suggest they are.(15)

Fuller's work on a group of West Indian girls in a mixed comprehensive school shows how gender and ethnicity may overlap and
doubly disadvantage those concerned, even though an awareness of
such disadvantages may lead to strong resistance of the implications
of gender and ethnic labels by the pupils concerned. As in
Llewellyn's study, present theories and research are shown to be
inadequate. Fuller demonstrates how existing research on ethnic
group membership and its effects in schooling tells us little about
the consequences for such members when they happen to be girls.
And indeed compared with the girls studied by Llewellyn, the West
Indians in Fuller's researches show a much greater awareness of the
contradictions and difficulties they are likely to experience both
because of their sex and because of their race. Unlike their male
West Indian peers, they do not retreat into cultures such as Rastafarianism as a means by which to achieve a psychological 'return'
to their homeland, but concentrate rather on taking their education
(although not school itself) very seriously, as their only route to
success in the labour market, where their race and sex would

otherwise handicap them considerably. On the other hand, their
behaviour and conduct in school (as distinct from their academic
work) would hardly have met the criteria for 'good behaviour' speci-
fied by the primary and secondary school teachers encountered by
Llewellyn and Clarricoates. Thus, Fuller is also able to expose the
fallacy perpetrated in much earlier educational research that academic achievement is necessarily correlated with acceptance of a
school's own cultural values and accepted standards of classroom
behaviour.

Shaw's article on the value of single-sex schooling as opposed to
mixed schooling raises as a controversial issue in education something which most educationalists have long since ceased to see as
problematic: that is, is mixed schooling really as advantageous as
research and argument have led us to believe? Shaw's contention is
that, for girls at least, the outcome of the debate over mixed
versus single-sex schooling has been unsatisfactorily resolved in
favour of mixed schooling. She suggests that where girls are concerned the social advantages of mixed schooling (and it must be
remembered that these in any case are only advantages in terms of
what is considered to be gender-appropriate behaviour) are far out-
weighed by the academic disadvantages, and by the processes of
gender categorization which cause girls to be seen by boys as a kind
of negative reference group which excuses their own comparative lack
of academic success, because at least they are 'better than girls'.
The academic failure of girls, on the other hand, is underwritten
often by the argument that they will in any case be getting married
and hence have little need for academic qualifications. Llewellyn's
paper demonstrates that such assumptions may also operate in single-
sex schools too, but the evidence advanced by Shaw indicates that
the processes of gender-stereotyping may operate less stringently in
single-sex schools than in mixed ones. Furthermore, as Shaw notes,
in single-sex schools girls are at least likely to be taught for a
majority of their subjects by women, thus removing beliefs prevalent
in mixed schools that subjects taught by men and taken by boys are
unsuitable for girls.

The question of a sexual division of labour which operates
between divisions of knowledge and which serves to reinforce other
beliefs and practices about gender-appropriate subjects for boys
and girls, is taken up also by Weiner in her analysis of girls and
mathematics, and by Harding in an exploration of the differential
performances by the sexes in conventional 'O' level and Nuffield
science examinations. Weiner surveys current research on sex differences in mathematical performance and assesses the validity of
explanations purporting to explain these in terms of genetic factors,
cognitive differences, differential socialization experiences, pupil
attitudes and schooling practices. The nature of the evidence is
such that it is difficult to reach clear-cut conclusions; but in
any case, as Weiner argues, even if we are not at present able to
pinpoint the exact reasons for girls' comparative lack of success
in mathematics, we can at least search for strategies which can help
to overcome those factors and difficulties over which we do exercise
control. The material provided by the ethnographic studies in this
volume indicates that the reactions of teachers, and of female
pupils, to subjects which girls find difficult are often the reverse

of seeking positive strategies to remedy those difficulties; that
is, girls are excused from good mathematical performance (or good
science results, or proficiency in 'male' crafts) on the grounds
that such performance is unnecessary to those who will spend their
lives in unskilled jobs, in carrying out domestic tasks and in
caring for children.

Harding's researches not only show that what is true of the way
many schools teach, or fail to teach, mathematics to girls is also
true of much science education, but also alert us to the importance
of examining methods of teaching particular areas of knowledge and
the modes of assessment which are utilized to test pupils' reten-
tion and understanding of areas of knowledge. Learning theories
and assessment techniques have tended to be treated as components of
the educational process which are gender-neutral, whereas Harding
points out that this may be a misconception. Educational innovations such as Nuffield science may well have a different effect on
the education of girls than they have on the education of boys, an
effect which may further disadvantage girls who take science subjects, in conjunction with the processes of gender-stereotyping
already taking place in the schooling of girls.

As MacDonald says in Chapter 1, it is important 'to develop an
analysis of women's education which relates the form and content of
schooling to women's position in ... societies'. The careful
exploration of the processes of gender and class reproduction in
schooling is not in itself a sufficient enterprise, unless we also
consider the impact of these processes of reproduction on the labour
market, on the family and on other aspects of the lives of women.
Keil's study of the processes by which young school-leavers learn
about the job opportunities available to them suggests that these
are not strongly influenced by gender, but does indicate that
despite the absence of 'overt sexism' there is 'an impression of
employers working in a familiar market recruiting to well-established
categories of work which had long been recognized as appropriate for
men or women'.

Similarities in the ways in which boys and girls sought work were
found to contrast sharply with their eventual placement in the
occupational structure. And here it is insufficient to consider the
notion of a dual labour market,(16) which, as Beechey reminds us, is
a rather simplistic way of understanding what happens to women in
the labour process, and which also fails to recognize as a factor of
fundamental importance in understanding the position of women in the
labour force, the family and the sexual division of labour which it
encompasses.(17) It is also necessary to remind ourselves that class
differences operate as much on the female labour force as they do on
its male equivalent. Furthermore, as Ashton and Maguire's work
shows, local labour markets are by no means similar in their structure of employment and demand for labour. And variations in demand
for products cannot be used to explain the patterns of women's employment present in the state sector, where 'consumer' demand is of no
importance, but where women still experience different kinds of work,
rates of pay and promotion prospects from those experienced by men.
Hence the importance of the reproduction of gender and class differences in schools; and the relevance of the sexual division of labour
and patriarchal relations must be fully taken into account when we

consider what happens to women on entry to the labour market.

Newton's work on the Engineering Industry Training Board's scheme to train girls as engineering technicians illustrates just how diffi- cult it may be for girls, for schools and for employers to overcome many of the constraints operating on the employment of women in an area of work traditionally carried out by men, and where the motiva- tion for a switch to the encouragement of female labour is not, as it has been in clerical work during this century, a change in technology and the nature of the work,(18) but rather the impact of legislation on sex discrimination and of a more generalized awareness of the dis- advantaged situation of women in the labour market. However, impor- tant though such schemes may be, we should remember that they cannot provide more than a token entry of women into male jobs, and that they do not fundamentally alter either the sexual division of labour or the system of patriarchal relationships which exist in capitalist economies. Female engineering technicians are, by virtue of their schooling and socialization experiences, and by virtue of their assi- milation of the gender-code, as well as because of the structures of male/female dominance operating in our society, still likely to experience contraints on their jobs and employment careers which are not faced by men in the same field of work.

Ashton and Maguire illustrate particularly well the limitations of developments such as legislation on sex discrimination in alter- ing established patterns of employment for males and females, especially in local labour markets where traditional areas of employment for either sex are in decline or where the units of employment are small. They also pinpoint something which does not apply to male workers (although in their case age may play a part): the situation whereby female school-leavers compete for jobs with older married women. That this competition exists exemplifies the effects of the sexual division of labour on women of all ages. Married women, because of their domestic responsibilities, provide both a more flexible (in terms of willingness to work part-time, or for short periods) and also a more stable work force (they are not likely to leave to get married or have children as they have already acquired these statuses and responsibilities) than female school- leavers, but school-leavers may be cheaper to employ and have more relevant skills or qualifications, especially in the public sector.

Many women have never either been offered the chance, or even perceived such a chance as something appropriate to females, to con- tinue their education beyond school level. Hence, in so far as it can be called a choice, when the outcomes are largely not only structurally but also ideologically determined, most women have been faced with the alternative of unsatisfying, boring paid work or marriage and domesticity, and often the even more unsatisfactory combination of both. But, as Griffiths shows us, for some such women the establishment of the Open University has provided an opportunity (albeit without the financial aid offered to full-time students) to do degree-level work even without the possession of formal university entrance requirements. Griffiths examines the variety of backgrounds from which female Open University students come, and considers the reasons which have motivated them to embark upon their courses. On the whole, those reasons are far from instrumental. Women students at the Open University tend to

congregate in those subject areas where most female students in
higher education are found: arts and the social sciences; and their
lack of confidence is displayed by their tendency to register for
fewer courses than male students. However, their academic performance in all subjects (even in mathematics and science) indicates
that 'they are doing rather better than men in all faculties'.
Clearly their performance in the Open University, as Griffiths
remarks, is affected by their domestic situations, or by their occupation of typical areas of female employment, as well as by their
previous schooling into the gender code, in a way that the performance of male students is not. But, as Griffiths says, for those
women who can overcome, at least partially, the effects of such
constraints, their courses may provide an enormous change in their
lives, their outlook and their identities.

The situation of women in more conventional forms of higher education presents a rather different picture, as Rendel's analysis of
women academics during the period 1912 to 1976 demonstrates. The
representation of women in universities as teachers over this
period has shown scarcely any improvement at all. Some may regard
the situation of women academics as an elitist one, irrelevant to
the interests of the majority of women,(19) but it can equally well
be argued that since universities play such as important role in
structuring the curriculum of secondary schools, in allotting
priority to areas of research and in evaluating areas of knowledge
as of high or low status, then if women are under-represented there,
it has a significant impact on what happens to and what educational
experiences are offered to, women in the remainder of the educational system. Furthermore, the small number of women academics
illustrates the success of most schooling of women in preparing them
for low levels of paid work and domesticity. As Rendel shows, the
lives and careers of women academics are hampered by exactly the
same kinds of factor relating to their status as women in a patriarchal society, as are the lives of their less 'fortunate' sisters.

Higher education may mean that women who have access to it enter
the labour market at a different level and with higher qualifications than other women, but, as the chapter by Chisholm and Woodward
points out in a summary of some of the findings emerging from their
study of what happened to a group of university students who graduated in 1960, such women do not after graduation share the same
experiences or fortunes as their male peers. Graduate women, as
much as non-graduate women, tend to move, if not initially then
quite quickly, into areas of employment traditionally occupied by
females, notably in education and the public sector of employment,
rather than into industry and commerce. Where women did choose
employment outside the female 'ghettoes', they were often forced to
retreat back into those ghettoes by processes of discrimination,
under-promotion, and lack of confidence, although there was reluctance to admit that such factors were at work. Chisholm and Woodward argue that the careers of graduate women may be affected more
by processes of discrimination in the field of employment, by perceptions of lack of ability and confidence, than by their marriage
and family commitments. But it is difficult to escape the conclusion that domesticity, the sexual division of labour and the structure of patriarchal relations still shape the processes which affect

the progress of women graduates, even if as individuals those factors seem to be of less importance than for non-graduate women.

By way of concluding this introduction to the volume, it seems important to reiterate what was emphasized at the beginning: that is, although we must not fall into the trap of seeing a simple connection between what happens in the schooling of women and what happens to women thereafter, it is clear from almost all the chapters that the reproduction in schooling of gender categories, of class, of the sexual division of labour, of the relations of patriarchy, plays a significant part in the maintenance of the subordinate position of women in our society, whether in paid work, public life or the family. Equally, it is evident that this situation cannot be radically altered without a significant change taking place in the mode of production, in class relationships, in the structure of male-female dominance relations, as well as in schooling itself. Until those changes occur, gender will continue to play a crucial role in the schooling of women and their preparation for work.

NOTES

1   See Tresemer (1977), p. 114.

2   Deem (1978) and Byrne (1978) both give more detailed accounts of how women are disadvantaged and discriminated against in schooling.

3   See Byrne (1979), p. 187.

4   Kuhn and Wolpe (1978).

5   This is mainly achieved in Chapter 1 by MacDonald.

6   See Spender (1978); Kelly (1978); Maynard (1979).

7   Maynard (1979).

8   See Wolpe (1978).

9   See the introduction in Kuhn and Wolpe (1978) for a discussion of this.

10 The power possessed by women is discussed briefly by Stacey and Price (1979b).

11 Some material about the position of women in socialist societies may be found in Broyelle (1977); Scott (1976); Davin (1976).

12 See Frankenberg (1979), p. 14.

13 From McDonough and Harrison (1978), p. 40.

14 See Willis (1977) and Hall and Jefferson (1976) for accounts of the ways in which male youth cultures and strategies of resistance develop.

15   See McRobbie and Garber (1976).

16   The theory of a dual labour market is discussed by Barron and Norris (1976).

17   See Beechey (1978).

18   The changing labour process and labour force of clerical work is considered by Braverman (1975).

19   Byrne (1979) makes this point.

Chapter 1

Socio-cultural reproduction and women's education

Madeleine MacDonald

Within a capitalist mode of production, patriarchal relations which are characterized by male-female hierarchy and dominance assume specific historical forms, at the economic, the political and ideological levels. Even though patriarchal forms of control existed prior to the advent of capitalism, the economic and social subordination of women has, nevertheless, become an integral element of the capitalist social formation. This is not to assume that they constitute an essential ingredient, necessary for the survival of that system, but rather to recognize that they figure as one of its central organizing principles. In the capitalist economy, patriarchal relations have a specific material base in, for example, the separation of the family from the production process, in the economic dependence of women on men. In this chapter, therefore, I shall attempt to develop an analysis of women's education which relates the form and content of schooling to women's position in such societies. The emphasis will be upon the way in which schooling produces both classed and sexed subjects, who are to take their place in a social division of labour structured by the dual, yet often contradictory, forces of class and gender relations.

Despite the diversity of material and forms of analysis now available for the study of women's education, some of which are represented in this volume, there is one consistent overriding concern. The essential unity of purpose in this research is the establishment of the sociology of women's education on the academic agenda. The pressure which this research exerts upon existing accounts of schooling takes the form of demanding recognition for the ways in which schooling constructs, modifies and transmits specific definitions of gender and gender relations to each new generation, within and across class boundaries. The challenge inherent in these analysis is to reassess current explanations of schooling, which have glossed over or ignored the existence of the sexual division of labour within the school and its impact in determining the relations between the family, schooling and the labour processes.

It is my intention in this chapter to reassess two major bodies of theory, to investigate their limitations, and to suggest how they may be reformulated in the light of new evidence. I shall

concentrate on what have been called the theories of social reproduction and those of cultural reproduction of the class structure.
Within the first tradition I shall focus on the work of Althusser
(1) and of Bowles and Gintis;(2) within the second, the work of
Bernstein;(3) with the aim of using these theories as the basis for
an explanatory model of the forms of women's education within societies which are both capitalist and patriarchal.

In the work of Althusser and Bowles and Gintis, one finds the
initial premise, that education plays a central, if not critical,
role in the reproduction of a capitalist mode of production. As
outlined by Althusser, there are essentially two aspects to this
process. First there is the reproduction of productive forces; and,
second, and perhaps more importantly, there is the reproduction of
the social relations of production.

In the analysis of the reproduction of productive forces,
Althusser points to the fact that if any social formation is to
reproduce itself, it must ensure not merely that its labour force is
available in sufficient numbers (through biological reproduction and
immigration), but also that it must be diversified, adequately
skilled, and competent to work within a given social structure.
Historically the reproduction of the work force was provided by 'on
the job' training and apprenticeship schemes. Under capitalism
outside institutions, such as the educational system, increasingly
have taken over the task of providing workers with basic skills
such as literacy and numeracy. Further, the educational system
equips future workers with the appropriate attitudes for work, which
include acceptance of the rules of good behaviour, 'respect for the
socio-technical division of labour and ultimately the rules of the
order established by class domination' (Althusser, 1971, p. 127).
Individuals, he argues, are placed in a certain relation to the
existing social order - relations of 'subjection to the ruling ideology or mastery of its practice' (p. 128).

These parameters may also be found with the analysis of Bowles
and Gintis's (1976) 'Schooling in Capitalist America'. Here they
stress the importance of educational structures as selective and
allocating devices for the social reproduction of the class structure. The function of school, they argue, is to produce a differentiated, stratified and conforming work force, adjusted in personality and character, equipped with the necessary skills and compet-
ences to work in the socio-economic division of labour.

In analysing the labour force found within the US economy, Bowles
and Gintis recognize, under capitalism, the tendencies for the
labour market to segment, and point out the segregation of the
primary and secondary labour markets. The primary segment they
locate predominantly in the corporate and state sectors, where jobs
are characterized by relatively high wages, job ladders and opportunities for promotion. Within this segment, there are likely to
be high levels of job security and workers' unionization. In the
secondary labour market there are relatively low wages, little
workers' unionization, low levels of job security, and little chance
of promotion and training. Within this labour market are to be
found the most oppressed groups, which in the USA are 'blacks',
Puerto Ricans, Chicanos, native Americans, women, the elderly, youth
and other minority groups (my emphasis, Bowles and Gintis, 1976,
p.67).

By classifying women as yet another minority group, Bowles and Gintis fail to analyse labour market segmentation as one of the most significant features of the integration of the sexual division of labour and in particular of patriarchal power structures within the very nature of the capitalist formation. They thus gloss over the presence of a sex-segregated labour force within and across the binary division of primary and secondary labour markets. Particularly in the USA there is a process of 'ghettoization' of the female labour force in the secondary labour market.(4)

Further, there exists a sexual division of labour within each segment, where women are typically employed in jobs that have subsequently been defined as stereotypically 'feminine' occupations, whether it is because of their assumed manual dexterity (e.g., textiles), their domestic interests (food processing, health care, cleaning, etc.), or their vocation in providing personal services (teaching, social work, etc.). What characterizes women's location both within and between these different labour markets is their inferior position with regard to wages, training prospects and promotion. Although Bowles and Gintis recognize that capitalism has adapted and utilized pre-existing 'social prejudices' such as racism and sexism, they neglect to give any material basis to what in their analysis appear to be exogenous ideological factors. Any theory of education which seeks to account for the form of schooling in terms of the mode of reproduction of the work force, I would argue, must recognize the structure of male-female dominance relations as integral and not subsidiary organizing principles of the work process.

Within this framework, it is essential that we recognize the pattern of specifically female employment as different from that of men. The changing definitions of jobs from 'masculine' to 'feminine' and vice versa are one aspect of the dynamic nature of women's position in society. At one level this is mediated, as shown by Ashton and Maguire (ch.9), by the attitudes, expectations and ideology of employers, who operate and realize historically specific conceptions of female employees, their abilities, and their personalities (diligence, lack of boredom with routine tasks, dexterity).

These conceptions, however, whilst appearing as an independent variable in the process of employee selection, are core features of the pattern of use of female labour within the economy. As Beechey (5) has argued, capital acquires certain advantages in the employment of female labour within certain sectors of the labour force. The two major advantages she identifies relate to the dual location of women within the family and the production process. First, when all members of a workman's family are employed, the value of labour power is lowered as the costs of reproduction (e.g., nurturance, household and health care) are spread over all members of the population. Second, the value of female labour is less than that of men since women have less training, and are not expected to pay the full costs of the household, as it can be assumed that they will be supported by their menfolk. Women are not expected to bear the costs of their own reproduction, therefore employers may also pay less than the value of female labour, since women are defined as subsidiary workers, financially dependent on men within a patriarchal family.

The hiring of female labour, while it has its advantages, also
poses dilemmas for capital, especially in the employment of married
women workers. The greater the use of married women in wage labour,
the more threatened is the effective performance of their work as
domestic labourers within the family. The separation of waged from
domestic labour, of production from consumption, of the economy from
family life is not merely a facet of the development of capitalism
but also constitutes one of the elements of the process of reproduction of that system. Women's services within the family as wife,
mother, servant, therapist, etc. are critical aspects of the reproduction of the labour force.(6) The tension therefore exists
within capitalism in maintaining an appropriate balance between the
need for certain types of labour power on the one hand, and on the
other, the continued functioning of the patriarchal nuclear family,
which services and reproduces the labour force outside the production system.

Any account of the relationship between schooling and the structure of the labour force must therefore take into account the
differing positions of women and men within the social formation.
It must furthermore take heed of the advice (Coulson et al., 1975,
p.60) that

the central feature of women's position under capitalism is not
their role simply as domestic workers, but rather the fact that
they are *both* domestic and wage labourers. It is this dual and
contradictory role that imparts a specific dynamic to their
situation.

It is important to recognize the existence of class differences
operating within the female labour force, which determines not
merely the sort of jobs which women are likely to find themselves
in, but also their relation to the means of production. Within the
working class, women workers bear the same relation to the means of
production as working-class men, since they own only their own
labour power to sell on the labour market. At the other extreme
women within the capitalist class might well have a different relationship to the means of production than their menfolk. Whilst
their fathers and husbands are more likely to own and control
capital directly, buying the labour of others, these women may indirectly benefit from and live off the accumulation of family
wealth without any necessity to work for an income. With the
breaking down of patrilineal inheritance and the rights of women to
own independent property, potentially more women of this class can
become actively involved in the production process as owners of
capital, shareholders and employers. They are still represented in
very small numbers in the structures of management and control. For
the majority of these women, the relation to the means of production
is one of indirect ownership and control. In the professional
middle classes, while the men are likely to become the ideologists
or the managers of capital, the women, located primarily in the
'caring' professions, may be a major source of what Bernstein
(1977d) called the 'agents of symbolic control', presenting the
'soft' face of capitalism in the welfare and educational agencies.
It is important, therefore, to recognize the difference between the
forms of women's education found in the private and state schools,
and further to relate the forms within them not just to women's

labour but also to their future class position.

What Bowles and Gintis have tended to assume is that, within the differential forms of schooling catering for different sectors of the wage labour force, both sexes experience on the whole similar conditioning. Carter (1976, p.180), in the same tradition of political economy, is more careful about assuming similarities, even though he does not attempt an analysis of the differences.

> The structural relation of school experience to subsequent labour market experience for women is very complex and does not exactly replicate the relation that obtains for men. For instance, many women achieve good grades, graduate from high school and still obtain only secondary jobs. To understand the relationship of women to existing job structures, we must consider not only the structure and ideology of schooling but also the structure and ideology of the family. To avoid confusing the analysis with too many details, we have ignored the circumstances peculiar to the experience of women.

What becomes clear from the study of forms of women's education, particularly in terms of curriculum and examinations, is the different routes the two sexes take through the educational system. For the working-class girl, often allocated to the curriculum streams of of the 'less able' requiring courses in 'everyday life' and 'citizenship', basic training in skills and non-examination courses, the experience is orientated towards a future domestic role rather than waged labour. Training is directed towards domesticity, with courses in household crafts such as cooking and sewing added to a diluted academic curriculum. As Wolpe has shown,(7) the 'common code' in British government planning in education has been founded on the assumption of gender differentiation with the belief that women's primary role in society is to become wives and mothers, despite the fact that large numbers of women become workers outside the home. There is an assumed dichotomy between the world of work which is taken as the primary goal and interest of boys, and the world of the family and marriage as the future desire of girls. The educational motto of 'preparation for life' takes on specific meanings in the ideological climate of patriarchy. The results can be seen in the alignment of forms of education for socially defined and attributed gender roles.

The patterns of working-class girls' schooling (though this may appear contradictory, given the presence of working-class women in the labour force) may have a certain logic. By regarding marital and maternal roles as primary goals in life, working-class women are likely to treat work within social production as a peripheral and secondary concern. This focusing upon domestic life for personal fulfilment, which is encouraged rather than discouraged by the educational system, may partially explain why women are prepared to accept employment in the worst, lowest-paid jobs within the secondary labour market. The provision of a form of schooling for domesticity may be one of the ways in which the conditions are ensured for the continued existence of a female reserve army of labour and an unskilled, cheap, female labour force. Such a form of schooling would also contribute indirectly to the reproduction of capitalism by encouraging a female domestic labour force, responsible for the biological reproduction and the nurturance of workers.

For the middle classes, school experience is different but no less contradictory. The overt ideology of equal opportunity and equality between the sexes, although realized by the equal range of curriculum options made available to both sexes and the expressed liberalism of the teachers, may well run counter to the hidden curriculum of the school, which perpetuates the ideology of femininity as synonymous with wife and mother. Even where the school is geared more towards careers, the assumption can often be identified in teachers' attitudes and their guidance on choice of school subjects, that these careers are best found in typically 'feminine' professions, such as medicine, education, social work, etc. Ironically too, these girls may well receive sufficient academic qualifications to proceed to higher education and full-time careers which later come into conflict with their concept of marital life. Particularly within the professional middle classes, one finds a strong belief in motherhood as a professional full-time job which requires the mother to be at home with her children, responsible for the reproduction of the class culture by her domestic pedagogic work, and capable of responding to the demands made upon her by the schools.(8)

In the case of working-class girls, the ideology of sex differences, and the naturalness of the sexual division of labour between home and work, is often overt, with only minimal recognition of the necessity for or the desire of, these girls to take up paid employment. In the education of the middle-class girl, the situation is reversed. There is often a recognition of the desirability that women should achieve academically, in order to obtain some work fulfilment and career prospects; this is set against the likelihood that once married they will have much greater financial security and less need to work either for money or for fulfilment, given motherhood. In both cases, the ideology of femininity and the acceptance of the sexual division of labour act as a filter for the continued presence of women in certain types of labour with specific expectations and attitudes to work.

If we turn now to the reproduction of the social relations of production (i.e., the class relations operating within the structuring of the labour process) we find the kernel of Althusser's and Bowles and Gintis's analyses of schooling. Both see the reproduction of the social relations found in the production process as the central function and determining force in the shape of schooling within capitalism. For Althusser, the educational system is the dominant ideological state apparatus which processes each school population in accordance with, and in preparation for, the class structure and class power relations. The process is one of selective socialization where groups of children, on the basis of their class origins, are given different types and amounts of education through which they acquire certain types of knowledge and know-how as well as particular ideological predispositions. Theoretically these acquisitions allow them to cope with and adapt to the work relations and authority structures in specific locations in their production process. Some children will thus be prepared for their future role as the exploited, with an apolitical, national, ethnical or civic consciousness. Others will learn how to give orders and enforce obedience, in expectation of their future role as agents of exploitation (employers, managers) or agents of repression (police, army). The third major category will acquire the ability to manipulate ideologies and forms of consciousness. Within the seemingly neutral context of the school, 'the relations of production in a capitalist social formation, i.e. the relations of exploited to exploiters and exploiters to exploited, are largely reproduced', by a 'massive' inculcation of the ideology of the ruling class (Althusser, 1971, p.148).

In this rudimentary framework, Althusser concentrates upon class domination with no mention of the ways in which patriarchal ideology is transmitted in the school, mediating and contextualizing the ruling ideology of class domination within the structures of sexual oppression. A question he forgets to ask is: are women ever inculcated with the ideology suited for the agents of exploitation or repression? If any ideology is most likely to be acquired by women, it is that of the exploited, with relatively few trained to become professional ideologists.

In the work of Bowles and Gintis (1976), the reproduction of the social relations of production occurs through their presence in structural equivalents in the social relations of schooling. The form of socialization, rather than being ideological, is one of experience of the social relations and authority structures of schooling which mirror those to be found in future work places. In elaborating what they call the 'correspondence principle', they identify a structural homology between the hierarchy of the teacher-pupil relations and that of the supervisor/manager over the worker, which reproduces the authority structures and forms of control characteristic of class relations (Bowles and Gintis, 1976, p.131):

> Specifically, the social relationships of education - the relationships between administrators and teachers, teachers and students, students and students, and students and their work - replicate the hierarchical division of labour. Hierarchical relations are reflected in the vertical authority lines from administrators to teachers to students. Alienated labour is reflected in the student's lack of control over his or her education, the alienation of the student from the curriculum content, and the motivation of school work through a system of grades and other external rewards rather than the student's integration with either the process (learning) or the outcome (knowledge) of the educational 'production process'.

Beyond this aggregate level, Bowles and Gintis point to the different forms of education and internal organization of schools, which prepare children for different levels within the occupational structure. Whilst the lowest levels are likely to emphasize rule-following and close supervision, the middle and higher levels of education provide greater space for initiative, moving from discipline and direct control to more independent activity. These levels are to be found not merely in the various tiers of the educational system but also within streamed schools. The implications of these structures are the attunement of each generation to the behavioural norms required by the levels of the capitalist production process, which are internalized in the 'types of personal demeanor, modes of self presentation, self image and social class identifications which are the crucial ingredients of job adequacy' (ibid).

In this analysis of schooling, there is little recognition of
the potential correspondence between patriarchal authority structures and the hierarchy of male over female within the social
relations of the school and of the work processes. This might be
due to the fact that Bowles and Gintis define sexual inequality and
prejudices as external to the operation of capitalism. They point
out that the 'smooth control over the work process requires that
the authority structure of the enterprise respect the wider society's
prejudices. In particular socially acceptable power relationships
must be respected' (p.98). They suggest, but do not develop the
point, that a strong case could be made that the form and strength
of both racism and sexism are closely related to the particular
historical development of class relations in the USA and Europe.

Furthermore, they do not analyse the ways in which sexual power
relations have become integral features of capitalist work structures. The control of women workers by male managers, for example,
may be found mirrored in the sexual hierarchy of the school's division of labour, with a male headteacher and inspectors and a large
female teaching force. Within the fragmentation of knowledge, one
can also find the stratification of knowledge reproducing the hierarchy of male over female with particular school subjects and disciplines classified as 'masculine' or 'feminine' (Harding, Chapter
7 and Weiner, Chapter 6), which contribute to the acceptance of
students of the sexual divisions within the labour force. In the
classroom the authority of the teacher may also be affected by sex.
In the primary school, the teacher's authority is more likely to
be similar to that of the mother (i.e. personalized), while at the
university level the model is one of paternal authority, based
upon status and position.(9)

This sexual division of labour in school knowledge and amongst
the teaching staff is perhaps one of the ways in which women
become attuned to the dual forms of control found within their
specific work locations. For example, within an office the form of
control between male bosses and their female secretaries is likely
to contain elements of paternalism. In industry, as Gee found,(10)
the form of control of the female work force was a combination of
patriarchal and capitalist management practices. She concludes
(Gee, 1978):

> The sexual division of labour underpinned by the patriarchal
> structure of the family and the division of labour in detail,
> brought together under factory discipline and management, means
> for women *a dual form of control* in the work place.

The implication of this dual form of control within the work
place is that women are expected to be both docile to management
and docile to men. Such a training in obedience and subservience
can be seen located in the educational system, which expects high
degrees of conformity not only to the school norm of a good pupil
but also to the definition of femininity, as the research on the
hidden curriculum of schooling has shown.(11)

Further, socialization into both class and gender identity is
also found within the family, where, as Bowles and Gintis (1976,
p.144) point out:

> Despite the tremendous structural disparity between family and
> economy - one which is never really overcome in capitalist

society - there is a significant correspondence between the
authority relationships in capitalist production and family
child-rearing.... The male-dominated family, with its characteristically age-graded patterns of power and privilege, replicates
many aspects of the hierarchy of production in the firm.

Interestingly here, they notice the existence of patriarchy as
one potential element in the authority structures of production.
While they have not accounted for the ways in which schooling may
reproduce, at an ideological and structural level, the sexual division of labour, they do analyse very briefly the role of the family
in this context. (p.144):

First, wives and mothers themselves normally embrace their self
concepts as household workers. They then pass these on to their
children through the differential sex role-typing of boys and
girls within the family. Second, and perhaps more important,
children tend to develop self concepts based on the sexual
divisions which they observe around them. Even families which
attempt to treat boys and girls equally cannot avoid sex role-
typing when the male parent is tangentially involved in household labour and child-rearing. In short the family as a social
as well as biological reproduction unit cannot but reflect its
division of labour as a production unit. This sex typing,
unless countered by other social forces, then facilitates the
submission of the next generation of women to their inferior
status in the wage labour system and lends its alternative -
child rearing and domesticity - an aura of inevitability, if not
desirability.

It would appear that if we are to understand the ways in which
women are prepared to take their assigned place within capitalism in
the family and in the labour force, we need to investigate the processes of gender construction in both the family and education. As
David has argued,(12) it is time to look at the family-education
couple as the dual determining agencies of reproduction of sexual
divisions within the social formation.

With this in mind, I shall now turn to the theories of cultural
reproduction and specifically to the work of Basil Bernstein (13),
who analyses education in terms of the contribution it makes to the
cultural reproduction of the class structure. This work emphasizes
the importance of the culture of the curriculum and the social and
moral order of the school. Unlike the social reproduction theories,
which stress the economic inequalities of class societies, Bernstein
emphasizes the mediation of the family between class origin and
school as the critical source of cultural inequality. Not concerned
with the inheritance of economic capital, he develops his analyses
around the concept of symbolic property (language, cultural tastes,
manners) and educational property in the form of certificates and
diplomas. Although Bernstein does not specifically address the
question of gender differentiation within schooling, his theory
makes available conceptual tools which can be usefully employed in
the analysis of gender relations in schooling. According to
Bernstein (1977b, p.85):

Educational knowledge is a major regulator of the structure of
experience. From this point of view, one can ask 'How are forms
of experience, identity and relation evoked, maintained and

changed by the formal transmission of educational knowledge and
sensitivities?'

In investigating this question, Bernstein concentrates upon the
ways in which schooling reproduces the social order through the
categorization of pupils by age, sex and social class. This categorization lies embedded in the structuring of knowledge and also
in the form of pedagogy, the spatial organization of the school and
the evaluation criteria. The two critical features of school experience are to be found in the form of classification (the construction and maintenance of boundaries between different categories,
their interrelations and stratification) and framing (the form and
degree of control within pedagogic relations, between teacher and
taught).

Using this theoretical framework, it is possible to investigate
the ways in which schooling transmits a specific gender code whereby
individuals' gender identity and gender roles are constructed under
the school's classification system. The boundaries between the
appropriate activities, interests, and expectations of future work
for the two sexes are maintained, and the relations and hierarchies
between the two are determined by such a gender code.

In traditional schools one may find a strong boundary between the
definitions of masculinity and femininity, which will be reinforced
by the application of this principle to the spatial organization of
the school, school uniforms, classroom activities and curriculum
subjects. This will be implemented through specific pedagogic
relationships where the framing is strong. The child's behaviour
will be evaluated according to sex-appropriate criteria (e.g., 'that
is quite good for a girl', 'little girls don't do that'). In this
type of school, the teacher in the classroom is most likely to operate distinctions between male and female children in terms of their
notion of a 'good pupil', their expectations of ability and educational success, and their form of discipline. This form of pedagogy
would most likely occur in societies or communities where the sexual
division of labour in the home and in the work environment was
strongly demarcated. As Clarricoates found in her research (Chapter
2), the classification of gender roles was strongest and most overt
in schools serving industrial or agricultural communities where
sexual differentiation at the economic and ideological levels was
strong.

In schools serving either the suburban middle classes or the
semi-skilled or skilled occupational groups on a council estate,
the classification of children by gender was weakened in the spatial
arrangements and types of education which girls and boys received.
It was nevertheless to be found within the classrooms, despite the
ideology of equal opportunity. While gender may not have been the
major organizing principle of the school structure, it was still
operative in the context of pupil control (i.e. strong framing).
In none of the primary schools studied by Clarricoates could one say
that the gender code was characterized by weak classifications (i.e.,
equality between the sexes) and weak frames (freedom to negotiate
the definitions of gender). Given that a strong sexual division of
labour exists within capitalism, it is not surprising that the dominant gender code of schooling in Britain is that of strong classification, which reproduces the power relations of male-female

hierarchy, and strong framing, where teachers play a large part in determining gender definitions and control. Within this dominant code, one may of course always find 'codings': particular expressions of the dominant ideology which may attempt to weaken gender roles.

The dominant code can be 'interrupted'(14) by single-sex schools in which, without the presence of one sex, the gender boundaries are blurred and the form of gender control weakened, as Shaw (Chapter 5) has shown. Nevertheless, children within this type of schooling will still acquire the principles of gender classification by the very existence of a division of schools based upon sex difference. Once such pupils have reached higher education, they will be confronted with the academic sexual division of labour (Rendel, Chapter 11) and the realities, after graduating, of the labour market and career prospects (Chisholm and Woodward, Chapter 12).

The constraints which limit the possibility of weakening gender classifications and patriarchal structures are manifold, especially since they are, as has been previously argued, integral elements of the capitalist mode of production. That is not to say that reforms are not possible. One starting point must certainly be the breaking down of gender roles within the family and the patterns of child-rearing. As Bernstein (1977c, p.129-30) argues:

> To the extent that the infant/primary school fails to utilize age and sex as allocating categories, *either* for the acquisition and progression of competencies *or* for the allocation of pupils to groups and spaces, the school is weakening the function of these categories in the family and the community.

In particular, such restructuring is likely to affect the mother's domestic pedagogic work. This process could be accomplished by a series of educational reforms including the re-education of teachers, the editing and selection of textbooks, the monitoring of classroom practice and curriculum guidance, and the availability of all curriculum options for both populations of school children.

Just as it is certain that these reforms would make an impact upon sexual inequalities, especially at the level of gender identification of children, it is also certain that the reproduction of sexual division is not a smooth, unproblematic process. The setting up and transmission of sex stereotypes as a form of social control does not necessarily imply that individuals become what the stereotype demands. As Fuller has shown in her contribution to this volume (Chapter 4), West Indian black girls strive for academic achievement and, by doing so, resist the stereotypes of 'blackness' and 'femininity'. Operating a delicate balance between resistance and acceptance of school norms, they walk a tight rope between conformity to school discipline and conformity to the racial and sexual stereotypes.

In the case of white working-class girls and boys, the mediation of class and gender categorization takes different forms. As Willis (1977) has shown in his research into the behaviour and attitudes of working-class boys, these 'lads' celebrate their masculinity against school norms of docile, conforming and diligent pupils. By labelling such pupils as effeminate and 'cissies', the 'lads' affirm their pugnacious and physical masculinity in an anti-school culture.

They thus confirm their respect for their masculine identity, derived from their families and peer group, and see its fulfilment in hard, physically demanding manual jobs. According to Willis, the 'lads' therefore invert the mental-manual hierarchy to match the male-female hierarchy. As he describes it, (p.148):

This important inversion, however, is not achieved within the proper logic of capitalist production. Nor is it produced in the concrete articulation of the site of social classes of two structures which in capitalism can only be separated in abstraction and whose forms have now become part of it. These are patriarchy and the distinction between mental and manual labour. The form of the articulation is of the cross-valorization and association of the two key terms in the two sets of structures. The polarization of the two structures becomes crossed. Manual labour is associated with the social superiority of masculinity, and mental labour with the social inferiority of femininity. In particular manual labour is imbued with a masculine tone and nature which renders it positively expressive of more than its intrinsic focus in work.

Mandy Llewellyn (Chapter 3), on the other hand, together with other researchers such as McRobbie (1978) and Sharpe (1976), reveals that the definitions of femininity can act as both a prison and as an escape route for working-class girls. Because they are female, their academic failure is legitimated, their success treated as unusual luck or a result of over-diligent, hence 'boring' effort. Femininity as constructed within the school does not encourage achievement or ambition in the academic world; rather it directs the girls to external goals of being good female companions to men. In this sense it runs counter to the prevailing ideology of education, which stresses academic achievement, intelligence and material success in later life.

On the other hand, the concept of femininity can provide working-class girls with the weapons with which to fight a class-determined education when the realities of working class life-chances are recognized for what they are. By searching for emotional and personal fulfilment in domestic life and motherhood, the girls can turn away from the frustrations of school life and meaningless employment. They themselves judge academic success not as masculine but rather as 'unfeminine' on the assumption that 'bluestockings' do not find husbands or boyfriends and therefore will fail as women. The effect, similar to the result of resistance of working-class lads, is to invert the hierarchy of productive over domestic labour, although they leave unchallenged the hierarchy of male over female. School resistance is individualized, unlike that of the working-class boys, yet it also derives from peer group culture and families' (particularly the mothers') definitions of femininity.

Paradoxically, then, while the school may not succeed in transmitting gender definitions which can merge easily with prescribed class identities, pupils may still acquire gender identities which prepare them indirectly for their future class position.

In conclusion, what I have attempted to show is that the theories of cultural and social reproduction, despite their limitations,(15) still raise interesting questions for the

sociology of women's education. By looking specifically at the
educational experience of women, we are forced to modify any simple
'correspondence' theory of the relations between schooling and work.
The contradictory nature of women's position in society, rather
than being resolved through schooling, is more likely to be accentu-
ated; and, if women are prepared for certain types of waged labour,
it is often only indirectly. Furthermore, we need to ask the
question, what relation, if any, does the 'gender code' of schooling have to the patriarchal relations in domestic life and in the
production process? We also need to find out more about the forms
of resistance to, and negotiation of, definitions of gender through
class cultures and peer groups inside and outside the school.

   Finally, while there is much more research required before we
can say we understand women's education, this work should not preclude any of the very necessary programmes for breaking down
sexual discrimination in our education system.

NOTES

1 Althusser (1971).
2 Bowles and Gintis (1976).
3 Bernstein (1977).
4 See, for example, Hartmann (1979); and for Britain see Barron
   and Norris (1976); Bosanquet and Doeringer (1973); Wolpe
   (1978); Ashton and Maguire in Chapter 9 of this volume.
5 Beechey (1978).
6 This area is now subject to what is commonly referred to as
   the 'domestic labour debate'. For good summaries of this
   debate, see Himmelweit and Mohun (1977) and Fee (1976).
7 Wolpe (1974 and 1978).
8 For an analysis of middle-class women's relation to 'progressive' primary schooling and the contradictions this poses for
   them, see Bernstein (1977c) and Chamboredon and Prévot (1975).
9 The distinction between personalized and positional authority
   is derived from Bernstein (1977a).
10 Gee (1978).
11 For a good summary of this research see Lobban (1978).
12 David (1978).
13 See specifically Bernstein (1977b).
14 This concept derives from Bernstein's analysis of 'progressive'
   primary schools (1977c), where 'interruption' is defined as a
   change in the form of transmission and reproduction of the
   dominant code.
15 For further analysis of the theories of cultural and social
   reproduction, see MacDonald (1977).

Chapter 2

The importance of being Ernest . . . Emma . . . Tom . . . Jane
The perception and categorization of gender conformity and gender deviation in primary schools

Katherine Clarricoates

Present-day research on primary schools in England has usually dealt with the descriptive field (i.e., curricular materials, inequalities of staff ratio by sex, subject specialism) rather than the analytical, although there have been some analyses of teachers' expectations.(1)

I should like to concentrate in this particular instance upon the constructs of 'femininity' and 'masculinity' within primary schools and how these differ according to class and the catchment area. In all four schools I observed, 'masculine' and 'feminine' are seen as immutable characteristics of normal proper behaviour. But contradictions emerge. Just as there is a capricious inconsistency of sex-role attributes accorded to males and females in varying cultures,(2) so what is considered normal in some schools is abnormal in others.

Differing patterns of sex-role socialization are by no means a new concept in feminist scholarship: Pauline Marks, in her paper on Femininity in the Classroom discussed the class-specific notions of femininity which underlie the existing educational model (1976, p.180):

It is fascinating to discover that their [girls'] 'femininity', that supposedly biological and absolute characteristic, is dependent on the viewpoint of the observer; different social origins and intellectual abilities alter the meaning of 'femininity', which is thus not a fixed concept in educational thinking.

Belotti, in her book 'Little Girls' also states (1975, p.126):

Those who have had the opportunity to make comparisons because they have taught in schools encompassing different social groupings, admit that this [masculinity and femininity] phenomenon is much more pronounced in village or small-town schools where masculine and feminine stereotypes are more rigidly differentiated.

Although I agree in principle with Belotti's hypothesis, I question her generalization. To begin with, the situation is more complex than she suggests and her contrasts (village and small-town schools) are oversimplified. I hope to show that, despite the variations in sex-role stereotypes, it is not that some schools are less authoritarian or discriminatory to girls; rather the pattern, not the degree, of socialization changes to accommodate so-called 'liberal' attitudes to women. This could be defined as a 'divide and rule' philosophy. Sue Sharpe points out that the values and attitudes of sex differentiation do not develop in an arbitrary way, but are influenced by the nature of the economic structure of a society and 'the division of labour that has been developed around it'.(3)

My research is based on eighteen months' observation in four totally different primary schools, encompassing diverse social groups (for the purpose of this report individuals and schools will be given fictitious names in order to retain anonymity).(4)

A   A traditional working-class school of Dock Side, set in the heart of an urban area and fishing port, due for demolition and usually termed 'a northern industrial slum'.(5) It is characteristically comprised of terraced housing - 'tunnels-to-backs' - which are poorly maintained by private landlords.

B   A modern suburban 'rural' middle-class school of Applegate, opened eleven years ago to meet the needs of an expanding population due to development of what Pahl called 'the rural fringe' (Pahl, 1965). Within easy commuting distance of the small Minster town, it serves mainly settled, prosperous, home-owning professional parents.

C   A council estate school of Long Estate which is an early example of the new, spacious primary school built in the early 1960s. It serves children of parents who have been rehoused from the old decaying urban areas, situated five to six miles outside the city centre.

D   A very small rural primary school in the village of Linton Bray in an agricultural area. House-types vary from the country stone cottage and farmhouse to the row of newly developed ranch-style bungalows of the 1970s. Although the basic economics of the community are no longer totally agrarian (lorry drivers, workers in light industry, garage mechanics, etc.), nevertheless family farms dominate the area.

The social class distinctions among the four schools are both observable and unseen. One can easily enumerate the school differences between the four settings: classrooms are arranged either as informal workshops or pedagogic 'absorption tanks'; and to classify one school simply as 'progressive' or 'traditional' is an over-simplification. One has only to think of the old wooden desks, scored by years of graffiti, and the Victorian architecture of the old schools compared with the plastic, new wood and tile flooring of the new suburban schools, to provide the visual class differences. Research has shown that social class can handicap children from early in their lives, for it is influential in such areas as streaming, helpful parents, and teachers' expectations. The neighbourhood and the sub-culture are all variables which have come under scrutiny and have been shown to be factors affecting a child's school career. Spatially all the schools are geared to a set pattern of movement, whether in open plan or traditional rigid structures, for children are behind desks, in lines, in queues, and always in the position of having to accept educational authority.

This somewhat bewildering variety of organised spatial practices and social expectations reveals the diverse attitudes to sex-role stereotyping; but there is some overlap and this makes it difficult to keep assumptions - and results - discrete.

It was through the recognition of divisions set up by the schools and the teachers (and in turn accepted by the children) that the polarization between the sexes was revealed. As stated before, though many aspects were similar in all four schools, a pattern did emerge revealing significant differences in gender deviation and gender conformity. By studying the appropriate behaviour required from each of the sexes within each school, I was able to make some judgments about the value structure of 'femininity' and 'masculinity' within the specific catchment area. My research has led me to believe that models presented to the children, with their demarcation between masculine and feminine, are based on ecological factors which pertain to that school, i.e. the value structure of the school in relation to the community values.

The urban traditional school revealed behaviour which was considered 'typical' of the two sexes, behaviour and norms that were sharply differentiated. This was due to the school's reinforcement of stereotypes and the children's learning and development experienced within the community. Dock Side has all the hallmarks of a male culture (this is not to say that middle-class communities do not), consisting of norms interpreted through a masculine-feminine polarization. O'Neill, in his research of the actual community, states: 'The tendency towards stereotyping and compartmentalization characterise the authoritarian elements of traditional working-class life' (1973, p.195). A rigid conformity existed in social relations, with a preoccupation towards fixed masculine qualities of strength, toughness, dominance and bravery; whereas women were seen in direct contrast: submissive, weak, with 'their place' emphatically in the home. There does, however, appear to be a contradiction here, for there was a large number of women who were employed.(6)

Segregation begins in the street outside, and one must assume that girls and boys have been socialized within families which express a sharply defined sexual division of labour, so that the children learn from an early age to steer clear of each other. Boys are aware of what is expected of them and avoid 'feminine' things at all cost; social deviance of any form in a pervasive working-class community is likely to meet firm resistance and to be finally suppressed.(7)

Girls will make their way to school in separate groups from their brothers, and through this process the stereotypes are solidified and reinforced. It is a land of working men's clubs, or 'men only' bars where landlords encourage sex segregation. To be seen too often with women would undermine a man's 'maleness'. The young males join their fathers at this form of social club, with women invited only on specific days.

School does not offer any alternatives. Separation begins in early infancy with separate playgrounds, separate toilets, separate lines, even separate lists on registers. This serves as something of a reminder of Victorian morality, and suggests that if boys and girls come together they somehow become immoral. Conformity to sex-roles is strictly adhered to, whilst deviation is rigidly avoided. The school, like its surroundings, is impoverished of grass, space and playing fields; the high walls bordering it are covered in graffiti announcing the ever-youthful optimism of the local football team (this despite its struggles in the lower half of the Third Division). Above the doorway are those ominously familiar letters: BOYS.

Appropriate gender behaviour is expressed in all aspects of school life. High academic achievement is neither highly valued nor expected; at best it is only hoped for by the teachers. For girls it is expected that they follow the traditional line of 'doing well anyway' as part of their conformity to institutional expectations; in fact their 'achievement' is seen as part of the 'feminine' stereotype.(8) When asked who tends to get the best results, the teachers' most common reaction is to explain in sex differentiated terms:

'Oh the girls, naturally; you can always rely on them to do their work properly.'

'The girls ask the right questions simply because it's expected of them.'

'Definitely the girls, but I think it's more to do with wanting to please rather than being intelligent.'

But the general expectations for these children were revealed in the following way:

'There isn't much opportunity round here for these kids anyway.'

'Change and opportunity hardly filter down here...parents want their sons to follow the traditional jobs like fishing.'

'Higher hopes are not the sort you would expect in this type of area.'

'To be realistic and when you think of the jobs and what 90 per cent of these children are going to do, you know, I'm very glad I've got the intelligence not to have to do that kind of job.'

'I think of the kind of life and the job that they're going to have just by having these parents.'

'I can't actually change the system; most of these kids will finish up in semi-skilled or unskilled jobs.'

Academic norms among the children can easily be distinguished when observing and listening to them:

'Girls always try to answer the questions first.'

'Yeah, they think they're a bunch of cleverclogs.'

'We sit quiet, we don't have to do anything 'cos the girls will answer the teachers' questions.'

'Boys always make a noise and try to stop you working.... I like doing sums.... I got three stars today.'

'They don't do their writing properly like we do.'

'See that girl there, Wendy Hagan...she's the best in the class.'

Tables by rote, and regurgitative 'singing' in order to memorize knowledge, were the order of the day. Girls were eager to 'succeed' in this one sphere that was allowed them, but even then they were not given the credit for creative potential.(9) Expectations (or lack of) exacerbated the divisions between the sexes; in a game of general knowledge girls and boys were constantly pitted against each other. If the boys won there was a loud triumphant uproar. The girls frowned upon Ian who was exceptionally good at general know-ledge: 'We would win if it wasn't for him,' stated Debbie, pointing at him. The academic expectations of the teachers towards this social group were reflections of a belief in the stereotypical qualities.

Physical aggression was much more accepted in this school than in others:

'It comes from home.'

'They've no idea of discipline in the home.'

'We have a lot of "humdingers" in this school; mind you, I blame it on the parents.'

'You can't expect anything better from these kids, coming from an area like this.'

But they did expect girls to set a good example in behaviour, and in fact they thought they got such behaviour (though this could well be a product of their own perceptions which dichotomize the behav-iour of girls and boys so that even the same activity may be evaluated differently according to the sex of the actor):

'Girls are better behaved, boys are louder.'

'The boys are more aggressive, whilst the girls are typically feminine.'

'Boys are the ideal of what males ought to be.'

'Girls are more bitchy towards each other.'

'Girls are more fussy.'

'I think boys tend to be a little more aggressive, and on think-ing about it the male is the same in the animal world.... We are animals basically.'

This was despite the fact that the girls were as verbally aggressive (particularly in terms of swearing) as the boys. When asked what lay behind these differences, most teachers agreed it was 'conditioning' or 'socialization' within the family, and there was general recognition that parents' expectations were different for girls and boys. But this did not prevent these same teachers from going right back into the classroom and reinforcing the sex-role stereotypes by their expectations and toleration of different standards of behaviour between the sexes, instead of trying to eradicate the previous conditioning.

Craig, a five-year-old, spent a good deal of his time in harassing his classmates. He took a great delight in breaking up their games, bombarding any hapless child who happened near him with marbles, and was a constant source of irritation to the girls, whom he maliciously attacked - either verbally or physically - and all this within the confines of the class and to the non-reaction of the teacher. On the other hand, Sarah was prone to outbursts of temper, either screaming or letting loose a barrage of insults at her offender. I was present at a time when she let fly a quantity of paint at Lynsey, who promptly burst into tears. Sarah's behaviour was met with severe rebuke in public by the teacher: 'Little girls do not do that,' amongst other things; and thereafter she was nicknamed the 'paint-dauber'.

The teacher then proceeded to justify her own behaviour by telling me how Sarah was a problem child; for example, annoying her classmates. It seemed to escape her attention that this was the very same behaviour that Craig was allowed to get away with. Not only were different standards of tolerance applied, but also the same behaviour was categorized differently depending on the sex. Many times I observed children involved in play, and in many instances I was aware of the use of this double standard:

Craig and Edward were involved in a game of Plasticine and both are seized with a fit of laughter. They are allowed to carry on. But, parallel to this, when two girls were caught up in a similar game and became noisy the teacher classed it as 'giggling hysterically' and told the girls to 'calm down'.

And yet in this particular instance there was no real distinction between the girls' or the boys' behaviour. It can be seen that there is a subtle interaction between the teachers' observations and the teachers' beliefs.

As stated before, the phenomenon of masculine and feminine behaviour differed between urban traditional, suburban middle-class, council estate and village school; this fact of necessity leads to a brief discussion of the value structure and norms of the catchment areas, indicating the different patterns of male dominance arising from the social relations of production and consumption.

Applegate reflected the space, green fields and high aspirations that Dock Side lacked. It was representative of middle-class, prosperous parents with young children, searching for the 'rural' family life: the new 'rural-urban frings'.(10) According to O'Neill, the middle-class stereotype of femininity is bound up with occupational status and social prestige.(11) Still implicit in

middle-class ideology, however, is the belief that it is preferable
for a wife not to work, and that the aspiring husband should be
able to earn enough to support his whole family. Most of the
children I talked to told me their Mums 'did not work' but stayed
at home. Pahl states that the middle classes have high aspirations
for their children's education since 82 per cent (against 15 per
cent of the working class) wanted their children to stay on until
18 or over. To the working class, extra schooling was seen as a
training of some sort, whereas the middle class saw it as a means of
urging their children to go to university. The veil of egalitar-
ianism between the sexes is soon lifted when one scrutinizes the
values and norms of such a community. Pahl also recognized the
significant theme that emerged from his research into the middle-
class 'commuter villages': parents tended to discriminate in favour
of their sons in regard to university education when they had to
pay for it, with the consequence that the education of daughters
could well be made to suffer. Justification for this lay in the
'belief' that daughters are not clever enough to study for a
degree.(12)

Male domination can also be revealed through social relations.
Babchuk and Bates, in their paper on The Primary Relations of
Middle Class Couples (subtitled A Study in Male Dominance), showed
that a large number of wives' 'best friends' were first met through
husbands, revealing that husbands had the greater influence in
initiating friendships and in determining who the 'best friends'
of the couple would be. Due to extreme polarization, working-
class women tended to choose their own friends through network
ties, such as work, for example. Noticeable differences were
apparent between the urban traditional and commuter middle-class
family life and home. The latter consisted of a small mobile
household, enabling the family to follow the husband as he moved
from town to town when promotion had been achieved.(13) Frequent
moves can increase the isolation of middle-class wives. 'Men
Only' bars and working men's clubs are replaced by a round of golf
with the 'chaps' and 'business lunches'.

Applegate primary school reflected the value structure of high
aspirations and academic achievement:

'Most of these children are capable of going to university.'

'We have a very high standard educationally...if you compare it
with an urban working-class school.'

The high academic goal was projected to the children:

'If you work hard now, chances are you'll get to university
without any trouble.'

Whilst at Dock Side pupils were taught 'dates' and 'things', in
Applegate rote learning was almost non-existent, and the emphasis
was on relationships and processes in most subjects. Boys were
required to have the academic norms which were so lacking in the
Dock Side boys. In fact they were regarded as the intellectual
elite (by both teachers and children), even though girls usually

had the highest marks in all subjects right throughout primary school. I was browsing through some poetry displayed on a class-room wall written by top junior children when a girl touched me on the arm. Pointing to a specific poem she told me, 'That's Peter Jenkinson's; he's the brightest in our class,' a statement of fact not said with surprise or envy - just relayed as a piece of informa-tion. The teacher informed me:

'On the whole you can generally say that the boys are more cap-able of learning.'

'Boys are interested in everything and are prepared to take things seriously.'

'Then tend to ask the deeper questions, while girls tend to be more superficial about subjects.'

'Although girls tend to be good at most things, in the end you find it's going to be a boy who's your most brilliant pupil.'

The teachers' perception of creativity was underscored by their beliefs in sex-roles. They saw the boys as having much more imag-ination, and having the real ability.

In this school a high standard of hygiene and dress was expected from both sexes, but particularly from the girls. There was also a verbal double standard, with teachers censuring girls more harshly than boys for using improper language:

'When Emma fought to retain a prized book from the school library her self-control faltered and she emitted verbal abuse to the boy who had endeavoured to take it: 'Give me that book back you rotten, lousy...' Her words reached the teacher: 'Emma, that is no way for a young girl to speak; go and stand at the back until you decide to improve your language.' Emma does so, and the boy gets away with his misdemeanour.

Aggressive behaviour in general was discouraged in Applegate but, again, more actively for girls than for boys. The teachers informed me (as in Dock Side) that they did not believe that there were any real innate personality differences between the sexes, and all stressed that in no way did they treat them any differently, except of course on an individual basis. They were emphatic that the children were not treated differently. The discrepancy between their stated behaviour and my observations is apparent, for why else would they actively discourage aggressive behaviour more often in girls:

'It's not nice to see a young girl fighting.'

'You would expect it from boys, although I myself wouldn't con-done it, rather than you would expect it from girls.'

'I expect a high standard of behaviour from my girls and fighting and swearing is totally inexcusable.'

The children in Applegate were steered to the norms of hard work,

self-denial and academic achievement with their ensuing rewards of
good prospects, university education and economic competition.
(Well, this was the context for boys.)

Sex-segregation was not so distinctively a part of organization
at Applegate as at Dock Side. It did not seem so important to keep
the two sexes apart, perhaps because other social forces were in
operation to do it for the school. It was obvious that there seemed
a flexibility and not the fixed polarization between the two sexes
which was evident in the urban traditional school:

> Paul, a six-year-old, does not need a reason to play with or be
> in the presence of girls. He consistently seeks their company
> and enjoys being involved in what is usually referred to as
> 'feminine' play: as indeed other boys do, but he does not falsify
> his behaviour as they do. He also withstands the ultimate in-
> sults which boys direct against each other expressed in female
> gender terms like 'sissy' or 'puffy'. Paul's status within the
> class is indeed quite good, his company being sought by both
> girls and boys. In Dock Side a boy like Paul would have been
> shunned, especially by the girls, who tend to deride 'deviant'
> boys as much as the boys themselves.

Boys who got involved in the Wendy House and were 'caught in the
act' took measures to reduce the likelihood of ridicule and belittle-
ment by assuming to comply with appropriate gender behaviour:

> Two boys are happily playing in the Wendy House: Edward is
> setting the table whilst Tom is ironing. The teacher comes
> forward: 'Aren't you busy? What are you playing?' Edward looks
> at Tom, both look sheepish. 'Batman and Robin', states Edward
> vehemently. The teacher smiles and moves away.

In order to cloak any behaviour that might be met with derision by
their classmates they falsified their activity, giving it a 'masculine' name. It was significant that this so-called flexibility was
much phased out in the older classes of junior pupils where sex-
segregation became once more an internal feature of organisation
within the school. But it was a less dogmatically expressed
division than within Dock Side.

Even in Applegate the young children faced many limitations as
to what was acceptable gender behaviour and 'deviants' were soon
made aware of this. The peer group's attempt to control and ridicule a deviant can be very powerful:

> Andy approached me wearing a long, tatty gold lamé dress, a
> woollen beret pulled down over his ears, and carrying an old
> handbag. It was obvious he had been in the 'dressing-up'
> corner. He stumbled towards me, 'I'm a policeman' he declared
> (I don't know what the sociological implications of this are.)
> During our ensuing conversation another boy dashed past and
> yelled 'sissy'. All this was being observed by the teacher.
> Surprisingly, Andy was slightly confused and asked his friend,
> 'What is a sissy?' 'Someone who dresses up in women's clothes,'
> came the reply. He hurriedly removed the now offensive clothing
> and retreated to the other side of the classroom with a hostile
> look in my direction. One can easily assume he will never don
> 'women's clothing' again.

The teacher, in allowing the incident to pass without a reaction
from her, informed the class that it was acceptable for Andy to be

'checked' for his deviant behaviour. Just as the teacher's interaction with the children (or a particular child) could be perceived
as enticing the child to engage or not engage in certain behaviour,
so her non-interaction would be construed in a similar fashion.

In my observations of Long Estate primary school the routines of
discipline, dress and language were again gender-differentiated.
The school caters for the children of parents who have been rehoused
from the area around Dock Side. To a certain extent a break comes
in the close family ties and, according to O'Neill, there is less
pressure to conform to the sharp demarcation between male and
female. The inhabitants 'question the existing norms of polarization of masculine/feminine'.(14) Husbands tended to help more in
the home, a thing hitherto unheard of in the Dock Side district,
which pointed to 'a democratic and participatory attitude towards
conjugal relationships'.(15) If one is to discuss egalitarian
relationships between men and women, then it is inevitable to
define what form power usually takes: how women are socially, mat-
erially, and historically dominated by men. The fact that a man
helps with the washing-up hardly means an equal relationship in
the making. Though there did not exist 'male only' bars, and there
was a decline in some of the practices observed in Dock Side, this
did not necessarily mean a decrease in male dominance but rather
just a change in pattern.

Long Estate school did reflect change: the school, with a female
headteacher, did not on first sight reflect the obsessive need to
keep the two sexes apart. This was partly due to the fact that the
architecture was not spatially organized in such a rigid design as
Dock Side. But this did not necessarily preclude the existence of
categories of gender deviation and gender conformity. The dis-
couragement of participatory activity between girls and boys was a
constant factor. The pattern did vary - in certain aspects it was
more contrived than in Applegate and less so than in Dock Side.

Long Estate's conditioned response to sex-role stereotypes was
revealed in particular with regard to Michael, a seven-year-old boy
in the third year infants' class:

Michael, much to the concern of his teachers and to the contempt
of his peer group, loved to play with dolls. He liked to bake,
and constantly sought the company of girls, despite their insults. He was constantly admonished by his teacher 'to try to
behave properly'. But to no avail.

During a conversation in the staffroom about his particular behaviour:

'Ah, yes,' said one teacher, 'bionic woman.'
'Don't be unkind,' laughed another.
A well-meaning teacher added, 'His brother is really a nice
little boy and quite normal.'
'Perhaps when he grows up he'll get straightened out.'

This behaviour is similar to what was accepted in Applegate.
Michael is excluded from his peer group and avoided by teachers
in answering questions for fear of 'making it more obvious'. When
I spoke of the advantages of Michael's behaviour - that he was not
a bully, and really an imaginative and pleasing child - I was
immediately corrected:

'Oh no, he has all those nasty little ways that girls have.'

'What do you mean?' I asked.

'He's ever so "catty", he bites and scratches and pulls hair.'
Michael's deviant behaviour is obviously very 'bad' for him. He is
publicly called 'bionic woman' and many attempts are made to
'guide' him away from his deviancy.

Ms T... reads Michael's 'diary' for the morning: 'On Saturday I
helped my Mum bake a cake and I made a dress for my doll.' The
teacher despairs: 'Couldn't you play football or something?'
Taking the doll he is clutching away from him she offers him an
'Action Man' [same toy, different label]. Michael stares at her
as if she's gone quite mad and moves over to the other side of
the classroom.

'I'm merely trying to protect him from the rest of the class;
you know children can be so cruel,' the teacher informs me.

Because it is conveyed to the class that Michael's behaviour is
deviant, he is the target of much bullying by some girls and most
boys. The headteacher, a kind and progressive woman, remarks that
Michael is confused between masculine and feminine roles and she
suspects that he has 'feminine genes'. If he is not 'cured' by the
time he leaves school, she suggested to me, then the only solution
to his 'problem' is that he enter the 'world' of the arts, drama or
music, where 'that kind of behaviour' is much more acceptable. The
obvious implications in this, is that 'deviant' behaviour is caused
by some personality disorder, i.e. a biological malfunction. It is
not that Michael is being attacked personally, but rather his
behaviour - his identification with the inferior sex, female.

I'd like to focus on the small rural school in Linton Bray, where,
as in most agricultural areas, the tendency is towards an enclosed
existence, traditional and hierarchical. Here the sexual division
of labour is pronounced, partly because farming is considered a
man's job and the only occupation for a woman is to be a farmer's
wife. Indeed, the children's attitudes to sex-roles were en-
trenched, due to the limited occupations within the village itself.
The only jobs available for women were shop assistant (very limited
as there were only three shops and two pubs in the village) or
cleaning woman; the only alternative was to travel to Market
Heathton some five miles distant to obtain any other job.

The school itself was very small and hence there was little need
for lining up or queueing (although this sometimes happened), a
practice which usually allows for the physical segregation of the
sexes. The lack of amenities required that all pupils had to
share, from toilets to sports equipment. But no matter how small
the school and how few the pupils it would seem that the all-
pervasive phenomenon of gender required segregation. I might have
walked into a small-scale Dock Side if it hadn't been for the
dramatic change in scenery. The children had specific lines of
demarcation: boys and girls did not sit at the same table, they
did not stand in the same files in assembly, they did not all play
for the football team (girls were mostly excluded). The irrationality of sex-typing the female was ever-present at this school: it
was believed that girls are weak, that they cry, that they can't
drive tractors (neither can boys at that age). In contrast, it was
believed that boys play football, they're tough. There was the
same boring, dogmatic and seemingly endless list of 'arbitrary

qualities' assigned to the social categories of 'masculine' and 'feminine'. The school in no way questioned these assumptions, and by not questioning it automatically provided implicit approval for such stereotypes.

The illogicality of such views is obvious when you realize that in the country girls are expected to help with the rough and dirty work of the farm:

'When I go home I change into my wellies and help with the chickens.' (Debbie)

'I help my Dad bring in the cows and then I "muck out" with the other helpers.' (Linda)

'There's not much else to do in the village on an evening so I generally help out on the farm like my brothers and sisters do.' (Jenny)

Academic norms are not high, and most of these kids have never even heard of university:

'Most of these children have only been as far as Market Heathton.'

'Their horizon is very narrow, limited within the village.'

And the school does nothing to widen this horizon. According to Eileen Byrne a less-able girl in a rural school has a triple chance of resource deprivation.(16)

In all the schools the constant exercise of separating the sexes on a consistent level serves to emphasize the assumed sex-role differentiation of girls and boys; and, whether intended or not, it serves to inculcate rivalry and antagonism between them:

'Why don't you boys do as you're told; you don't find the girls behaving like that.'

'Let's have a game of general knowledge: boys against girls.'

When asked why they segregated the girls from the boys most teachers tended to reply with stock answers, which in reality did not even address the question:

'Well, it's easier to mark off girls from boys.'

'It's a common division, isn't it?'

'I'd get confused if they were mixed...you know, if another form of division was used.'

'Well, it's the easiest...with children they know which are boys and which are girls.'

These statements are from the very teachers who constantly told me that they:

'don't treat girls differently from boys.'

'I treat them all the same.'

'They'll play with each other and not realize they are a girl or a boy.'

In all the schools even the punishment system works against any solidarity between the sexes. The slipper or cane is mainly used on boys for 'serious' misdemeanours, (although it is used more often in working-class schools), whilst girls are sent to the senior female teacher for a 'good talking-to' or given some other form of institutionalized school punishment, like being made to stay in at playtimes:

'Girls never get the slipper.'

'They always get away with more things than us.'

'They always get us into trouble.'

In the working-class schools the boys tend to brag about how many times they've 'had the slipper' for it is a sign of being tough. The girls do not share this norm:

'Boys are naughtier than us; they get the slipper from "Sir".'

'They're silly, they show off about getting the slipper.'

The teachers rationalize this demarcation by stating:

'Girls are not as bad as boys.'

'It's not quite right somehow to give girls the slipper or the cane.'

'I would give a swift kick up the boy's backside more than I would a girl's.' (male teacher)

'I suppose on the whole I'm stricter with the boys than with the girls.'

'A lot of trouble comes from the boys than the girls.'

'Girls never seem to be mischievous as do the boys, so I suppose I do overlook the few misdemeanours the odd girl may get up to.' (male teacher)

The speed at which teachers will enumerate the many differences between girls and boys is startling:

GIRLS	BOYS
Obedient	Livelier
Tidy	Adventurous
Neat	Aggressive
Conscientious	Boisterous
Orderly	Self-confident
Fussy	Independent
Catty	Energetic
Bitchy	Couldn't-care-less
Gossiping	Loyal

By providing such ready, stereotyped lists, the teachers betray
their own habit of classifying children according to their sex.
Any girl who is 'aggressive' or 'independent' and any boy who is
'effeminate' or 'sensitive' are the exceptions, the so-called
deviants. The children must change, for there seems little chance
of the teachers' stereotypes changing when presented with contradictions.

The girls' internalization of the beliefs that boys are superior whilst they are inferior manifested itself when I talked to
both girls and boys about their hopes and aspirations for the
future. Girls actually believed that boys were naturally ordained
with a profusion of masculine esoteric skills such as being able
to drive a car, tractor or helicopter; significantly boys revealed
a pattern of oppression already in their young lives, against
girls:

Applegate:

    Jennifer informed me her father was a helicopter pilot.
    'Would you like to be one?' I asked.
    'Oh no. Women would fall out of a helicopter whereas men
    wouldn't - they're stronger.'
    'But don't men fall out?'
    'No, they hang on better than women.'

    Damian informed me his father was a doctor. He wanted to be a
    scientist. I asked him:
    'Don't you think women should be able to do the same jobs?'
    'No, I don't think too many women should be scientists as they
    might get hurt.'
    'What do you mean?'
    'Well women are more likely to touch things they're not supposed
    to.'

Linton Bray:

    'A woman wouldn't be able to drive a tractor; it is too heavy
    for her.' (Mark)

    'A man would work on a farm but a girl cannot work on a farm;
    she is not strong enough.' (Laura)

    'I would not let my Mum drive a tractor; she would get it dirty
    and break it.' (Chris)

    'Women drive the tractor and trailer too fast.' (Samantha)

'A woman can't be a farmer, she can't drive a tractor,' said
Sean.
'But men can't either; like everybody else they have to learn,'
I replied.
'Yes, but it would take much longer to teach women to learn.'
Irrational they may be, but to these kids these reasons are concrete. They had simply accepted that if a job was categorized as
men's work it was obviously not right for a girl to do it. It was
tragic to recognize the realism within Dock Side, when asked about
their future:
'I suppose I'll work at Birdseye like my Mum and get home in time
for when my kids leave school.' (Stephanie, 8 years old)
Stereotypes are not only different for each sex, but also vary
according to class, and the symbolic separation between girls and
boys is manifested in varying ways. Once women appear to be strong,
self-willed, or assertive, they immediately displace the prevailing
norms defining what it is to be a man. The two main points of this
chapter are: that 'femininity' varies, and does so according to the
area in which the school is situated (occupational structure); and
that, despite such variations, the subordination of women is always
maintained.

Most women are pressured towards the feminine role; there is
little alternative. For working-class girls this will be forced
upon them earlier because they are not encouraged towards extending
childhood by opting for educational achievement. The nexus of community values and school expectations works against them. Patriarchy imposes more limitations upon their future lives as working-
class women. Expected to marry and have children, they will do
this earlier than their bourgeois sisters in an attempt to escape
the tedium of their boring, mundane jobs. They will also face
enormous discrimination in the paid labour market and difficulties
in integrating work and home, with the lack of free nurseries and
the rigid school schedule which exercises constraints and social
control over women. For them there is no question of alternatives.
One would assume that bourgeois women escape the ultimate greyness
of working-class women's lives; and indeed it would seem so, with
their 'au-pairs' and cleaning women who can release them from the
domestic burden. But they themselves are inevitably faced with
the enormous contradiction of 'liberal' equality when they attempt
to move into the professional elite.(17)

All women, whatever their 'class' (economic class for women is
always in relation to men - fathers and husbands) suffer oppression. It is patriarchy - the male hierarchical ordering of
society, preserved through marriage and the family via the sexual
division of labour - that is at the core of women's oppression;
and it is schools, through their differing symbolic separation of
the sexes, that give this oppression the seal of approval.(18)

NOTES

1 See Frazier and Sadker (1973); Lobban (1978); Weinreich (1978).
2 See Mead (1935).
3 Sharpe (1976), p.62.

4 This research is from a larger project funded by the SSRC.
5 According to the Inland Revenue's assessment of rateable value.
6 There has been a long tradition for women to work outside the home in this seaport area.
7 O'Neill (1973), p.87.
8 Clarricoates (1978).
9 Ibid.
10 Pahl (1965).
11 O'Neill (1973), p.81.
12 Pahl (1963), p.244.
13 See Bell (1968), especially his work on 'spiralists'.
14 O'Neill (1973), p.97.
15 Ibid, p.97.
16 Byrne (1973).
17 Sharpe (1976).
18 I should like to thank my research supervisor Colin Creighton, Dale Spender and the Editor for helpful comments on an earlier draft of this chapter.

Chapter 3

Studying girls at school
The implications of confusion

Mandy Llewellyn

I want to consider initially in this chapter the ways in which existing expirical studies and theoretical formulations in relation to education and youth systematically neglect gender and render it invisible: both as a category and a determining force in structuring social reality.

The implications of this neglect and invisibility of women are twofold. First, we don't actually know what girls do either at school or outside it. We haven't got any ethnographies of girls at school in the Hargreaves/Lacey mould,(1) or any small-scale studies to set alongside Willis's lads.(2) Likewise the sociology of adolescent girls' participation in present-day youth culture is virtually non-existent.(3) They are just not there in the litera-ture, or if they do appear it is through male eyes as 'birds', 'scrubbers' or 'hangers-on'.(4) However, this is not simply a pity because, second, it also means that the theoretical insights gener-ated by such work are sociologically inadequate when the entire school as adolescent population is being considered. Gender - 'the fact that they are boys' - is assumed self-explanatory and unprob-lematic in that it is not seen as something which needs to be under-stood, even though in a different context or when challenged most sociologists would acknowledge that gender is a social product and that it is given different meanings cross-culturally and histor-ically.

So because these studies have not considered the significance of gender, never mind explored it, the explanations for actions and behaviour offered are at best partial and at worst inadequate and misleading.

Although there are crucial explanations for this systematic neglect of gender within sociology and the sociology of education, (5) in some senses there are no defensible reasons. Sociology is, after all, about 'questioning what we previously took for granted' (Berger). Developments in the 1970s within the sociology of educa-tion should have opened up the possibilities of recognizing the significance of gender along with class and race in determining social processes and structures. The 'new' directions (6) should have made us even more critically aware of existing assumptions and perspectives as we questioned what counted for legitimate knowledge.

Also, face-to-face relations have been raised to levels of new consciousness in the research and literature through the various interpretative perspectives,(7) which should give scope to recognize the gender of the actor engaged in constructing his or her own reality. Yet the fruits of much labour are disappointing. For example, the spate of classroom interaction studies have focused on pupil as pupil and teacher as teacher: neutralized and neutered categories which can only be fully understood in relation to pupil and teacher also as girl/boy/woman/man; working class/middle class; black/white; young/old.(8)

Marxist perspectives in education (9) have necessarily broken down formerly reified boundaries between school and the outside world, particularly the labour market. Yet these have too often neglected to recognize the invisibility of women due to their primary positioning in the home and the domestic labour market, which is crucially subordinated to the labour market.(10)

So, whereas the sociology of how class permeates every dimension of social life from thought and language patterns to life chances has reached an incredible level of sophistication - often such that it becomes paradoxically inaccessible, even to most sociologists - gender is still not considered problematic in similar ways. Consequently it is often hived off as something which is either only about women or something that only female sociologists are concerned with.

Recognizing the sociological significance of gender thus involves being crically aware of the gaps and inadequacies of the existing analyses; but we also need to suggest ways in which gender does operate within educational processes and structures.

I want now to explore some of these ideas in relation to my own research, which consisted of an intensive participant observation study of 230 girls at two urban single-sex schools: a grammar and a secondary modern.

Initially, in the summer of 1975, I selected this focus and style of research for two main reasons. First, as a sociologist and a teacher I was interested in school processes, and the relationship between what formally went on at school and the crucial informal levels of the 'hidden curriculum'. I wanted to understand the dynamics of pupils' friendship groups and the polarization between academically orientated pro-school pupils and the anti-school sub-cultures. Second, I was rather naively concerned with the lack of studies on girls, either in school or in the youth culture literature.

I thus gained access to two girls' schools: an unstreamed grammar which selected pupils from all areas of the city, including a predominantly white working-class post-war council housing estate from which the secondary modern school of my choice drew its girls. The two schools were a mere hockey pitch away from each other, and there seemed a certain amount of hostility between them, suggested by contemporary reports in the local newspaper whereby both schools had opposed recent plans concerning comprehensive reorganization into one community college. Thus there seemed plenty of scope for sociological inquiry both within and between the two institutions. I wanted to explore adolescent girls' involvement in, and commitment to, their school environment across the range of those 'succeeding' and those 'failing' academically. I was aware of the class-based nature of this division within the educational system, although obviously unsure of the specific dynamics.

As the focus of my study was to be the adolescent girl as 'successful' or 'failing' pupil, I wanted to enter the field as 'one of the girls'. This proved to be considerably more problematic than I could have ever envisaged. Despite the difficulties,(11) which unfortunately I have no space to describe or analyse, I persevered and attended the two institutions throughout the girls' fourth and fifth years at school. I spent five days a week (two or three days at each) for the entire school year September 1975 to July 1976, and two or three days a week regularly throughout the subsequent academic year. I was involved in every aspect of school life with the girls from quick fags in the lavvies to inter-form hockey tournaments and being humiliated in French lessons for only getting three out of twenty for my test. Although the girls were aware that I was undertaking some sort of project on girls in school, I spent so much time with them that they tended to forget this, and they did not relate their personal contact with me to me trying to find out and question them about aspects of their lives. Throughout the two years I maintained this contact with the entire range of girls both from the various cliques of friends in the three grammar school forms and the seven streamed classes of the secondary modern. I was thus able to gain access to almost the entire range of activities available to and engaged in by the girls: from reading magazines, listening to records and chatting in bedrooms; to evangelical church services and coffee evenings; and hanging around the streets of the estate, and the occasional fair.

Obviously I collected a vast amount of data. Primarily this was in the form of daily journal notes and recordings of informal conversations and interviews with girls and teachers. I also collected detailed diaries for a week from all the girls and two questionnaires: a lengthy one at the end of the fourth year, and one on leaving the school at the end of the fifth year.

I want to return now to illustrating and pursuing some of the ideas I outlined at the beginning of this article. Once I had entered the field I encountered a mass of problems and dilemmas, some of them generally related to this style of research, others more specifically concerned with the focus of my study. These latter involved the difficulties of gaining some sort of purchase on the privatized, fairly excluding spheres inhabited by adolescent girls.(12) All participant observers must be initially overwhelmed by the mass of potential data surrounding them, but I felt particularly confused by the actions and behaviour of the girls around me. How could I understand their relations with each other, with their teachers, the relationship of school-based activities and behaviour to the wider social context of estate life, suburbia, and the home and family setting? Partly this is explained by the complexity of social reality. But more importantly I would argue that it was because I was unconsciously trying to understand what was going on around me in relation to existing concepts and frameworks of analysis, whilst not recognizing or questioning the limitations due to what they were based upon: empirical work on boys at school and male youth culture, and a neglect of gender as a sociologically

significant dimension of analysis. Whilst there is nothing inher-
ently unsociological about selecting an area of interest to research,
the assumptions and implications of this process do need to be
clearly stated and understood. However, the fact and significance
of the focus of these studies being boys, not simply pupils at
school, and lads, not simply working-class adolescents hanging
around the streets, has been lost - considered too obvious to be
worth mentioning. Because it was empirically unproblematic, it was
not theoretically acknowledged or conceptualized in terms of what
part does gender centrally play in structuring everyday experiences
as well as life chances?

   In studying girls you cannot get away so easily with neglecting
gender, because you are forced to acknowledge that what happens to
them is determined within certain boundaries by the very fact of
their being girls, and not only by their being pupils or working
class or academically successful. These latter dimensions are
crucially interrelated with the very complex concept of 'being
female'.(13)

   Thus I would argue that there are always distinct 'female' and
'male' experiences of any situation, as well as shared levels of
meaning through being working class or successful within the classroom.(14) Furthermore, it is not simply a matter of charting the
girls' side of the picture or combining it with what we already
know about boys, because it is necessary to understand and concep-
tualize the whole. This involves complex articulations between
male and female experiences of gender and other cross-cutting dimensions of class, race and age.(15) Crucially, girls' and women's
experiences are structured in response to male definitions, and
therefore data relating to the previous invisibility of females can
not simply be 'filled in' because it raises crucial questions as to
how the previous work has been understood.

   So, for the remainder of this article I should like to indicate
some of the more specific confusions of my fieldwork in relation to
friendship groupings amongst the girls, and suggest ways in which
the actions and behaviour described can be meaningfully understood
only when gender is centrally incorporated into the analysis.

   During the process of observing, participating and trying to
understand the informal groupings amongst the entire range of girls,
many significant facts and patterns emerged which needed explanations. From these I want to discuss four observed illustrations of
how gender affected the girls' friendship groupings. These are:
the inflexible nature of these groupings; the stereotyped images
which arose between groups; the individual isolation of the non-
exam secondary modern girls; and the contradictory pressures exerted
on the girls, as illustrated by the paradoxical position of Sandy.

   First, the groupings of girls tended to be fairly static or
exclusive, irrespective of the formal organization of the school;
i.e., whether it was rigidly streamed or not. It seemed that the
criteria for friendship groupings were not determined primarily or
even very significantly by academic and school-based factors.

   However, the organizational divisions obviously shaped the daily
lives of the girls to some extent. Where these divisions created
and maintained boundaries separating the girls, such as between
the three unstreamed forms of the grammar school, and the exam/non-

exam classes of the secondary modern, this distance enabled certain
stereotyped views to be developed and perpetuated. The nature of
these images relates not simply to the school context which produced
them. So, to the top exam stream of the secondary modern the non-
exam streams were 'thick', 'daft', 'dillons', and also 'gangish',
'loud-mouthed':

'You wouldn't catch us clomping round the place like them.'
'Ee - you hear the language on 'em.'
'Eh-up, the way they stick together - it ain't natural, yelling
at lads across park.'

Likewise the non-exam girls perceived the top stream girls as
'clever', 'snotty', 'keenos', 'stuck up', but also:

'Exams won't get them nowhere, they'll be out with their prams
next year - if anyone'll have 'em.'
'You seen the way they dress? - wouldn't be seen dead like that.'
''Taint never seen them with a lad.'

So the various stereotypical images employ notions of gender and
of appropriate feminine behaviour. This was one of the most per-
tinent dimensions - albeit a very complex one - on which the girls
judged themselves, each other and their teachers (male and female):
the extent to which they conformed to certain internalized - from
birth onwards - notions of appropriate gender behaviour and characteristics. It was not the only criterion by which the girls
judged the people around them which simultaneously informed and
defined the way they behaved towards females and males in social
situations; but it was a crucial, much glossed over and invisible
dimension, especially as it was so well internalized and personalized. The following conversation indicates the range of criteria
employed by a group of top-stream girls as they discuss Diane.
This girl had been placed in the top stream on her arrival at the
school in the second year, but by the end of the third year she had
been demoted to a non-exam stream.

M.L.   I didn't realize Diane Snail used to be in your form?
Debra   Yes, it was awful. Fomper [Deputy Headmistress] must
          have been stupid to put her in with us. She was useless,
          do you remember? She couldn't do the work, she asked
          dumb questions, and just sat there - well, you know
          what she's like.
M.L.   Well, yes, but what was she like when she first came?
Debra   The same - she just didn't fit in - we were the best
          form, still are, and we didn't want Snail spoiling that
          - she was no good, she smelt.
M.L.   Oh come on, she doesn't smell that much.
Lesley   Look at the way she dresses, Mandy.... Those horrible
          old jumpers all orange and whatsit - purple - and skirts
          nearly down to her ankles or above her knees. Reckon
          her Mum goes round the jumble sales - or the neighbours
          give her their left-overs, or maybe Diane just finds
          them when she's walking round the streets!
M.L.   Oh - maybe her family ain't got much money for clothes.
Debbie   I wouldn't go out looking like that, I'd stay in.
Debra   Me Dad's off work and me Mum don't buy me things - but
          you can manage with what you've got. She could wash her
          clothes and iron 'em....

Debbie	And her hair's a mess - it sticks out all over the place ... and her face - when she comes to school with all her make-up on - oh, it's horrible - all blue and her skin's all blotchy.
Lesley	Yer - and she can pluck her eyebrows. That don't cost nowt.
Debra	Trouble is she's too stupid to realize what she looks like.
Debbie	No wonder all the lads run away from her.
Lesley	Have you seen her ... she goes over the boys' field and waits for 'em - she has to up to them and ask 'em out! (Laughter.)
Debbie	Yer ... and pay for 'em! (More laughter.)

Thus Diane was truly ostracized, because she was 'failing' and 'discredited' on every dimension that was important to these girls: (1) In relation to school, Diane was (a) an academically 'failing' pupil, and also (b) a 'non-conforming' to the norms of that class-room pupil. (2) As an adolescent, she didn't conform to the precise teen-scene fashion norms as regards dress, hair-style, use of make-up. (3) All the girls were working class, yet intra-class differences are also crucial referents, and Diane and her family were seen as rough, inadequate in relation to the norms of working-class respectability. (4) She was also seen as a 'bad girl' in that she engaged in non-appropriate feminine behaviour, such as taking the lead in relation to boys.(16)

It is important to realize that Diane was not accepted with open arms by the non-exam girls in the fourth year, as an outcast from the top stream. She was further rejected and ostracized by them for the same sets of reasons because these criteria cut across the school-based factors. The only difference was that within the context of the classroom she was utilized as an obliging scapegoat to pass the time more interestingly, and therefore momentarily accepted.

A further area of confusion, which emerged after prolonged con-tact with all the girls, was that, despite the perceptions of the top streams of the secondary modern school towards the non-exam groups, there was very little contact, friendship or solidarity between the non-exam girls, even though to outsiders (other girls, teachers) they appeared to go around in a tightly knit gang. The composition of this group was constantly changing (partly due to truancy and non-attendance), and friendship and loyalty links were virtually non-existent. This was manifested very clearly in the spatial arrangements of lessons, where girls sat apart, separated and isolated from each other, a fact which contrasted vividly with the frenetic seating arrangements of the grammar school girls. As a result of this separation (17) the girls' resistance to their lessons and teachers was either individualized and personalized: day dreaming, filing and painting nails, writing initials on desks and books; or invisible: they 'skived' off school. These patterns of behaviour make interesting comparisons with the anti-school model of groups of pupils (boys!) challenging en masse the teacher's authority.

The different social and personal realities available to

adolescent girls, the lack of power they had to define themselves
and the situations around them, and the inadequacies of existing
(male) explanations, were well illustrated by one girl, Sandy. In
many conventional ways, Sandy was the high-status girl of the low
streams at the secondary modern. Everyone knew her, her sisters
had preceded her through the school, she was one of the school's
personalities. She was considered a problem by the staff, a
trouble-maker, coming from a difficult home background. Further,
her parents didn't support the school's attempts to contain her, so
within the classroom Sandy had considerable power to define proceedings.

Yet she was very isolated both at school and outside it, unlike
her male counterpart who would have reigned supreme with an admir-
ing group of lads in tow. Outside of the classroom - where
Sandy's antics constituted light relief and amusement - the other
girls didn't have to go along with Sandy's definition of situations
and appropriate behaviour: because they were not the dominant
forms, of which a crucial component is gender-specific. Thus Sandy
was not only a failing, non-conforming pupil coming from a rough
working-class family, but she also deviated from accepted definitions of appropriate feminine behaviour: for example, by initiating
contact with lads and being publicly sexually explicit when she
yelled out to them. As such, she was a threat to the rest of the
girls and the boys in the challenge she represented to their widely
and firmly held norms. Contradictorily, she was also a source of
comfort to the girls. The unenviable picture of her constantly
reminded and reinforced their notions of what constituted 'female'
status: a goal which they could all attain, irrespective of class
location and educational performance. Thus there was very much a
feeling amongst them that they had the last laugh. As two girls
commented to me as we watched Sandy striding ahead across the park:

Gill   Look at 'er, yelling at them lads. She thinks she knows
        it all ... silly cow - what a mouth on it.
Ann   Don't make no difference, though ... you should hear
        what me brother and his mates say about 'er.
Gill   I know ... all 'er talk and more besides ... don't get
        her nowhere. (Laughter.)

Similar ideas were reproduced by those in power and authority.
Crucial messages were transmitted to the listening audiences of
girls as well as Sandy in the below incidents:

'Just calm down, Sandy; with a temper like yours, my girl,
you'll be lucky if you get a husband ... and if you do, you
won't keep him if you treat him the way you do your teachers.
Come on, calm down, do you really want to end up like your
sister? ... back home no sooner out of it with two kids and
bruises ...' (Senior master placating Sandy after a classroom
flare-up)

'Come on, Sandy, in you come, don't want to talk about your
family's "business" in the corridor. Come on, stop picking on
the others ... just because they behave sensibly and act like
young ladies ...' (He puts his arm round her shoulder.) 'I
don't know - I would have thought you'd enough sense to settle
down - you're too old for fighting now. Look at the mess your

hair and clothes are in. The least you could do is to try and
look nice, even if you can't behave nicely.... Come on, let's
see how things are going at home ...' (Educational Welfare
Officer talking to Sandy prior to informal 'chat')

The 'tone' of the teacher and welfare officer are different, and
to understand the two situations fully more needs to be explored in
terms of the class-based nature of the interaction between teacher
and pupil, and concerned officer and 'client', within the context
of an estate secondary school. However, in such considerations the
gender dimension is often neglected, or taken for granted and ren-
dered invisible, and yet these are important 'moments' in the
transmission of appropriate feminine ideologies. And this is much
more central to the process of schooling than is recognized. As
one concerned and distressed senior mistress confided to me:

'I wouldn't mind, Mandy, ... to be honest, I can understand the
girls kicking their heels against the lessons. They're boring,
the teachers don't bother, and it won't bring them better jobs
... whatever we say ... but some of those girls - Sandy - the
language she uses - but it's not that, it's so much more, oh ...
I don't know, I just feel we've failed. She's no decency, I
can't see her ever settling down and making a loving home ... I
don't mean she should only be a wife and mother ... but she
won't get anywhere as she is ... we haven't given her a chance
... we've failed ...'

The school had 'failed', not simply at the formal, but crucially
subordinated, level of providing basic skills and qualifications,
but also at the informal 'hidden' dominant level of transmitting
ideologies of appropriate values and behaviour to the adolescent
working-class girl.

Within the context of this chapter, I have only been able to
draw briefly and rather sketchily upon my own research data. I
hope that enough has been explored to indicate how the implications
of confusion in empirical studies of girls at school, or out of
school, are not simply the product of muddled thinking, but are
rather demonstrating that we need to understand the complexity of
how gender shapes social reality, as well as studies of it. Feminist perspectives in all these areas are central to the task.(18)

NOTES

1 Throughout the 1960s and 1970s there have been numerous studies
   of boys at school, their academic performance, involvement in
   and commitment to school, friendship groupings, etc. Probably
   the most interesting are Hargreaves (1967) and Lacey (1970).
   For a detailed summary of such research see Banks (1976).
2 Willis (1977).
3 As Mungham and Pearson (1976) comment: 'There is an appalling
   neglect in the considerable literature on adolescence of
   young women and girls. Youth culture is held to be synonymous
   with male youth culture.' Nevertheless they still entitle
   their edited collection of articles 'Working Class Youth
   Culture'.
4 This is briefly and very interestingly discussed by McRobbie

and Garber (1976). It may well be that this is how adolescent
girls are seen by their male counterparts, but that is no
defence for the male researcher to reproduce those views uncrit-
ically, thus making them implicitly his own.

5 This is an important area for feminist sociologists to tackle,
and the literature is growing. See, for example, the introductory chapter in Oakley (1976); Fuller (1978); Lightfoot (1975).

6 See the so-called 'new' sociology of education literature,
sparked off by the publication of articles edited by Young
(1971). A central characteristic of these new directions was
to challenge (some) existing assumptions and approaches in the
methodology and findings of the studies of the 1950s and 1960s.

7 The various ethnomethodological and phenomenological approaches
filtering through the sociology of education during the 1970s
have been most noticeable in the classroom interaction studies.
See Delamont (1976) and Woods and Hammersley (1977).

8 One of the most striking examples of this is in Furlong's (1976)
work on interaction in the classroom. In his own research he
stresses the fluidity of pupils' interaction patterns and
rightly asserts that existing analyses have failed to grapple
with these complexities and have not given sufficient credi-
bility to participants' own accounts of behaviour. Yet he
himself neglects to incorporate into his analysis the crucial
factors that the 'pupils' he studied were girls and West
Indian. He thus cannot adequately account for the complexity
of behaviour he observed and recorded.

9 I am referring here to recent contributions by Bernstein (1977),
Bourdieu (1973), Sharp and Green (1976), Bowles and Gintis
(1976) and Willis (1977), although the first two are not,
strictly speaking, Marxists. While there is some scope within
these writings for understanding the 'special' position of
girls and women in the educational process, this is never specifically addressed.

10 An important contribution within a Marxist feminist framework
has been made by Wolpe (1977).

11 These ranged from coping with vexed teachers' responses to my
uninvited presence as one of the girls, to dilemmas concerning
how far I should take involvement at adolescent parties.

12 This crucial aspect of any research on girls has been well
noted by McRobbie and Garber (1976). The failure of much
research to overcome these difficulties or appreciate them is
self-evident in Ward's (1977) comment in his introduction: 'One
curious feature of this study as it turned out: we find ourselves saying rather little, certainly much less than might
have been expected, about the girls' attitudes to boys, relationships with them, and feelings of importance about this.'

13 The complexity of the concept of 'femininity' is thoughtfully
discussed in Marks (1976). Ideas concerning 'femininity' vary
not only over time, but between different social and ethnic
groups at any one time. Thus, amongst my sample of girls there
was a differing range of appropriate behaviours expected from
each other and themselves as girls.

14 This concept of 'female experience' as distinct from 'male
experience' was most vividly illustrated to me on a school trip

to York with a small group of the grammar school girls. We had
spent days chatting, within the safety of an all-girls-together
classroom, about what we were going to wear, what we were going
to do there, and which sights to see. Yet from the minute we
arrived and started walking about - a group of six or seven
young females - we were followed and chatted up and even
touched by groups of lads; and we spent the entire day running
down streets, going in coffee bars to get away, keeping a look-
out in the shops and cathedral to see if they followed us in.
My entire 'female' perspective recollection of York is of eyes
lowered at pavements and steps, and shops where we pretended
to separate and look at souvenirs!

15 This point is discussed in the introduction to articles written
    by the Women's Study Group, Centre for Contemporary Cultural
    Studies, 1978.

16 These criteria, polarized in terms of: successful/failing pupil;
    conforming/non-conforming pupil; girlish/adolescent; rough/
    respectable inter and intra class differences; 'good'/'bad'
    girl, are crucial in understanding the ways in which the
    entire range of girls judged themselves and their peers.
    Although interrelated, the various dimensions are significantly
    identifiable as separate strands.

17 Here I would want to suggest that the significance being
    attached to solidarity between girls and the notion of best
    friend by McRobbie (1978) is idealizing and oversimplifying
    the complex reality of social relations between girls. Some
    girls are very involved and self-sufficient with their female
    friends and others are not - all for important and explicable
    reasons. The specific group of girls I am discussing here were
    involved in an important transition phase: school had ceased
    to have much meaning to them, they looked towards the adult
    world of work and social relations, and they were disdainful
    of the childish antics of the girls who hung around together;
    they had moved on to 'better' company - men!?

18 This chapter is based on a paper originally given at the BERA
    Seminar on 'Women, Education and Research', 14-16 April 1978.

Chapter 4

Black girls in a London comprehensive school

Mary Fuller

In the areas of housing, the law, employment, education and welfare, black people and women continue to be disadvantaged in comparison with men and whites. The facts of racial and sexual disadvantage in Britain mean that, whatever their social class, black women and girls are in a doubly subordinate position within the social formation.

With regard to education, those people in Britain writing about academic aspirations and achievement of pupils have compared black and white pupils, and made similar comparisons between females and males. At the time when I began my research (in 1975) I was unable to find any instance of work which attempted to analyse simultaneously the bearing which pupils' sex and race might have in this area. With the single exception of Driver (1977), writing about the academic achievements of black pupils continues to treat them as a sexually undifferentiated group (see, for example, Little, 1978). Other writers, working in the interactionist and/deviancy tradition, and concerned to document and analyse the experiential world of the adolescent, inside and outside school, have been equally limited in their focus. Their efforts have been almost exclusively concentrated on white sub-cultures - with Sharpe (1976) being a notable exception - and the balance being heavily towards male (and white) adolescent experiences and cultural expressions. In other words, not only does this tradition in sociology treat the world of adolescence as essentially male, but it also considers adolescents to be racially undifferentiated.

What seemed to be clear was that black pupils were under-achieving academically,(1) and that black youth (and some parents) were increasingly disaffected from schooling (Dondy, 1974). It seemed equally clear from the studies by Hargreaves (1967) and Lacey (1970) that similar anti-school and what were termed 'delinquent' sub-cultures among white boys were related to the pupils' social class. In the cases of both race and social class, disaffection from school and relatively poor scholastic performance were connected.

In the absence of specific work about them it was difficult to know where black girls came into this schema. If one assumed the primacy of social class and/or racial category in developing an

anti-school stance, black girls could be straightforwardly accommodated, since there would be little difference between them and
their male peers. But the fact of being female might alter this
picture - by virtue of their sex girls are in a particular subordinate position. There are no a priori reasons for assuming a
greater importance for either sex or race in this respect, and no
certain guidelines as to the effect of an interaction between the
two. From logic and guesswork only, the fact of being female
could have rather different implications for black girls' sub-
cultural response to schooling. Given an additive model of subordination, it would seem that black girls would be essentially like
their male peers, only more so; i.e., even more disaffected than
similar male pupils. On the other hand, and in line with the
common view that females as a group are more conformist, less
likely to rebel and generally less 'troublesome' in the school
context (Levy, 1972), black girls could be expected to demonstrate
similar but less strongly manifested alienation from school. This
is not something to be decided by logic; rather it is an empirical
question, though not, as already indicated, one which has actually
been given prominence by previous writers.

In this chapter I shall describe a small group of black girls
(of West Indian parentage, though mostly themselves of British
birth) who formed a discernible sub-culture in the comprehensive
school in which I carried out research during 1975 and 1976. As
part of a much larger study (2) involving male and female pupils
from Indo-Pakistani, West Indian and white British family backgrounds I spent two terms in the school in daily participation and
observation of pupils' school lives. At that time and subsequently,
observational material was supplemented by interviews, questionnaires and the analysis of various school documents. The larger
project aimed to examine in what ways pupils' and teachers' sex-
structured their position within the school as well as the ways in
which teachers' and pupils' relations with each other were structured by their respective notions of gender (i.e. masculinity/
femininity). Hence the work took place in a mixed school. To confront adequately the question 'How much does sex matter in school?'
some additional and equally important referent is required, so
that inferences about sexual differentiation may be subject to
alternative explanation.(3) For this reason the school selected
was multi-racial, and the possibility of social class and race as
alternative or additional explanations for differentiation among
pupils was integrated into the analysis. This point has been
laboured because in the ordinary way a study based on only eight
people could hardly expect to be taken as a serious contribution
to the sociological literature; although in our present state of
ignorance concerning black girls and schooling, such considerations
might be waived.

As I shall go on to argue, the existence and specific defining
features of this sub-culture of black girls call into question some
of our present assumptions and thinking, not only about black
pupils but also about the development of school-based sub-cultures.
I make this argument with greater confidence because what follows,
while relating to a small and particular group, is informed by
constant comparisons with other same-age peers within the school:
male and female, white, Asian and black.

TORVILLE SCHOOL

The school was a ten-form entry comprehensive in the north London
Borough of Brent, and the students, in their final year of compulsory schooling, were aged 15 to 16 years. The fifth year was
divided into two parallel bands, one containing 128 pupils who
followed a mixed curriculum of practical/vocational subjects with
some more academic ones, and who would be expected to take some
'O' level or CSE exams; the other band (the one with which I worked)
containing 142 pupils following a more thoroughgoing academic
curriculum, with the expectation that they would take a rather
larger number of 'O' level and CSE exams than those in the practical band.

The academic band contained significantly fewer girls than boys
(with the reverse sex-ratio in the practical band). There were
fewer West Indian girls in the academic than the practical band,
as was true also of white British and Asian girls. Although there
were in general more boys in the academic than the practical band,
a greater proportion (and absolute number) of West Indian boys was
to be found in the practical band. Relating this to other writers'
work (e.g., Coard, 1971; Troyna, 1976), it is clear that the situation with regard to West Indian boys, but not with respect to
girls, confirms the view that West Indian pupils are found in disproportionate numbers in the lower streams (or equivalent groupings)
within school.

Within the fifth year nearly a quarter of pupils was of West
Indian parentage, a further one in four were of Indo-Pakistani
parentage, and just over half were white and British-born with
only a very few other white Europeans. Within the academic band
the majority of West Indian pupils was British-born, whereas the
majority of Asian students was immigrant (with by far the majority
of these being of East African rather than Indian sub-continental
birth).

THE GIRLS

Five of the eight girls were British-born, three having migrated
to Britain from Jamaica, two when aged 3, and one when aged 11.
One of the British-born girls had spent four years in the West
Indies as a small child (aged 2 to 6). Six lived in a two-parent
family and two in mother-headed families. All had at least one
brother or sister living with them, and in most cases considerably
more than one. The mothers of six of the girls were permanently
employed outside the home in full-time jobs, one girl's mother had
a permanent part-time job, and in one case the mother took seasonal jobs according to availability. All six fathers were
normally in permanent full-time jobs. The girls came from predominantly manual working-class homes (five) with two having a
father in a manual but a mother in a non-manual job; one girl had
both parents in non-manual employment.

Although the sub-culture comprised girls in the same age-group
attending the same school, in many important respects it was not
simply or mainly a school-based sub-culture, for in order to make

sense of its structure and values it is necessary to look outside
the school, to the situation of black minorities in Britain generally and also to the situation of women in comparison with men.
The girls consciously drew on these when discussing themselves and
the other girls in their group. In particular they drew on their
knowledge and experience of the West Indies.

WEST INDIAN ROOTS

Most of the black students whom I interviewed had themselves
visited the West Indies in the relatively recent past; all were
closely connected with others who had also returned from visits,
and were in other ways kept apprised of life in the West Indies.
In large part it was their awareness of their Caribbean roots and
the inferences which they drew concerning themselves as females in
that society which underlay and provided the basis both for the
existence of the sub-culture and for an understanding of its values
and particular style. The other part is contributed by the girls'
interpretation of the fact of their female sex in British society.
   From what they had themselves observed and gleaned from others'
accounts the girls had constructed a picture of a physically
demanding and financially unrewarding life for women in the West
Indies, in comparison with which their present and future lives in
Britain seemed favourable.
   'Women back home were really masculine. They had to be. They
   had to go and fetch water, come back and do their washing and
   it was really dirty because they don't have washing machines.
   And they had to get down and really scrub, then after that they
   had really old fashioned irons and had to burn coal to do it,
   plus you've got to starch it, then wet it again and iron it.
   And the men just expect them to do that. So, I mean, they can't
   be really careful what they do.' (Monica)
Foner (1976) suggests that older immigrant women whom she interviewed in London shared this perception. The girls drew a comparison between the life-styles of women and men in the Caribbean,
typifying that of men as pleasanter and less arduous, even though
male unemployment was high. Boys, during interview, also indicated that they believed this to be the case.
   One very important ramification of this picture was that the
girls did not easily envisage a future for themselves in the West
Indies; on the contrary their awareness of their West Indian roots
led them to believe that they would be better off in Britain. On
the other hand a return to the homeland (by which was meant the
West Indies) featured prominently in the boys' thoughts about the
future, sentiments which were frequently given coherence by their
understanding of Rastafarianism. Within the fifth year at Torville
only boys displayed some of the externalia of Rastafarianism - the
wearing of woolly hats in orange, green and black, modified 'locks',
etc. - and had adopted its rhetoric. It may be that because the
option of returning was less (psychologically) available to the
girls that they found a Rasta identity that much more difficult to
contemplate.
   It should not be inferred from this that the girls dissociated

themselves from their Caribbean origins or wanted to be anything other than black. None of the girls indicated in any way that she would prefer to be white, and indeed they were proud to be black. For example, Janice having explicitly defined herself as 'pure black' on several occasions in the interview returned to the theme of blacks who 'go on as if they are a white person', who are the opposite of 'pure black'. She also suggested that '...if a black goes over to white we regard them as traitors, but if a white person comes over to us, we accept them as a black'.

This positive acceptance of themselves as black echoes Ladner's (1971) findings in relation to Afro-American female adolescents. As was the case with many of the Asian and white girls interviewed, the black girls expressed considerable resentment towards their brothers because of what they saw as discrimination in favour of boys within their own families. The basis of their argument was that domestic tasks were unfairly allocated, so that the main burden of the shopping, child-minding, laundry and cooking not undertaken by their mothers fell on the shoulders of the girls in the family. Boys were not expected to contribute to these domestic tasks, or only intermittently, whereas commitments of this kind absorbed considerable amounts of the girls' time out of school. (The boys confirmed that they were not expected to help and only rarely undertook such 'womanish' work.)

The girls in Driver's (1977) study were also undertaking quite onerous domestic commitments. In his discussion of conflict with parents he seems to suggest that relations between girls and their parents are relatively harmonious despite these demands made on the girls. At any rate he does not mention conflicts except in the context of boys and parents. Among the girls at Torville this was the most frequently mentioned topic of arguments with parents, and it was patently a source of considerable friction between girls and their parents as well as between girls and their brothers.

In many cases this resentment extended to boys in general. And yet at the same time the discrepancy in the demands made on girls and boys seemed to provide one of the bases of the girls' greater confidence in their ability. They were inclined to interpret the boys' behaviour as evidence of inability to do even simple things, as signifying 'childishness', 'laziness', and so on. This interpretation seemed all the more plausible to them since it echoed the division of competence, as they perceived it, between their parents within the home. Thus Marcia:

'My dad helps around the house, he only helps with the good things - he never does the washing up.... He's not very good practically, my mum doesn't really approve of him when he's doing his decorating. My mum did the back room actually because my dad did it in this paint and my mum didn't like it so ... she's quite independent really. She's a lot better than my dad at things - he's good at the theory, but not on practical things.'

Though they might envy the boys their greater freedom from domestic chores and freedom of movement the girls nevertheless expressed no desire to be boys, other than in 'idle talk'.

The girls were aware of racial discrimination, recounting

incidents involving themselves and people whom they knew, and were
conscious that such discrimination would probably continue. They
were also aware from a number of sources of the high levels of
unemployment locally and nationally which had double implications
for them as young blacks. They had, as already described, experienced what they themselves interpreted as less favourable treatment because of their sex. The conjunction of all these - their
positive identity as black but knowledge of racial discrimination
in Britain, their positive identity as female but belief that both
in Britain and the Caribbean women were often accorded less than
their due status - meant that the girls were angry at the fore-
closing of options available to them as blacks and as women.

Such a conjunction might be supposed to engender apathy and
despair, but quite the reverse was the case. Discussing working-
class pupils, White and Brockington (1978, p.111) also note that
'Anger and frustration, consolidated and supported, is not wasted
but can motivate to action'. The girls' forms of action and the
import of their stance within school need to be understood as
strategies for trying to effect some control over their present
and future lives. Because they considered their futures were
necessarily to be in Britain, these attempts included finding some
modus vivendi with whites which did not undermine their identity as
blacks.

FEATURES OF THE SUB-CULTURE

The sub-culture emerged from the girls' positive acceptance of the
fact of being both black and female. Its particular flavour
stemmed from their critical rejection of the meanings with which
those categorizations are common endowed. Their consequent anger
and frustration, unlike that of their black male peers, was not
turned against themselves or translated into an automatic general
dislike of whites or the opposite sex. Rather their feelings and
understandings gave particular meanings to achievement through the
acquisition of educational qualifications.

The girls were all strongly committed to achievement through
the job market (cf. Ladner, 1971; Slaughter, 1972), being marked
out from the other girls not so much by the type of jobs to which
they were aspiring as by the firmness with which they held their
future job ambitions, and by their certainty that they would want
to be employed whatever their future domestic circumstances might
be:
    'I want a proper job first and some kind of skill so that if I
    do get married and have children I can go back to it; don't
    want just relying on him for money, 'cause I've got to look
    after myself. There must be something I can do.' (Michelle)
and Monica's view of herself is very similar in this respect:
    'I should go out to work because, really, if I don't start
    learning to get on with it, I maybe will just have to leave
    home, get married and depend on the husband and I don't want
    that at all ... the picture of myself is an active one, always
    doing something, I don't know what. Mybe I'll be a housewife
    or something like that, but I always picture myself working.'

They were also strong believers in the value of education and educational qualifications as a necessary preparation for the 'good' jobs which they hoped to obtain - or more accurately, perhaps, they took such a belief for granted. They were confident of their ability to achieve the academic qualifications which they were aiming for, both in the short term (i.e. 'O' level and/or CSE) and in the longer term ('A' level and/or a variety of examinations to be taken at college, polytechnic or university).

This optimism extended to their wider life-chances. Conscious of actual incidents of racial discrimination and the possibility of discrimination against them because of their colour and sex, and aware of the high levels of unemployment locally and nationally which had double implications for them as young people and blacks, the girls nevertheless believed that in the job market there was much that they could do to forestall ending up in low level, dead-end jobs, or finding themselves unemployed on leaving school. They spoke of this in terms of being 'ambitious', but equally, ensuring that whatever ambitions they had were not deflected.

As will be clear, acquisition of academic qualifications was an integral part of this sense of control over their future. What was less immediately obvious was the underlying relationship of academic qualifications to the girls' sense of self-worth. In a very real sense they perceived the obtaining of academic qualifica-tions as a public statement of something which they already knew about themselves but which they were also certain was given insuf-ficient public recognition: that they were capable, intelligent, and the equal of boys.

> 'I think people trust you more when you're a boy; they say
> you're more reliable, you're more trustworthy. Because my dad
> always says that, he says you can take a boy and you can show
> him a trade, but you can take a girl and the next minute their
> heads are all filled up with boys, that she just doesn't want
> to know. So I'm going to show him, you see!' (Beverley)

That is, their sense of self-worth did not derive from the acquisi-tion of academic qualifications nor, in the future, from obtaining a 'good' job; rather their pursuit of these ends was given meaning by their existing knowledge of their own worth and their under-standing that this was often denied. During interviews most of the girls said they thought boys considered themselves superior to girls, an idea which they viewed with amused disbelief or scepticism.

> 'Most West Indian boys definitely aren't going to let a woman
> dominate them or tell them what to do, they firmly believe that
> they're the boss and she has to do everything.... They just
> have this thing that they are the superior ones and women are
> inferior. This equality business - I don't think that it would
> ever work in the West Indies, don't think they'd accept it,
> might here. And I don't think the West Indian boys growing up
> here, I don't think they're going to accept it either because
> they always talk about it as a load of rubbish anyway, because
> as far as they're concerned they're superior and they're not
> going to be equal with a woman, or anything like than.'
> (Christa)

The written word does not readily convey the tone in which Christa spoke, but what was clear was that she, together with most of the other girls, did not take it as self-evident that males were superior or deserved to be taken more seriously than herself.

To this point in their careers the girls' confidence appeared well-founded; they had passed a greater number of 'O' level and CSE exams, and at rather higher grades than had the black boys. The black girls achieved a mean of 7.6 passes at this level compared with 5.6 for the black boys, an achievement which put them second only to Asian boys in performance in 'O' level and CSE. Similarly, while all the girls had remained in full-time education for at least one year beyond the statutory school-leaving age, only two of the black boys had done so. Where girls had left school or college to take up employment, all mentioned that they were also continuing their education by day release or block release schemes or by attending college in the evenings; only one boy mentioned that he was continuing his education in any way.

So far the picture drawn seems to be that of the girls as archetypal 'good' pupils - ones who have high aspirations and achieve well in public examinations - but this was far from the truth in most other aspects of their lives in school. Unlike other pupils who were similarly pro-education, the black girls were not pro-school. That is to say, their intolerance of the daily routines and their criticisms of much that went on inside the school were marked. They shared with some other pupils a view of school as 'boring', 'trivial' and 'childish', and yet at the same time were markedly different from these same pupils in that they had high aspirations and a high degree of academic success. Despite their critical view of school the black girls did not define it as 'irrelevant' (as did other pupils who found school boring, etc.), because of the particular importance which they attached to academic achievement. Quine (1974) discusses a similar orientation among the boys in his study of two Midland comprehensive schools.

Most high aspirers and achievers in the school were concerned to demonstrate their seriousness of purpose to teachers and other pupils by certain kinds of classroom behaviour: punctuality, a modicum of attention to lesson content, and a 'respectful' (by no means always deferential) attitude towards teachers, in addition to actually doing the work set. Whether they actively courted a good reputation in other ways or not, such pupils tended to be seen as 'good' pupils. The reverse of this behaviour was taken by both teachers and pupils to indicate a lack of interest in school and was associated with a reputation as a 'bad' pupil.

The black girls conformed to the stereotypes of the good pupil only in so far as they worked conscientiously at the schoolwork or homework set. But they gave all the appearances in class of not doing so, and in many other ways displayed an insouciance for the other aspects of the good pupil role. They neither courted a good reputation among teachers nor seemed to want to be seen as 'serious' by the staff or other pupils. Eschewing behaviour which would bring them into serious conflict with teachers (for example, truanting, direct challenges to a teacher's authority, grossly disruptive behaviour within the classroom), the girls were frequently involved in activities which exasperated the staff and which were yet not quite clearly misdemeanours requiring comment or action on their part. The following examples drawn from field notes represent incidents which occurred with some frequency: openly engaging in some 'illegitimate' activity (reading a magazine, chatting, doing homework for another subject) so that it appeared that the girls were not listening or not working, yet when questioned by the teacher they could show that they had, in fact, taken in what had been said or had actually completed the work assigned; arriving technically late for a lesson but actually seconds before the teacher, who could see their late arrival; handing in work for marking when it suited them rather than immediately it was asked for; complying with a teacher's request somewhat slowly and with a show of complete uninterest, and so on. Studying delinquent pupils (some of them black) in an American high school, Werthman (1963) describes somewhat similar behaviour. Neither meek and passive nor yet aggressive, and obviously confrontationist in their stance towards teachers, the girls were something of a puzzle to some of their peers and teachers.

Three themes emerged in their discussions of the stance they adopted within school. First, to be seen as a 'good' pupil, i.e., showing too much eagerness in class, appearing to take school too seriously, risked the discovery of their academic and job ambitions and consequently invited ridicule and possibly more from those peers with whom the girls most frequently compared themselves - black boys.

'I find that most boys do have ambitions but they're influenced by their friends, so they never get put into practice anyway....
I think the girls are more ambitious but if they want to do something they don't feel embarrassed about it except when boys, when they hear you're doing 'O' levels, they won't come out with it and say you're a snob but they treat you a bit differently and you can feel it.... I think West Indian girls might feel a bit funny about that.' (Joan)

'I've always got my head in a book. I don't think they [boys in school] like it because they are always commenting on it and they say "You won't get anywhere", and sometimes I think they don't want me to learn or something like that, you know; but I spoke to my mum about it, and she said I shouldn't listen and I should keep working hard.' (Marcia)

In this way their classroom behaviour may be seen as a conscious smoke-screen to confuse others and enable the girls to retain the friendship of their peer group without giving up their aspirations.

Second, to be viewed by teachers as a 'good' pupil was inconsistent with the girls' own view of themselves. 'Good' pupils were boring, were unable to have 'fun', and were in other respects 'immature'. To behave in class like them would invite comparison with people from whom the girls expressly distanced themselves.

Third, the girls believed that other highly aspiring pupils placed too great an emphasis on teachers' opinions in relation to pupils' success: in so far as public examinations were marked by people who did not know the candidates personally, pupils could expect to pass exams on the quality of their work rather than on the quality of their relationship with the teachers who taught them. Very few other pupils discussed pupil-teacher relationships in this way.

The black girls' behaviour within the classroom is, I suggest, intimately connected with their positive identity as black and female. It seems reasonable to suppose that in coming to a sense of their own worth the girls had learnt to rely on their own rather than others' opinion of them. Their weighing up of the potential relevance and importance of teachers was part of a more general stance towards others. The girls were relatively sophisticated in judging who did and did not matter in their pursuit of academic qualifications, for example, so that one could say they adopted a somewhat 'strategic' political stand in relation to other people, including whites generally and white authority in school specifically.

To some extent this can also be seen in their social relationships with other pupils. The girls appeared to treat poor relationships as a resource of essentially individualistic achievement aims rather than as a source of pleasure and/or confirmation in its own right. The girls came together as a result of each of them trying to cope with the difficulties of proving their own worth. This was to be expressed through the acquisition of paper qualifications, not through the living out of a particular peer-based life-style. In a sense the confirmation of the girls' sense of identity could not come from either their peer group or from adults, but only from their own efforts. For this reason the sub-culture was not a readily discernible entity, marked out from others by a particular and visible style. Or rather their style was not the raison d'être of their coming together.

Unlike pupils in other 'academic' sub-cultures described in the literature (e.g., Hargreaves, 1967), the girls did not confine their friendship choices only to other academically inclined pupils, but showed a fluidity of friendship choices among other black but 'non-academic' girls in the school. This indicates, I suggest, that the girls had discovered or assumed that they had little in common with other pupils (white or Asian) who, like them, had high aspirations. That the black girls in the academic band at Torville made their choices of friends from among both academic and non-academic black girls, is partly due to the relatively small number of black pupils from whom to choose. (Similar ethnocentrism in friendship choices is reported by Durojaiye, 1970; Bhatnagar, 1970; Troyna, 1978). The girls' choice of friends does also underline the central importance of both their sex and ethnicity in the girls' identity.

This can also be discerned in their assessment of certain teachers. As already indicated, the girls did not automatically define teachers as adversaries, despite the fact that they behaved in ways which might have been interpreted as giving insufficient respect to teachers, and despite the fact that the girls were critical of many aspects of their daily life in school. Alone among the pupils, a few of the black girls indicated that they greatly admired certain teachers, whom they would like to emulate. As can be seen from the following passage from an interview with Beverley, the reasons for this admiration stem from the fact that the particular teachers in question are thought to demonstrate qualities (of persistence, struggle against convention, etc.) which have a particular resonance with the girls' own current situation. In other

words, the teacher is admired not because she is a teacher or
because she is white, nor even despite these factors, but only
because she has succeeded in the job market. In this respect the
teacher's sex is the salient point.

In reply to my question 'What is it about Miss G that you admire?'
Beverley replied:

'Because she's a careers woman. She succeeded in life at a time
in her days when women were expected to sit around ... she
rebelled against that and she's got what she wanted, got her own
car, got her own flat, completely independent, goes where she
likes when she likes, she's got her own money, you know, she's
well paid. And now she's succeeded and got what she wants out
of life, she's getting married - everything has kind of worked
out for her... she can be very serious and hard-working but at
the same time she can be good fun, you see.'

What is also clear is that this particular teacher is a living
demonstration that success and femininity can be reconciled, and
that success and solemnity are not synonymous. No matter that the
girl's perception of the 'olden days' may be inaccurate and the
difficulties to be overcome exaggerated, the teacher's example is
taken to heart since struggle and resourcefulness (Ladner, 1971)
are important aspects of the girls' ideas about themselves. As the
following incident illustrates, the girls' persistence is already
well-developed:

'When I first went for the job, I was very crafty when I wrote
the letter. I put that I was a student and they thought I was
coming from university, and I did it in perfectly good English
so they wouldn't think that it was a foreign person. And then
when I went and they actually saw that I was coloured I think
they were a bit shocked, so they kept stalling and said come
back tomorrow. They said the person isn't in, can you come
back next week, and I wouldn't give in. Every time they said
come back I'd go back and I'd go back. My dad was backing me
all the way and in the end I got through.' (Christa)

This kind of persistence is much admired and is a source of considerable pride:

'Michelle and I are the same really, we have this thing to
succeed, determined, you know. If anything gets in the way we
kick it out the way and get on.' (Annette)

SUMMARY AND DISCUSSION

In trying to describe and understand the sub-culture of black girls
in a particular school it has been necessary to make frequent comparisons with other people in and outside Torville school itself.
There are two reasons for this. First, as is common in the development of an in-group identity, the girls saw themselves as a
separate group by comparing themselves with other blacks (Rosenberg
and Simmons, 1972) and contrasting themselves with others. Second,
very few features of the sub-culture on their own were unique to
the firls, although the specific configuration of values, attitudes,
behaviour and self-perceptions did mark them out as quite distinct
from other pupils in their year.

Because this sub-culture of West Indian girls contrasts with the general picture of West Indian disaffection from school and low attainment, it would be helpful to know just how prevalent or typical such a sub-culture is of West Indian pupils generally. The majority of writers do not differentiate between boys and girls, and from internal evidence it would appear that much of the work has been based on males, with perhaps the implicit assumption that what is established for males is more or less an accurate representation of the whole group. Because of this lack of differentiation or failure to specify the sex-class of those being studied, it is not possible to give an accurate estimate of the typicality of the sub-culture described of black pupils in general. For very similar reasons, that in the literature on adolescence, schooling, and sub-cultures very little specific attention has been paid to girls in their own right (a lack noted by McRobbie and Garber, 1976; Ward, 1976; among others), it is not possible to gauge just how frequently such a sub-culture may be found among girls. However, Lambart's account of her work in a girls' grammar school is particularly instructive, since her description of the Sisterhood (a group of third-year pupils) suggests a very similar conjunction of academic attainment and non-conformity to the rules, regulations and routines of school (Lambart, 1976, pp.157-9):

They had a sense of fun bordering often on mischief; and they were careful of the 'respect' they have to teachers...despite its deviance, the Sisterhood existed as a focus for girls with more than average ability.

The relationship between academic performance and behaviour within school of the black girls at Torville and Lambart's Sisterhood contrasts with that described for boys by Hargreaves (1967) and Willis (1977). I would argue that this calls into question the necessary equation of academic striving and success with conformity, an equation which the work of Werthman (1963), Holt (1964) and Jackson (1966) in any case indicates is not universal.

Since it is frequently argued that teachers' expectations (4) serve to depress the attainment of certain groups of pupils (including females and blacks), it is particularly interesting that the black girls' achievement was not related to whether teachers saw them as good or bad pupils. Nor was there any relationship between teachers' perception of the girls as pupils and the girls' classroom activities, which contrasts with Driver's (1977) finding of a considerable overlap (particularly in relation to black boys) in the West Midland school he studied.

A radical analysis of schools and schooling points to an underlying ethnocentrism and middle-class bias in the structure, organization and curriculum of all schools. As Reynolds (1976) points out, this leads to viewing school as a battleground of opposing values in which pupils demonstrate their resistance to alien and oppressive race and class values by refusing to conform. It becomes only too easy to assume that academic striving and achievement are synonymous with subscribing (conforming) to these values, and to see school failure as necessarily indicative of rejection of those same values. Apart from the fact that neither Reynolds nor Quine (1974) could find evidence of such polarized stances in the schools they studied, conformity and deviance within the school are rarely

global, but are situation-specific (Werthman, 1963; Furlong, 1976).
Moreover, if further research confirms the disjunction between
academic orientation and within-school behaviour, noted by Lambart
(1976) and in the present study of Torville school, it may be that
the pro-education pro-school connection and its polar opposite
(anti-education, anti-school) emerge as somewhat specific rather
than universal tendencies - specific to boys (and perhaps only a
proportion of these) and/or more typical of particular types of
school.

In this chapter I have described a group of black girls whose
acute awareness of their double subordination as women and black was
accompanied by a refusal to accept the 'facts' of subordination for
themselves. As a strategy for present and future survival the girls
had adopted a programme of 'going it alone' in which those aspects
of schooling to do with acquiring qualifications had an important
part. No more tolerant of the 'irrelevant' aspects of schooling
(e.g., the daily routines) than their black male peers, the girls
were in some ways a good deal more effectively independent of adult
authority than any other group of pupils (male or female) in the
school.

Wilkinson (1975, p.305) argues that

[Black] youth are unlike their white counterparts not only with
respect to placement in the social structure and their definitions of the dynamics of inter-racial relations, but also with
respect to the type of attitudinal orientation which emerges
from their cultural experiences. They are different in the
collective symbolism and self-oriented definitions of who they
are and what they wish to become. For they still must contend
with social issues that never confront white youth.

Miles and Phizacklea (1977, p.495) elaborate this theme, arguing
that 'it is the unique experience of blacks of racial exclusion that
is the essence of black ethnicity'. As I hope has been demonstrated
in this chapter, when racial exclusion is overlaid and combined with
sexual exclusion, it becomes necessary to begin to recognize that
black ethnicity may take different forms and point to differing
strategies for females and males.(5)

NOTES

1   The extensive literature in this area is treated in Fuller
    (1976) Experiences of Adolescents from Ethnic Minorities in the
    British State Education System, in P.J. Bernard (ed.) 'Les
    Travailleurs Etrangers en Europe Occidentale', Mouton, Paris/
    The Hague.
2   See Fuller (1978).
3   The same argument would apply whether the main focus were
    social class or racial category. In other words, analysis of
    sexual differentiation is not a special case, but the use of
    constant comparison is desirable in most research.
4   The classic text here is Rosenthal and Jacobson (1968).
5   The research on which this chapter is based was carried out
    while I was employed at the Social Science Research Council
    Research Unit on Ethnic Relations. This chapter does not

represent the views of SSRC, nor does it necessarily reflect those of the members of the SSRC Unit. I should like to record my thanks to Annie Phizacklea for comments on an earlier draft of this chapter, and to Sarah Pegg who typed the manuscript.

Chapter 5

Education and the individual
Schooling for girls, or
mixed schooling – a mixed blessing?

Jennifer Shaw

In a society where most children of either sex attend the same
schools an exclusive discussion of girls' education could seem a
little bizarre. Implicitly, at least, all such discussion is tied
to standards set by current levels of boys' achievements, and this
chapter is no exception. Explicitly, it is particularly concerned
with the social conditions of girls' schooling within co-educational
comprehensive schools.

Concern with arrangements that may encourage or hinder equal
opportunities for self-fulfilment or development invariably leads
towards a consideration of comprehensive planning and comprehensive
schools. By now most local authorities in England and Wales have
submitted plans for the re-organization of their schools along comprehensive lines and, though sceptics may doubt whether many of
them adhere to the spirit of comprehensive education, most of them
have managed to follow the letter. It may mean different things to
those who implement it, those who work within it and those who
receive it; but as a policy it represents a major attempts to secure
better educational opportunities for the socially disadvantaged.

Researchers have not been slow to follow the reorganization of
schools with evidence that unequal education lives on, under a new
guise, or to point out what a flawed ideal comprehensive education
is. A variety of interests, left and right, are expressed in the
numerous criticisms that can be cited, and much of what I have to
say could be taken as adding to the argument against comprehensive
schools; so I wish to make it clear at the outset that this would
be a misinterpretation. The issues that concern me are so basic
that they are probably inseparable from all forms of education with
which we are familiar; yet, on the whole, they have not earned much
attention from those eager and willing to fault the comprehensive
schools.

It is not my intention to carp at the relative failure of comprehensive schools to solve educational or social problems. What I
want to carp at is the pattern of relative failure of girls, which
has been continued and even enhanced by comprehensive education.
For a policy of mass co-education entered British secondary schools
on the coat tails of the campaign to abolish selective schooling,
and, on the available evidence referred to below, this has been

66

harmful for girls. Clearly co-education was only a secondary aim of
the campaign and, if much thought was given to the subject, it was
assumed to be progressive and hence quite compatible with comprehensive education. In most areas the programme went unchallenged,
although some campaigns to save certain grammar schools were inevitably also ones to save single-sex schools. Bradford was one
notable exception, for there the Muslim community objected to the
loss of all girls' schools, and there, despite a rhetoric of respect
for cultural and community integrity, the authority ignored the
organized opposition to its plans and went ahead with changing the
schools. Because of the ethnic implications it is difficult to know
whether this instance was typical of local education authorities'
commitment to co-education, and their likely response to local
pressure opposing this form of educational provision. Similarly, it
is hard to assess whether any part of the force behind opposition to
comprehensive education derived also from a recognition of its
secondary policy of co-education.

Opposition to women usurping the power and privileges held by men
is a common enough theme in everyday life. On the simplest of
theoretical assumptions, when education is deemed or designed to
change the social composition of those in power (for example, by
creating access to certain elite sectors) then this opposition will
be manifest within education. The history of girls' education is
largely the history of straightforward opposition to women getting
a good education; and the highlights of that history include the
establishment of schools set up expressly to provide for those girls
who were excluded from the foundations reserved for boys. Opposition remains, though often in less blatant forms. It is most overt
in higher and private education where women have come closest to
entering positions of power and authority; and it is important in
this respect to understand that the opposition voiced in those
sectors to, say, the continuation of all-female colleges stems from
exactly the same attitude as opposition to the admittance of women
to the all-male colleges did in a previous era. Interpreting both
forms of opposition as essentially identical is not as contradictory
as it may seem, for both are responses to the threat that women
might, through some particular means, take over some of the advantages reserved for and enjoyed by men.

In the earlier stages of education the associated processes of
separation and subordination take more general and less specific
forms. A good many of these have been documented, and illustrations
include the invidious sex-role stereotyping in many school textbooks, highly traditional 'vocational' guidance (a bad joke), and
the manipulation of curriculum choices so that it is hard to avoid
taking sex-typed subjects. Although it would be possible, I do not
want to continue the catalogue of all the beastly things that are
done to girls just because they are female, such as preventing those
who are pregnant from remaining at school. Rather I hope to show
how informal processes of division survive and have a pernicious
effect under the supposedly more liberal setting of mixed schools.

In principle, the position of girls' education should have
improved as a result of reorganization. There had always been more
single-sex grammar schools for boys than for girls, so if these
schools were to be incorporated into the pool of educational

resources open to all secondary school children, girls should not have suffered as a result of mixed comprehensive schooling. Yet ways to avoid equalizing opportunities have been found. The Sex Discrimination Act (1975) had a paradoxical effect, for in permitting the continued existence of single-sex schools it allowed more than one local authority to refuse to make a girls' school co-educational on the grounds that it would cost too much to bring it up to the standards required for the education of boys by building the necessary workshops.

At a general level the exact re-ordering of educational opportunity that goes with mixed schooling is somewhat hard to assess. Enthusiasm for some form of more egalitarian education has led both to more comprehensive schools and to a preference for seeing the results in a particular way. Hence, the crude indicators of performance now used in official statistics have the unfortunate effect of obscuring other sorts of residual and persistent inequalities. Schools are classified in the DES publication 'Statistics of Education' according to type; i.e., comprehensive, grammar etc., but not according to whether they are mixed or single-sex.(1) Girls' and boys' respective educational performance is listed but not according to whether they achieved their results in single-sex or mixed institutions. This makes for difficulties in relating the trends in overall performance of boys and girls to changes in educational organization.

The problem is further complicated by the fact that the change-over from single-sex education to co-education was spread over a long period, which included a number of other educational changes or reforms. Very few schools simply switched from single-sex to co-educational without also increasing in size or becoming non-selective. Initially many of the advantages of comprehensive schools were thought to lie in the breadth and range of subjects that large schools could offer. In order to assure many of these advantages older, smaller and single-sex schools were merged. Rural districts have always had more co-educational schools because, proportionately, they had more mixed secondary modern schools and fewer single-sex grammar schools, although, for a combination of reasons, the older inner city secondary modern schools were usually single-sex. Latterly, with the decline of the birth rate, especially evident in the inner city areas, demographic and geographic factors have led to increasing numbers of children receiving their education within a co-educational setting.

Great care has to be taken in comparing the performance of pupils, of both sexes, in either mixed or single-sex schools, because of the reasons just given. After all it would not be surprising if girls in a co-educational ex-secondary modern school in an authority which bought places at the local independent school did less well than girls had done when educated in single-sex grammar schools, or than boys who were in an ex-grammar school. However, three separate pieces of evidence undermine confidence in the assumption that educating boys and girls under the same roof is the same as giving them equal educational opportunity. The first is provided by the research of R. Dale (2) into the overall merits and demerits of single-sex or co-educational schooling, and research by M.B. Ormerod into subject choice in both types of school.(3) The second is given

in the 1975 report by HM Inspectorate on 'Curricular Differences for
Boys and Girls in Mixed and Single-sex Schools'.(4)   The third is
the accumulated evidence of differences in performance of girls and
boys seen in terms of examinations passed, or entry into higher and
further education.

I shall concentrate on the implications of the first two areas,
which both concern the greater subject and social polarization of
boys and girls in mixed schools than in single-sex schools. This
observation, which has been confirmed by virtually all the research
in the field, runs directly counter to most of the beliefs and
assumptions supporting co-educational schools. In fact, Dale, the
most prolific and prominent writer on the subject, argues that it is
a sign of improved social adjustment or maturity. He concedes that
whilst boys' academic performance is improved in co-educational
schools that of girls deteriorates. In defence of this outcome he
rightly insists that schooling is not only about success in examinations, but also social learning. Yet this particular social learning is a sexist programme in the extreme. Not only are a 'better
adjustment' and a more 'mature' attitude to members of the opposite
sex seen to be a fair exchange for girls' academic achievements, but
those measures themselves embody a commitment to and reinforcement
of the most traditional and limiting sex-roles. The acceptable
trade-off is supposed to be a poorer education for girls in favour
of 'happier' marriages for both sexes and even more sex-role
stereotyping.

In choosing not to focus the argument centrally on either comparative pass rates in examinations or entry into higher education I
run the risk of appearing to have insufficient grounds for concern
for girls' education. There are reasons for this decision. First,
good summaries of patterns of educational inequalities exist both
in official publications such as 'Social Trends' (5) (see, for
example, the introductory article in 1974 as well as the annual
statistics) and in easily accessible articles such as Tessa
Blackstone's chapter in 'The Rights and Wrongs of Women', edited by
J. Mitchell and A. Oakley.(6)   Second, by concentrating on the more
successful section of the school population we can miss out all those
who leave school without any qualifications at all (in 1975 over
122,000 boys and girls left school without even attempting GCE or
CSE examinations).

Third, there is a temptation in reviewing the respective pass
rates to believe that if the differential is narrowing slightly, as
it is in 'O' levels, 'A' levels and degrees obtained, all in good
time the discrepancies will wholly disappear. Such a view is not
only unreasonably optimistic; it is also based on a refusal to see
those social processes which serve to block the gaining or consolid-
ation of advantage by girls and women. After all, in certain basic
skills such as reading, girls have a marked lead over boys throughout primary school years, but the important issue remains a question
of exactly why such a lead is reversed by their experience of
secondary schooling. To expect that trends will simply continue
uninterrupted is as politically and socially naive as it is to fail
to see that if girls now achieve about the same number of 'O' level
passes as boys it is also the case that 'O' levels are becoming increasingly irrelevant to pupils' future careers. It is short-sighted

to be content with improved pass rates at CSE and GCE level in the light of knowledge that girls still end up in the worst paid, least secure and least interesting jobs available.

The HMIs reported that girls were less likely to choose a science subject if they attended a mixed school than they would if they went to a single-sex girls' school, even though in a mixed school they are generally more likely to be offered science. They went on to show that any correlation between the sex of the pupil and the popularity of a subject was markedly greater in mixed than in single-sex schools. The full significance of these, and Ormerod's, findings are to be seen in the light of Celia Phillips's work, which showed that the child who took science had a greater chance of remaining within formal education than the arts specialist at every level of schooling.(7) To some extent this is a result of successive government's attempts to encourage science education and hence discriminate in favour of it, and those who take it. A further point needs to be made concerning those girls who do take some science at 'O' or 'A' level. These candidates tend to offer hybrid combinations of subjects rather than 'pure' packages of science. Though they study some science, usually biology, they may be prevented from following certain careers in science because they lack the supporting subjects of chemistry, physics or mathematics.

Further consequences of these processes can be seen in the firmly segregated labour markets and in the use by employers and unions of the threat that women might 'take men's jobs'. Manipulation of such fears would not be possible unless they were widely regarded as reasonable, a situation supported by the Equal Opportunities Commission's dictum that differentiation is not necessarily discrimination although it quite clearly constitutes the preconditions for it. Furthermore, whilst I have no doubt that overall the sexual division of labour precedes divisions of knowledge along the lines of gender in an individual's life, it is division within the knowledge made available that largely determines one's place within the structure of society.

So far I have argued that the policy of comprehensive co-education has produced the possibly unanticipated consequence of greater differentiation and segregation between girls and boys and, to the extent that this is seen as a failure one could conclude that it merely exemplified the dangers of attempting progressive reform within a fundamentally unprogressive society. Alternatively, if the DES was thought to be persuadable, that pressure should be mounted to retain single-sex schooling as a significant part of the British school system. However, adopting solutions such as these without further examination of the social bases of division and separation is as likely to reinforce as remedy the situation. Judith Okely, in a perceptive though largely autobiographical account of a girls' boarding school, illustrates well the point that it is the ideological interdependence between the identities of girls and boys that is important, and that this process can be managed as well by single-sex institutions as by mixed ones.(8) For these reasons it is important to stress that it is the mechanisms of polarization that deserve attention rather than the detail of differences.

Whilst boys and girls may occupy the same physical space it would be wrong to assume that they therefore occupy the same social

space or receive the same educational experience. It is a commonplace to observe that boys and girls are not always taught together
even when they go to the same school. Certain subjects, the best
known being games and certain vocational subjects, are taught in
single-sex groups even when both boys and girls are permitted to
take them, and hence the impact of that teaching is correspondingly
different. Nor is it rare to find that within co-educational
schools some subjects are reserved, either formally (e.g., mother-
craft) or informally (e.g., as a result of earlier curriculum
choices), for children of one sex only. These practices cannot fail
to convey to pupils that sexual divisions are in some way part of
the absolute bedrock of society or to reinforce their acceptance of
them.

Arguably children do not experience the same teacher even when
they are in the same room, as research into the effect of teachers'
expectations on children's performance by Neil Keddie (9) and by
Robert Rosenthal and Lenore Jacobson has indicated.(10) However, it
would be crude as well as unfair to lay the blame for all the sexual
divisions in the classroom at the teacher's door. No doubt
teacher's perceptions include expectations that are orientated by
the children's gender, but it is a form of scapegoating to concentrate on these exclusively. Children socialize each other and
teachers' powers are strongly circumscribed, not least by certain
conventions which they share with children. One such convention is
a dual ranking system, one for girls and one for boys, which finds
expression in both social and intellectual dimensions.

The processes underlying subject choice comprise a complex set
of ways of thinking about oneself and about others. One such way
employs what social psychologists call a reference group, which, in
this context, is based upon an open acknowledgment that girls' and
boys' behaviour is quite incommensurate. Ten or fifteen years ago
research into higher education supported the idea that female undergraduates were reluctant to compete with men in their classes out
of some kind of joint respect for the male ego. Under-achievement
and 'playing dumb' was thought to be a neat way of solving the
'problem' of doing better than men. Similar arguments have been
applied to social relations in secondary schools. Put quite bluntly,
I suspect that one consequence of co-educational schooling is not
that girls retire gracefully from educational competition but that
they are pushed out by being turned into a negative reference group
for boys. By this I mean simply that boys define themselves as
being, whatever else, at least not a girl. This has many consequences, not least of which might be that in certain circumstances it reduces boys' inclination to work hard precisely because
of their security. Before discussing in any detail the possible
effects of such reference groups, the general point is that schools
may be able to underwrite the 'failure' of most of their pupils in
two particular and linked ways. If the possibility of marriage as
an alternative mitigates the sense of personal failure in educational terms for girls, then, by a similar sleight of hand, the
very presence of girls both ensures the minimum conditions for boys'
self-esteem and makes what is ascribed seem achieved.

In a competitive and selective educational system such as our
own, being better than someone else is of vital importance if

children are to believe their success. They have to be able to
recognize themselves in the processes of selection and examination,
and they do this by being able to identify those who are not as
successful. As a group boys have an advantage over girls simply
because their success is more public, more applauded, and leads on
to a future which more obviously records that success. A similar
process is repeated at the individual level, for there too male
success stands out more than that of girls. It seems that when boys
and girls who follow the same subjects are tested in any way they
tend to divide the scores into one for boys and one for girls.
Plausibly, if boys compare themselves only with other boys then
they are less downcast if the only person to do better is a girl.
The thirteen-year-old boy who brought this to my attention made it
clear that the girls in the class simply added bulk to the class.
He described himself as having come 'top of the class' except for,
and then he mentioned a girl's name. Impressionistic though this
is, it leads one to ask what the effect on girls is if they are
tacitly accepted as a baseline or benchmark of misfortune? Are they
more likely to undervalue their own achievements or see them as
flukes rather than as sure signs of their ability and worth? If
they treat them just as 'luck' then they will be less likely to
expect them to be repeated or to use them as a basis for planning
ahead, which might explain the puzzle of why so many girls drop
their best subjects.
    Clearly this is an area that urgently demands further research,
research which might re-interpret and link Keys and Ormerod's (11)
suggestion that the close correlation of sex sith subject choice
was a function of girls choosing their subjects according to perceived easiness, unlike boys, who were less affected by such
criteria. Compare this with Lomax's surprising finding that in an
ultra-disadvantaged context the most disadvantaged girls had the
least negative self-images, whilst, conversely, the girls who were
in fact relatively advantaged thought the worst of themselves;(12)
and Deaux's results, where temporary and unstable factors such as
luck were consistently applied to women's successes, whilst these
were invoked by men only to explain their failures.(13)
    At best girls and boys live in adjacent, not shared social
worlds. Where children sit and who they play with is but one
expression of this. There are others which are both more deforming
and harder to identify. Boys do not like being called a cissy or
being compared to girls in any way; indeed the foulest abuse thrown
at either sex invariably uses female terms. Girls' retaliation
uses the same format but rarely achieves the same force. In the
later years of girls' schooling observers have often commented that
they seem to switch their interest (and their desire to esteem)
from academic matters to the more traditionally feminine ones of
personal appearance and a carefully managed reputation of success
with boys. This is usually deplored and thought, though regret-
table, to be inevitable. Yet, far from this being the result of
some genetic or social maturation process, it follows from the
socially supported opposition to girls that boys both represent
and pursue.
    Take, for example, the school activity of teasing and joking.
All children are liable to be ridiculed and abused in this way, but

weaker children are the most exposed. Commonly this means younger
children, but in our culture it also includes girls. Ann Whitehead's
work has shown that sexual innuendo is the common basis of a large
number of jokes in our culture (as in many others).(14) These jokes
depend upon shared assumptions, including the innate risibility of
women, the sexual prowess of men, and the willingness of the audience to affirm these principles by laughing. At one level these
comments can be taken as an illustration of the theoretical point
made by Freud and others that people joked about are usually of a
lower status than those who make the jokes.(15) At another level
the observation that girls, as a category, are laughable and become
ever more so as they get mature, especially sexually, may go some
way towards explaining the increasing polarization and 'voluntary'
segregation of girls from boys that characterizes the later years
of schooling. As boys of the same age are easing themselves into
their futures by adopting styles and manners of the shop floor,
girls similarly have little option but to withdraw from the danger
zones where their presence simply invites abuse.

Support for co-education is central to the liberal tradition
which has characterized most thinking about educational reform, and
turns on a particular version of liberal pluralism. Differences
are recognized and supported; indeed, variety is seen as a positive
good, and the creation of an arena in which all of its forms are
present is thought to lead to the best of all possible worlds.
Implicitly, if not explicitly, conflicts are reconcilable and evils
will be cancelled out. As I hope I have shown with regard to co-
education, this view ignores the process of competition within such
arenas; it is subject to the same criticisms as those levelled at
concepts such as the 'family' or 'community' which function to
obscure the different experiences of men, women and children, or
young and old. The achievements of the most advantaged are equated
with the collective good and once more a conflict of interests is
disguised. For my purpose this is nowhere better demonstrated than
in the case of the opposed interests of girl and boy pupils or
better expressed than by the work of R. Dale.

It has been my intention to show that strong social pressures
and opposition to girls sharing the advantages conferred by education lie behind the apparently voluntary subject specialization
that occurs between girls and boys and is most marked in co-
educational settings. These are operated by boy pupils as much as
by teachers, by the curriculum or by the organizational features of
schools, and they are possible because the values and attitudes
thus expressed are endorsed on a mass scale by the culture in which
we live. I have concentrated on fairly informal methods of constructing and managing competition between the sexes; but the central point remains that mixed schools are essentially boys' schools
in so far as they are dominated by boys' interests. Education is
one of the few areas where the possibility of positive discrimination has been raised if not actually implemented. Inevitably the
parents of boys will feel that such a move is at their child's
expense; but, as many will also be the parents of daughters, we can
hope they will not wish to prefer their sons' chances over those of
their daughters. This might be a pious hope, for it was pressure
by the parents of boys that led one local authority eventually to

change one of its girls' schools into a mixed school.

Unfortunately, the very suggestion of a return to single-sex schooling touches at the core of many deep-seated beliefs, and most educationalists are not eager to adopt such a policy. Many received their own education in such schools and claim that it was a de-forming and depressing experience. Women so educated often assert that they are sure it was unnatural, and obstructed the development of good relations with members of the opposite sex. Such feelings are, of course, real, but they derive from the fact that the indiv-iduals concerned had been made to feel uncomfortable by being at the centre of conflicting pressures and not simply from belonging to a single-sex institution. From one side came all the usual pressures on girls to be feminine and focus their futures on romance, marri-age and men, yet from their school they also got encouragement to disregard that for the time being and concentrate on academic matters. It is no wonder they felt uneasy, the apparent risks were large: spinsterhood and that awful label, the bluestocking. No boy is ever asked to choose his identity in such a way and we should not ask girls to do so. In particular, the criticism of single-sex schools that they delay the process of 'coming to terms with the opposite sex' is misconceived. This, surely, is their strength, not their weakness, when the terms are so unequal.

Two final points need to be made to counter the view that approving of a return to single-sex schooling is necessarily regres-sive and politically reactionary, or that the burden of this chapter is primarily to promote such a return to single-sex schools rather than to question the liberal assumption underlying co-education. First, schools run by women for women can provide a model of educational excellence to be adopted more widely, and need not be put down and parodied. Institutions where women hold posi-tions of authority and responsibility can provide an alternative example to the more common one where such positions are the prerog-ative of men. Eileen Byrne, amongst others, has shown that mixed schools actually reduce the chances of women teachers holding senior and powerful positions.(16) Without insisting on any mech-anical notion of modelling or reproduction of the self, to have in one's repertoire the experience of an organization run well by women can constitute a resource to be used as girls and boys grow up, when such a possibility is increasingly undermined or made to seem ridiculous. Furthermore, instead of being frightened at drawing the conclusion that single-sex schooling is desirable and preferable for girls, especially as the converse is likely to hold for boys, support for contemporary all-girls schools can, in a sexist society, be viewed as a mode of affirmative action. The schooling provided under such a programme would not be the same as in the single-sex schools set up in a different era, to respond to sexism also but from a rather different set of assumptions, and would, at the very least, mean that the parents' right under the 1944 Education Act to choose whether their child was educated in a single-sex or mixed-sex school could in fact be exercised.

Finally, we should be aware that the current situation reflects exactly the split within feminist theory over the priority of gender or class in the subordination of women. Parental choice within education has always been something of a chimera, and though arguments for it have most usually come from the right there is no ligical reason why this should be so. For parents concerned with sexual inequality within education and convinced that single-sex schooling would be best for their daughters, there is only one way of getting it, and that is to buy it from the private sector if they can afford it. For those who also care about other forms of in-equality other than gender are in practice being asked to rank their commitment to the eradication of class or sex-based inequality. Such a choice is not necessary in this manner and it should be remembered that gender-linked disadvantage is unlike other forms of inequality in education (such as that based on race or class, which get progressively worse throughout the period of formal schooling), for girls in primary education have a marked lead over boys. It is at the secondary level that their fortunes suffer a sharp reversal. I have attempted to understand this by looking closely at some of the social conditions of secondary schools and would urge that, if whatever benefits we might think education confers are to be more equally distributed than at present, then the policy of co-education must be seriously questioned.

NOTES

1   Department of Education and Science (1976).
2   Dale (1974).
3   Ormerod (1975).
4   Department of Education and Science (1975).
5   Central Statistical Office, 'Social Trends', no.5 (1974), and
    annual statistics.
6   Blackstone (1976).
7   Phillips (1969).
8   Okely (1978).
9   Keddie (1971).
10 Rosenthal and Jacobson (1968).
11 Keys and Ormerod (1977).
12 Lomax (1977).
13 Deaux (1977).
14 Whitehead (1976).
15 Freud (1960).
16 Byrne (1978).

Chapter 6

Sex differences in mathematical performance
A review of research and possible action

Gaby Weiner

A great deal has been written and spoken in recent years on the apparent decline in standards of numeracy and literacy among this country's schoolchildren. Working parties have been set up within local authorities; the DES has set into motion a comprehensive monitoring system for the curriculum, which includes mathematics; and employers have remarked on the poor performance of school-leavers in computation and spelling.

At the same time, educationists have begun to look at the performance and achievements of girls and women as a distinct group within the education system (rather than as an invisible minority). Research has suggested that there are distinct sex differences in performance, conceptual development and attitude across a whole range of curriculum subject areas throughout the school life of boys and girls.(1)

This chapter is not concerned with the standards issue except in so far as the mathematical performance of boys and girls was selected as an important topic of interest in the now defunct 'Great Debate' on education, and is a major concern of an increasing technological society. It has rather more to do with examining existing research findings on sex differences in mathematics, attributing cause and effect where possible, and then suggesting what consequences these findings might have for future action. If areas of serious under-achievement of girls are disclosed and remedial action quickly taken, this eventually may have profound effects on national mathematical standards.

Performance in any curricular area is dependent on a number of interrelating factors. When we consider the performance of girls and boys in mathematics regardless of age or stage of schooling, we find that there are four important spheres of influence:

(a) Cognitive factors: the extent to which genetic/biological features affect mathematical performance.
(b) Socialization patterns: this includes pre- or extra-school activities, child-rearing patterns, the persuasion powers of the media and advertising, and peer group expectation.
(c) Impact of schooling: though not too much is known about the way in which any sex bias in curriculum areas or in text-books and reading schemes influences the true ability of

children, increasing literature on sexism in schools suggests
that the organization and expectation involved in classroom
life is a crucial contributor to the perceptions and attitudes of pupils and consequently their performance.
(d) Pupil attitude towards mathematics.

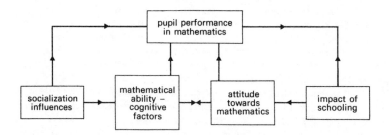

FIGURE 6.1   The major influences on pupil performance in
mathematics

COGNITIVE FACTORS

It is unnecessary here to consider the nature-nurture controversy
concerning academic performance in all but the briefest way, since
the literature on the subject is wide-ranging and comprehensive.
Essentially sex differences arise from the presence of a Y sex
chromosone possessed by male but absent in female human beings.
Long before birth this chromosone delivers a message which organ-
izes male development and sexes the brain.   In the absence of a Y
the foetus develops according to the female pattern.(2)   The extent
to which biological maleness or femaleness affects certain skills
and abilities and the degree to which they are modified by heredity
and environment have not yet been resolved.   Measures of conceptual
development and academic attainment have been inconclusive in all
but the most general of terms.   Summarizing research into sex-
differences of general ability:
(a) Girls (and women) perform better on average than boys (and
    men) on verbal, clerical and arithmetic tasks.   Girls on
    average are more advanced verbally.
(b) Boys (and men) perform better on average than girls (and
    women) on spatial mechanical and visual tasks.   Boys on
    average are more advanced spatially.
(c) On all of the tests the overlap is very large.   For instance,
    in certain vocabulary tests given to school-leavers in 1973,
    the girls scored higher than the boys overall yet 45-50 per
    cent of the boys scored higher than the girls.
(d) There is evidence that certain observed sex differences in
    ability may be a function of masculinity/femininity concept;
    i.e., adherence to sex appropriate roles, rather than of
    gender.(3)
   When we consider specifically sex differences in mathematical
ability, we find a similar pattern to the patterns for general
ability.   Maccoby and Jacklin found certain differences proven, but

also documented educational 'myths'. They found the following
variations established:

    (a) Boys excel in mathematical ability, though not until adol-
        escence. Beginning at 12 and 13, boys' ability in maths
        increases faster than girls'.

    (b) Boys excel in visual spatial ability. This is found consis-
        tently in adolescence and adulthood but not earlier.

In their very comprehensive review of the current literature they
refuted the 'myths' that girls are more accomplished at rote
learning and simple repetitive tasks and are less achievement-
orientated; or that boys are superior at tasks requiring higher-
level cognitive processes and are more analytic.(4)

    There are two conflicting views on how these findings should be
interpreted. It has been argued that sex differences in performance reflect the influence of social sanctions and rewards rather
than genuine ability, and therefore are just indicators or inequalities in social status and provision. If educational equality is
to be a meaningful precept, educational weaknesses need to be
strengthened rather than ignores or exacerbated. An alternative
view is that since academic inequalities derive from biological
dissimilarities between the sexes, girls and boys ought to be
treated differently to fit their essential complementary roles in
society. Whatever interpretation is adopted, all would agree that
bald statements of what certain children are able or not able to do
give insufficient information for a full explanation of why these
differences occur.

SOCIALIZATION PATTERNS

Child-rearing patterns and pre-school activities

From their earliest years children's ideas about appropriate roles
and behaviour have been influenced by the actions and attitudes of
their parents and other adults in their environment. Many facets
of pre- and extra-school experience combine to form in children
concepts of mothering, fathering, sex-appropriate behaviour, manli-
ness and womanliness. These pressures are so pervasive that toys
and activity preference of children according to sex is significantly evident as early as the age of four years,(5) and increasingly so as children move into adolescence. Similarly, Sears
found that four-year-old girls chose stereotyped feminine activities and four-year-old boys typically masculine.(6) These may be
purely imitative actions, as it has been argued that at this age
children do not have a well-developed notion of sex-constancy; i.e.,
at this age children still think that the sex of an individual can
change if dress and hairstyle are changed.(7)

    Maccoby and Jacklin come to the conclusion that there is a
remarkable degree of uniformity in the socialization experiences of
the sexes.(8) In so far as differences do emerge, boys appear to
have more intense socialization experiences than girls, and endure
greater pressure against engaging in sex-inappropriate behaviour.
Boys receive more attention, more punishment and also more praise,

and adults respond as if they find boys more interesting and more attention-provoking than girls. Both these points have important implications for the relationships between teachers and their pupils.

There are several alternative yet perhaps interrelated hypotheses to explain how children acquire sex roles. Imitation is the most favoured explanation; i.e., that little girls copy their mothers and little boys their fathers. This does not entirely explain why, for instance, the play of little girls is so dominated by domestic and nurturing activities when many of their mothers go out to work, drive cars, and so on. It has been suggested that boys experience a more complicated socialization process since they are forced to change from their initial contact and earliest model formulation, their mother, in order to adhere to the required male role, whereas girls' sex-typing is much simpler.(9) This early need to change may be the reason why, in later years, boys appear to be less afraid of change and challenge than girls.

ADVERTISING, MEDIA, AND PEER-GROUP INFLUENCE

As girls approach adolescence extra-familial influences increasingly assume importance. Pop-culture and magazines directed towards the teenage group introduce new stereotypes of masculinity and femininity, often very dissimilar from the safe parental image so far experienced, yet often just as restrictive.

'They [the pop magazines] are written in special teenage language, which encourages young people to become part of the pop-culture teenage group, resenting interference from other forms of authority'; yet 'the magazines support, confirm and perpetuate the restricted lives and ideas of the typical reader: the 15-year-old girl school-leaver who is engaged, perhaps by 16 or 17, married at 20'.(10)

Most of the magazines reviewed by Alderson enthused about romantic love in much the same way as many of the currently popular teenage songs. However, in the last few years popular musicians such as Julie Covington and Tom Robinson have provided a critique of social patterns and taboos in their music. Their continuing popularity may indicate that teenage stereotypes are indeed changing.

Members of the women's movement and other radical groups have long criticized the advertising industry for its general stereotypical portrayal of the average consumer. Consistently individuals are depicted as members of a nuclear family, having extremely modest aspirations; e.g., for men to be entirely bewitched by a particular brand of beer, or for women to spend most of their time trying to get the kitchen floor cleaner than that of the neighbours.

When advertisements show girls helping their mother with the washing up whilst their brothers play football with their father; and then they include such statements as 'Because girls dream about being a ballerina, Mattell makes Dancerina... a pink confection in a silken blouse and ruffled tutu' and 'Because boys were born to build and learn, Mattell makes Tod'l (a set of building

bricks for creative play)'(11), they are sending clear messages to
girls and boys and their parents that girls ought to spend their
leisure time either fantasizing (e.g., about being ballerinas) or
undertaking housewifely tasks, whereas boys ought to build, learn
and do.

Complaints about the more pernicious of these advertisements
have had little impact on the creators of the advertisements, since
they in turn argue that the advertising industry portrays life as
it usually is; e.g., white, prosperous and consumer-orientated; and
after all, it is not the place of the advertising industry to
encourage change. Thus the message of the media is powerful, and
in general most individuals wish to adhere as closely as possible
to the suggested ideals.

Several years ago an attempt was made, in a survey of 190 housewives in Texas, to detect types of housewife in terms of their
response to commercial products. Responses were statistically
analysed to produce clusters of items. The authors named the main
cluster as 'homemakers', since the preferred items were all of a
domestic nature. Other smaller clusters were described as matri-
archs, variety girls, cinderellas (sic), glamour girls.(12)
Clearly when girls and boys are initiated into society, this is
not done on an individual basis but through a filter of prescrip-
tions of sex-appropriate behaviour and aspirations.

Whilst it is only possible to hazard a guess at the extent to
which the patterns of socialization which have been mentioned
persuade girls that mathematics is 'unfeminine' or that they should
withdraw from 'difficult' subjects, it must be accepted that in
general typical boys' play (e.g., construction, physical games)
engages boys in more intense mechanical and spatial experiences
than girls gain from typical girls' play (e.g., playing with dolls,
chatting to friends).

IMPACT OF SCHOOLING

So far I have looked at sex differences in academic performance
and in socialization patterns, in isolation from the schooling
process. Since mathematics owes much of its significance to the
fact that for most people, their first contact with maths takes
place at school, where it is given high priority, the impact of
the school on boys and girls should be recognized as an important
element in the analysis of mathematical attainments.

There is evidence that mathematics is regarded by pupils of all
ages both primary and secondary (and by teachers) as a subject at
which boys excel. However, since Maccoby and Jacklin found few
sex differences in mathematical performance before adolescent,(13)
a closer look at the attitudes and assumptions of schools and
teachers (particularly at the primary stage) may make explicit
persistent but hidden prejudices. Why it is that, though girls are
just as good at maths as boys at primary level, boys like maths
more than girls and more often choose it as a favourite subject?
When questioned, boys have reported that they like mathematics
because it is difficult, and girls express dislike precisely for
the same reason.(14) Can an explanation for this be found in

patterns of schooling? Do teachers treat girls and boys in different ways?

If it can be shown that schooling encourages sex-stereotyping,
thereby conditioning girls to reject perceived 'male' subjects or
to shy away from challenging experiences, connections must then be
made between the impact of school and the reasons why girls reject
mathematics (and science).

School structure and organization

It has been established that schools use sex categories for ease
of organization. In a study of London primary schools, Lobban
found that the sexes were separated on many occasions for purely
organizational reasons. Girls and boys were listed separately on
the register: they were separated when lining up to go in and out
of school, for quizzes in the classroom and games outside the
classroom. Boys, in general smaller and lighter than girls before
adolescence, were expected to carry heavy PE equipment, whereas
girls tended to be given flowers, teas and displays to arrange.(15)

Up to the age of seven years children are taught almost exclusively by women and between seven and eleven years women teachers
predominate, although the headteacher and teacher responsible for
science are likely to be men.(16) At secondary level the balance
between male and female teachers is more equal, although there are
more men in authority and only 5 per cent of headteachers of mixed
comprehensives are women. All the support staff except the care-
taker are likely to be women: e.g., the dinner ladies, ancillary
staff and office staff. It is possible that the school organization so described affects girls and boys in terms of both what
they feel able to tackle and also their future career expectations.

The curriculum

Whilst it is difficult to expose and remove sexism in the social
structure and organization of the school (often described as the
'hidden' curriculum), the Sex Discrimination Act (1975) (SDA)
should have removed sex discrimination in official curricular
areas. Before the Act the differentiated primary curriculum
resulted in girls doing cooking, sewing and netball whilst boys
were occupied in woodwork, metalwork and football.(17) In secondary schools pre-SDA, girls and boys were unashamedly channelled
into different subjects with girls specializing in languages,
biology and homecrafts whilst boys followed courses in physics,
chemistry, woodwork and metalwork.(18) Also there was discrimination reported in the allocation of resources to girls' single-sex
schools compared with boys', particularly in the case of adequate
science laboratories.(19)

The Sex Discrimination legislation has not been in operation
long enough in Britain to allow its effects to be monitored. When
sufficient time has passed, it will be interesting to note whether
the primary and secondary practices of assigning subjects and
resources on the basis of sex will have been thoroughly eliminated.

Pupil-teacher interaction

The interaction between teachers and their pupils is bound to be a powerful determinant of pupil self-concept and confidence. Studies of teachers' attitudes to the sexes and to sex roles in the USA show that teachers endorse traditional attitudes. At pre-school and primary levels, teachers value female and male pupils equally, but describe their typical behaviour as being different.[20] A recent English study of primary teachers supports the hypothesis that girls and boys are perceived as being different by their teachers: 'the primary teachers saw girls as being more sensible, obedient, hardworking, co-operative, quiet, mature, bright, like-able... whereas boys were more excitable, talkative, needed more supervision and attention.'[21] It has also been reported by Clift and Nash that both male and female teachers perceive girls more favourably than boys.[22] However, whilst primary teachers may prefer to teach girls, possibly because they are more con-formist and well behaved, boys gain greater interaction with their teachers 'for approval, disapproval, instruction, being listened to', and 'teachers prefer boys to be self-sufficient and confident whilst girls are expected to be friendly, agreeable and good'.[23]

At secondary level evidence suggests that teachers do an about-turn and prefer to teach boys rather than girls, in the belief that male pupils are more interesting and critical and that their education is more important than that of girls.[24] There is also some evidence that teachers are unaware that their attitude towards boys and girls differs.[25] Whilst it is unclear why teachers behave in the way they do, it may explain why girls lack so much confidence in their abilities to undertake subjects perceived as difficult, e.g., maths and science, whereas boys find difficult subjects challenging.

'There is a cumulative increase in independence and autonomous behaviour in boys as they are disciplined, praised, listened to and taught more actively by the teacher.' By comparison there is 'a lowering of self-esteem generally for girls as they receive less attention and are criticized more for their lack of knowledge and skill.'[26]

Curriculum materials

The analysis of curriculum materials has figured prominently in the discussion on the extent of sexist practices in schools. Sexism in reading schemes and young children's book has been well docu-mented.[27] In her seminal analysis of English reading schemes, Lobban found that the schemes rigidly divided the sphere of people's activities into masculine and feminine compartments, that the number of male options depicted far exceeded the female ones, that there were twice as many heroes as heroines, and that parents were always portrayed in conventional roles.[28] Secondary text-books have also been found to be sex-biased, with books for girls focused most exclusively on dating and romance, and a pattern of neglect of women appearing in science and history books.[29]

As far as I am aware, there has been no similar comprehensive analysis of mathematics textbooks in this country. In an analysis of 24 mathematics textbooks reported in 1977 in the USA Kepner and Koehn (30) found that:

Males and females were seldom treated equally in illustrations and problems in these texts. The number of males identified was greater than the number of females in twenty of the twenty-four texts examined. Males participated in a greater variety of activities and occupations than females. Typically female roles were passive rather than physically active, except when they participated in household activities.... When specific mathematicians were identified ... these individuals were exclusively male.

A small survey of popular English primary mathematics texts has disclosed a similar pattern of sexism. Adult males are depicted in a greater variety of occupations than females, who tend to be portrayed in one of only three stereotype roles; the familial role (mother, sister, grandmother), the housewife, and the teacher.(31)

It is difficult to estimate the impact of sexist textbooks on the attitude and performance of girls in mathematics. However, this is one more way in which mathematics is represented primarily as a male activity and therefore not for girls.

SEX DIFFERENCE IN ATTITUDES TOWARDS MATHEMATICS

Research into sex differences in pupil attitude towards mathematics has been sparse, fragmentary and therefore difficult to analyse. Additional problems in analysis have been caused by the differential ages of the researched. In her view of research on attitudes towards mathematics, Fennema reported that, though studies of attitudes that included sex as a variable have produced no consistent pattern to show that one sex has more positive feelings towards mathematics than the other, these have shown that measures of attitudes and anxiety are better predictors of mathematics-learning for girls than boys.(32)

In a survey in South California of 1,324 students in grades 2 to 13 it was found, contrary to the expectations of the researchers, that 'in terms of liking the subject, mathematics was the only subject which exhibited no sex differences'.(33) (My own research findings in English primary schools indicate maybe that the situation is different in this country.) Another survey in the same locality (34) found unexpected differences relating to student attitudes towards mathematics failure:

Most students gave lack of effort as the reason for receiving a poor grade in every subject. However, when it came to maths 26 per cent of the females gave lack of ability as the basis for a poor grade, as compared with 15 per cent of the males.

If belief in one's ability to learn and use mathematics is essential in order to progress and if girls display more anxiety and less confidence than boys in their mathematical ability, then it is likely that they are going to make less progress in maths than in areas where they are more confident.

Fennema (35) found that research consistently indicated (though the number of studies was not large) that girls feel inadequate when faced with a variety of mathematical situations.

Is it not reasonable to conclude that because girls feel inadequate in mathematics, they will avoid mathematics whenever possible? Learners become more skilful in what they practise. It is reasonable to think that girls' mathematics achievement suffers because they may avoid practising mathematical skills.

SUMMARY AND CONCLUSIONS

In this review of research on sex differences in mathematical performance, I have suggested that there are four major areas of influence; i.e., cognitive factors, socialization experiences, the impact of schooling, and pupil attitudes towards mathematics.

As it is difficult to quantify the extent to which any one of these factors modifies the expectation, attitude and ability of girls and boys in mathematics and, as in all attempts to explain human behaviour, there are a great many variables to consider and causal links to be made, there is no simple answer to why sex differences in mathematical performance occur. It is, however, counter-productive to reports on the under-achievement in mathematics of girls or to offer reasons for its existence, unless this in turn leads to positive action.

I suggest that the following paragraph accurately describes the situation of many girls within the schooling process, and that teachers are not able or do not wish to halt a familiar female developmental pattern:(36)

Some primary school children, usually girls, show indications of anxiety and an extreme desire to conform and please. Frequently they develop skills of memory and automatic responses that hide a lack of understanding of basic concepts [the fact that girls are quieter and less likely to cause trouble in the classroom may contribute to their lack of understanding - author's insert]. Later in school life, as understanding rather than automatic response becomes of greater importance, they begin to fail.

Certain strategies of action have been suggested, and guidelines produced to alter this situation. In a pamphlet entitled 'Ten Quick Ways to Analyse Children's Books for Racism and Sexism' (37) it is suggested that teachers (and parents) should carry out an evaluation on children's literature in an effort to prevent exposure to racist and sexist attitudes.

1 Check the illustrations for stereotypes, tokenism, who is doing what (are males the active doers and females the inactive observers?).
2 Check the story line for the role of women.
3 Look at the life-styles.
4 Weigh the relationships between people.
5 Note the heroes and heroines.
6 Consider the effects on a child's self-image.
7 Consider the author's or illustrator's background.
8 Check out the author's perspective.
9 Watch for loaded words.
10 Look at the copyright date; was it written before people became aware of sexism?

Specifically related to girls and mathematics, it has been argued that by using the following guidelines,(38) teachers can combat the decision of many girls to withdraw from or reject mathematics at an early age.

(a) Maths and science teachers should give special encouragement to girls.

(b) Maths and science problems should be drawn from all aspects of culture, not just male ones.

(c) Information should be disseminated encouraging girls to go into maths and engineering.

(d) The spirit of enquiry should be encouraged, especially in girls, who should not be left to get on quietly in the corner.

To go back to the first page of this chapter: if by following guidelines such as those given by CDC the maths attainment of girls is so improved that it helps to raise the standard of mathematical ability in the nation's children as a whole, this will be a 'pay-off' which only the most prejudiced anti-feminist can afford to ignore.

NOTES

1   See Hutt (1972); Maccoby and Jacklin (1974).
2   Brierly (1975).
3   See King (1974); Maccoby and Jacklin (1974).
4   Maccoby and Jacklin (1974).
5   Ibid.
6   See Sears (1965).
7   Kohlberg, L.A., in Maccoby (1966).
8   Maccoby and Jacklin (1974).
9   Ibid.
10 Alderson (1968).
11 Komisar (1971).
12 Greene et al. (1973).
13 Maccoby and Jacklin (1974).
14 Weiner, unpublished research.
15 Lobban (1975).
16 Department of Education and Science (1975), Education Survey 21.
17 Lobban (1975).
18 Byrne (1975).
19 Ibid.
20 Maccoby and Jacklin (1974).
21 Clift (1978).
22 Nash (1973).
23 Sears (1965).
24 Ricks and Pyke (1973).
25 Maccoby and Jacklin (1974).
26 Sears and Freeman (1968).
27 Lobban (1974). See also Moon (1974).
28 Lobban (1974).
29 Davies and Meighan (1975).
30 Kepner and Koehn (1977).
31 Weiner, unpublished research.

32   Fennema (1974).
33   Ernest (1976).
34   Dornbusch (1974).
35   Fennema (1974).
36   Curriculum Development Centre (1975).
37   Council on Interracial Books (1974).
38   Curriculum Development Centre (1975).

Chapter 7

Sex differences in performance in science examinations[1]

Jan Harding

Comment on the small number of women, relative to men, working within science and technology is now commonplace. The origins of this may be complex, but the pattern is irrevocably established at option-choice time in our secondary schools.

THE PRESENT POSITION

A DES survey,[2] published in 1975, indicated that whereas nearly 50 per cent of boys studied physics in the fourth and fifth forms, only 12 per cent of girls did so. In biology the pattern was reversed, with more than 50 per cent of girls, but only 27 per cent of boys studying it.

Statistics of 16-plus examination entry [3] show that this behaviour is relatively stable, with steady increases in entries for science subjects, by both boys and girls, over the years since 1964. The most rapid increase is in boys' biology entries (which now, each year, exceed those in chemistry in both the CSE and GCE 'O' level) although the percentage increases in girls' physics and chemistry, from lower base lines, were more spectacular to 1974.[4] Since 1974 the entries for girls in physics have tended to level off, while those for boys continue to increase. The ratio of boy: girl entries in physics is of the order of 4:1 at 'O' level and 8:1 at CSE. The ratios for chemists appear less biased, but largely because fewer boys study chemistry. It appears that sex biases in the study of physics and, to a lesser extent, biology become more marked with less able children.

Explanations

Conventional wisdom has laid blame for inadequacies in girls' science education at the door of girls' schools, with their assumed poorer level of provision of laboratories, equipment and staffing. Mrs Renée Short argued in the House of Commons (5) that all would be well when mixed schools replaced single-sex schools.

87

But the DES survey (6) revealed that girls who were offered physics in years 4 and 5 were one and a half times more likely to choose it if they were educated in a girls' school rather than in a mixed school.

Other explanations involve differential interests and abilities, but the former, too, seem to be contextually related. Ormerod's work (7) showed that boys' and girls' attitudes to physics, similar in his sample of single-sex schools, became polarized in the mixed schools; and for the girls, in particular, liking for physics was not closely related to their choosing to study it.

What of abilities? Alison Kelly (8) has reviewed studies of intellectual abilities and their relationship (often supposed rather than demonstrated) to performance in science. She discusses sex differences in tests of numerical and mechanical skills, problem-solving, and spatial abilities, and sees the last as a possible source of differential success in science. She points out, however, that overlap between the sexes occurs in the results of all these tests; and if differences in spatial ability were the sole cause of the imbalance in numbers, then there should be two women in, for example, engineering for every three men.

Teachers' opinions

Science teachers' perceptions of pupils' abilities may be significantly related to their performance.(9) The writer interviewed such teachers during case studies carried out within a research project (10) which enquired into the use of new science curricula. Some maintained they found no overall difference between boys' and girls' performance in science and, indeed, claimed that girls were among their ablest pupils; but others mentioned greater problems experienced by girls, especially when using 'the Nuffield approach' or enquiry-based methods in learning science.

Entry and percentage pass data for the three years 1971-3 appeared to support the latter group of teachers, for whereas the boys showed considerably higher percentage passes in Nuffield 'O' biology and physics over national figures, this was not true of girls. Both sexes showed superior performance, in terms of percentage passes, in Nuffield chemistry.(11) There were proportionately fewer girls in the Nuffield groups than in national entries, but no further data on the nature of the groups were available, although it was known that the large entries from boys' public schools were not matched by similar entries for girls.

FURTHER ENQUIRIES: THE GIRLS AND SCIENCE EDUCATION PROJECT

Subsequently, research was initiated (12) to attempt to relate boys' and girls' comparative performance in science to the type of school they attended and to skills and knowledge required for success, using data already available in GCE examinations. Co-operation was obtained from GCE Boards and six examinations were chosen: the three Nuffield 'O' level sciences and one further examination, in each of biology, chemistry and physics, that represented

a more conventional course at the time (1974). For reasons
relating to the administration of the Nuffield examinations, the
'Nuffield' sample was selected from the candidates entering through
one Board only and, for geographical comparability, this Board was
identified, in each subject, as that administering the 'conventional' examination.

Within total populations of candidates, defined as above, a
disproportionate, stratified, systematic sample was drawn, for
each examination, to give about 1,000 individuals within 10 categories, identified by sex of candidate, intake of school (whether
single-sex or mixed) and selectivity (whether the school was identified by the DES as grammar, comprehensive or direct grant or
independent). Initially, comparisons of percentage passes and mean
marks for separate papers were made within each examination and,
for the former, between Nuffield and conventional examinations for
each subject.

Percentage pass analysis

No overall differences between percentage passes for boys and girls
were found in any of the six examinations. However, further analyses of the performance of sub-groups showed interesting trends
and some significant differences. Most noticeable was the vari-
ability in the percentage passes of groups of girls. In each
examination, the range of values obtained for girls was greater
than that found for boys. For example, only 13 percentiles separated groups of boys in Nuffield biology, whereas for girls the
figure was 34 percentiles. In only two of the examinations did
the range for boys exceed 20 percentiles, while that for girls
fell below 30 percentiles in only one.

Hypotheses were generated and tested for support or refutation;
differences of less than 5 percentiles were discounted as showing
'little difference'. For each hypothesis twelve sub-group comparisons were available from the six examinations. The hypotheses
are numbered and stated below, and a summary of the outcomes of
testing them is shown in Table 7.1.

Hypotheses generated from data

  1 Boys from mixed schools gain higher percentage passes than do
     girls from these schools when comparisons are made within
     grammar and comprehensive categories separately.
  2 Girls from girls' schools gain higher percentage passes than
     do boys from boys' schools when comparisons are made within
     grammar and comprehensive categories separately.
  3 Boys in grammar schools gain higher percentage passes than do
     girls in grammar schools when comparisons are made within
     single-sex and mixed schools separately.
  4 Boys in comprehensive schools gain higher percentage passes
     than do girls in comprehensive schools when comparisons are
     made within single-sex and mixed schools separately.
  5 Boys in boys' schools gain higher percentage passes than do

boys in mixed schools when comparisons are made within grammar and comprehensive schools separately.

6   Girls in girls' schools gain higher percentage passes than do girls in mixed schools when comparisons are made within grammar and comprehensive schools separately.

7   Boys in grammar schools gain higher percentage passes than do boys in comprehensive schools when comparisons are made within single-sex and mixed schools separately.

8   Girls in grammar schools gain higher percentage passes than do girls in comprehensive schools when comparisons are made within single-sex and mixed schools separately.

TABLE 7.1   Outcomes of hypotheses testing on sex differences in science exams

Samples within which comparisons were made	Hypotheses	Outcome of comparisons			
		Supporting	Refuting	Little difference	
Mixed schools	1 B > G	6	0	6	Supported
Single-sex schools	2 G > B	5 + 4 DGI	3	4	Weakly supported
Grammar schools	3 B > G	3	2 + 4 DGI	7	Refuted and reversed only within DGI
Comprehensive schools	4 B > G	6	3	3	Supported
Boys	5 SS > M	3	5	4	Refuted and weakly reversed
Girls	6 SS > M	5	2	5	Supported
Boys	7 Gr > C	11	0	1	Supported
Girls	8 Gr > C	12	0	0	Supported

B = boys, G = girls, S = single sex, M = mixed, Gr = grammar, C = comprehensive, DGI = direct grant + independent

Hypotheses 7 and 8 were anticipated, and were assumed to be largely dependent on the stage of secondary reorganization reached in the early 1970s. As the effect operated in the same direction for boys and girls, and within most examinations, it was assumed to have little direct bearing on this research and the comparisons were not pursued further.

Comparisons of Nuffield and conventional examinations within separate subjects

Percentage passes for corresponding groups of boys and girls were compared for the Nuffield and more conventional course examinations in each subject.

No clear pattern of direction of differences was obtained; and, because the number of schools providing the Nuffield samples was relatively small, any generalizations must be treated with caution. Boys showed more variation as whole groups, gaining a higher percentage pass in Nuffield chemistry than in conventional chemistry ($p < .05$), but a lower percentage pass in Nuffield physics than in conventional physics ($p < .01$). These differences held also for the boys in mixed schools. The variation for girls emerged when the comparative performance of girls in mixed schools was set beside that of whole groups of girls. Only in physics was the performance of all girls significantly different, with the higher percentage pass being obtained in the conventional examination, but this difference was not displayed by the samples of girls from mixed schools. In contrast, girls from mixed schools were less successful in Nuffield biology than in the conventional biology examination ($p < .01$), although for girls as a group there was no significant difference.

Comparisons within separate parts of each examination

Each of the six examinations used in this study contained more than one part. Although no significant differences between the sexes were apparent in percentage passes, some differences were found in mean scores obtained by boys and girls in parts of some of the examinations.

The papers included, broadly, three types of item: multiple choice (the two biology examinations contained none of these); structured questions (sections containing questions consisting of several parts were included in this category); and essay-type questions (only conventional biology included questions of this type).

All the physics and chemistry examinations included a separate multiple choice paper or section, two of them including as many as 70 items. In all but conventional chemistry, sex differences appeared. In Nuffield chemistry the boys, overall, obtained a higher mean mark than did the girls ($p < .001$) and this was maintained in the mixed schools, but at a lower significance level ($p < .01$). The boys again performed better as a group in Nuffield physics ($p < .01$), but this disappeared in the mixed schools comparison. The conventional physics showed no overall differences, but the boys gained a higher mean mark than the girls in mixed schools ($p < .001$); the girls in girls' schools were more successful than those in mixed schools ($p < .01$).

In the three Nuffield examinations and conventional chemistry the structured parts showed no sex differences. In both Nuffield biology papers the differences displayed in the percentage passes comparisons again occurred: girls being more successful when educated separately.

The boys did better than the girls in conventional biology, both overall and in mixed schools (p < .001). In the conventional physics, mixed schools samples, the boys were also more successful than the girls (p < .01), who did better if they came from girls', rather than mixed, schools.

These differences raise all kinds of questions. First, how reliable are they? Ferguson (13) has shown similar outcomes to have occurred when the London University, GCE 'O' level biology format changed to include a multiple-choice paper with an extended answer paper: the boys gained higher means in the former, while girls did better in the latter.

The boys' lesser achievements in extended answer questions may derive from a lower facility with language. Although more girls than boys enter for GCE 'O' level English language examinations, the girls achieve percentage passes around 10 percentiles higher than do the boys, but we have no means of knowing whether it is the same inadequacies that result in loss of marks in written English as in written science answers.

The extension of multiple-choice assessment techniques, which has accompanied the greater availability of computers, should lead us to question the skills required for successful performance in them. Do they favour the logical thinker or those who can argue from restricted data? Do they penalize the divergent thinker or those more aware of possible contextual dependence of outcomes? Do they require a greater independence of judgment? Is a dependence on learnt material a disadvantage? Do learning styles developed in school affect performance? Because assessment plays crucial roles in creating feedback to the learners and in determining future life chances, it is essential that we understand what different techniques assess and how any possible bias occurs.

The greater equality in performance of girls compared with boys in mixed schools in the Nuffield physics and chemistry examinations does not support teachers' perception that girls are less able than boys to cope with this type of course; and in the study reported by Wood and Ferguson,(14) the girls were markedly more successful than the boys in Nuffield chemistry. That these studies do not display a lesser success of girls in mixed schools suggests some factor or factors (e.g., in the course, the schools, or the teachers) may be responsible and merits further investigation.

DISCUSSION

No support for the overall superiority of performance of boys over girls, in science, emerged from this study, in the design of which equal populations of boys and girls were included from different types of school. However, the differences found within sub-groups are discussed below and their possible significance assessed.

The direct grant and independent samples (DGI)

For two of the Nuffield examinations no DGI group was included, as the number of schools entering pupils for the examination through

the Board chosen was too small to provide a viable sample. Hence
the DGI groups were excluded from all main analyses.

But, where they occurred, the DGI girls were outstandingly
successful, obtaining passes of around 80 per cent or more. This
is not true of the boys in the equivalent schools. There were,
however, fewer boys' DGI schools, in the original populations of
candidates, than girls' DGI schools. The numbers of these schools,
nationally, for the 13- to 16-year-old pupils are approximately
equal; moreover, it was known that many boys' public schools enter
candidates through the Oxford and Cambridge Joint Examinations
Board (not used in this study), whereas few girls' schools do so.
It appears, therefore, that the samples of DGI boys were deficient
in some of the ablest candidates in these schools as a whole.

Although comparisons with the boys may not be justified, the
performance of the girls remains. It may reflect a school policy
of entering only those girls who were likely to pass; but even so,
the entries per school were comparable with, and even exceeded,
those of the maintained grammar schools, which were often larger
in size.

Single sex and mixed schools

Dale's classical work (15) reports on studies of the relative
success in examinations of boys and girls. All were carried out
in grammar schools, and the only studies attempted since the
introduction of the General Certificate of Education in 1950 were
located in Northern Ireland, where the administration of schools
and of the public examination system differs considerably from
those in England and Wales.

Dale claims that:

The general pattern established over a period of some 45 years,
with very large numbers of schools and of pupils, and in many
and different parts of the country ... shows that the co-
educated boys are slightly superior to those boys in boys'
schools ... and girls in girls' schools are approximately equal
to the co-ed girls.

In several of the cases cited the girls' school pupils were significantly more successful than girls from mixed schools, especially in the physical sciences; but Dale emphasizes that the girls
in the latter schools were handicapped in two of the studies by
age, social class and the burden of subjects they studied for
examination. He assumes that differentials in these characteristics continue to apply to girls in the different types of school.
The only recent work to throw light on this,(16) found that, when
ability was controlled, girls entering for a larger number of
subjects gained the higher percentage of passes in them, thus
refuting Dale's assumption and suggesting an aspiration effect on
performance.

The research reported in this chapter weakly supports Dale's
findings for boys (hypothesis 5), but reinforces that girls from
girls' schools are more successful in science than those from
mixed schools (in spite of the possibly higher level of selection
in terms of ability, in the physical sciences, of the latter).

Where boys and girls were educated together, the boys tended to be more successful than the girls; when educated separately there was some support for girls' greater success over the boys. In comprehensive schools there was a tendency for boys to gain higher percentage passes, while there was no evidence of the overall superiority of either sex in grammar schools (Dale's populations). It appears that girls studying science may be at a disadvantage in the mixed school, especially if this is a comprehensive school. Therefore, those mixed comprehensive schools in which girls perform well in the sciences, and do so in relatively large number, are of particular interest.

Objectives for girls' education

Lavigeur (17) has drawn attention to two conflicting ideologies of girls' education: one, that they should receive an education equal to that of their brothers; and the other, that each sex should be educated to fit the role they assume in society, which, for the girl, is that of homemaker, wife and mother. The former was expressed in the curriculum of the early grammar schools established for girls in the last quarter of the nineteenth century (although Delamont (18) argues that even these schools did not escape pressures to educate their pupils to be 'ladies'), while the latter was most succinctly expounded by Newsom (19) in the context of secondary modern schools.

Many of the women teachers in the grammar schools of the twentieth century were themselves educated in those early schools and would be found in greater numbers in girls' schools, thus influencing the expectations within them. A large proportion of the girls in the grammar schools (both single-sex and mixed) came from professional, middle-class homes, where parents would be more likely to support their aspirations. On the other hand, the male and female sex roles, very clearly defined in working-class cultures, found reinforcement in the secondary modern school.

When schools are reorganized to become larger, mixed and comprehensive, the objectives of teachers, and the messages conveyed to the girls, become pluralistic; but as 70 per cent of all pupils are the average and less able, about whom Newsom wrote, the relevant ideology of homemaker, wife and mother role is likely to predominate for girls and lead to lower academic aspirations.

Such arguments may be used to account for the differential performance of girls described above, but point to the importance of the expectation found in the school, rather than the type of school in itself.

Girls' choice of, and performance in, science

In any discussion of girls' achievement in science two factors must be recognized. One, that school subjects (as well as adult occupations) carry a sex bias in terms of the relative numbers of males and females who are involved in them (and this has been shown above to be more extreme in mixed schools). Physical scientists, both teachers and those made visible in the media, are more likely to be men than women; physics textbooks contain many more references to males than to females,(20) and the type of example chosen for discussion is more likely to refer to a traditionally masculine interest than to a feminine one.

The other factor is the vocational role that the sciences have assumed in the school curriculum. In spite of the cultural claims made for science education, the physical sciences have been chosen largely by pupils who wish to use them in future occupations and not by others. There is a sense, also, in which biology (including, as it does, the working of the human body and aspects of hygiene and nutrition) has vocational relevance for girls, preparing them for the home-based role.

A common view in our society is that employment outside the home is indispensable for men, but not for women, who work merely to supplement the family income, or for 'pin-money'. From research carried out in the USA, Douvan and Adelson (21) claim that the job he will do serves both to make sense of present experience for the boy and to integrate his developing personality as he moves through adolescence. For the girl, the job merely fills in between school and marriage; the integrating principle she uses is a developing femininity, emphasizing the person she is becoming, rather than what she will do.(22)

Bearing these factors in mind, one can argue that there are at least two dimensions influencing girls' choice of the sciences and possibly their achievement in them. These are the distribution of school subjects or occupations along a masculine/feminine dimension, and commitment to work outside the home. The first may be constructed from the relative numbers of boys and girls choosing to study each subject or to follow an occupation; but, while the second may be conceptualized, it is more difficult to measure. Its importance, in the argument that follows, is in the increased motivation to succeed that commitment to work confers.

Theoretically, the two dimensions may be placed at right angles to define four cells, as shown in Figure 7.1. Individuals may then be placed within the cells in terms of their position on the work commitment dimension and their involvement in sex-typed activities.

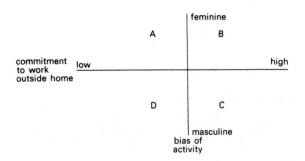

FIGURE 7.1 Dimensions relating to the choice of science subjects

Cell A will be populated by those who pursue 'feminine' activities (i.e., those which traditionally have been undertaken by women), with low career expectations. These will be largely women.

Cell B will be populated by those who pursue 'feminine' activities, but with higher career expectations. These may be females following careers in teaching, nursing or other paramedical fields, or by males who are at the top of their fields in, say, haute-couture, haute-cuisine, music, dance and, more recently, in nursing. Cell B is acceptable for females if the career has caring or service characteristics, but acceptable for males if they assume leadership roles within the activity.

Cell C contains those working in male-dominated fields (largely males, of course). A female in this cell must be prepared to defy convention along both dimensions, and it is this we ask a girl to do when she chooses to study physical science.

Cell D provides no acceptable location for the male, as he would be opting out of work or lacking in ambition. It may contain girls who have chosen to study, say, physics because they like it or are good at it and then are uncertain how to use it, being conscious of the male bias to activities that involve it. Such a girl may decide to teach and therefore move to cell B, as physics teaching is a more acceptable female occupation than practising physics in some other form.

Although what a girl learns in the home and absorbs in many subtle ways from her contacts with the media and the structure of society may contribute strongly to determining her position on the two dimensions, this chapter argues that the research reported above suggests that schools are powerful mediators of expectation during the crucial years of adolescence. Their influence is felt through careers advice, the presentation of options, and in many unrecognized ways in classroom interaction. The grammar schools, in which Dale and this research detected only small disadvantages for girls, are rapidly being replaced largely by mixed comprehensives, within which a lesser expectation of girls may prevail and in which, as this research suggests, girls are under-achieving relative to boys.

The distribution of girls, within a school, in cells A, B, C and D may be a measure of the degree to which a school succeeds in enabling girls to avoid a constraining conformity to stereotypes of female behaviour. Because the physical sciences carry a masculine image, the way girls behave within them may be regarded as an indicator of how that school processes its girls.

CONCLUSIONS

The under-achievement of women in science-related careers at all levels, but especially in the more technological fields, has its roots in the school, where few girls obtain the relevant qualifications and where many acquire sex-stereotyped attitudes to achievement in work outside the home.

The research into boys' and girls' performance in 'O' level science examinations reveals no overall difference in success in terms of percentage passes. In maintained schools, the most highly selective groups of girls in physical science (i.e., those in mixed schools) appear to be the least successful when compared with corresponding groups of boys and other girls. There is evidence also that relative success of boys and girls in examinations may be influenced by the modes of assessment used: multiple-choice items favouring boys and essay-type items favouring girls.

Because of the increasing importance of success in public examinations for future educational opportunities, we need greater understanding of the skills boys and girls bring to their responses to different types of assessment item, and how these relate to performance in real-life situations.

Although special attention to the content and presentation of science lessons may be needed, it is suggested that further research should be carried out into the ways girls' expectations and performance are shaped overall in the mixed comprehensive school, the most common school of the future.

NOTES

1   This chapter has been adapted from a paper read at the BERA Seminar, 'Women, Education and Research', at Lougborough University, 14-16 April 1978.
2   Department of Education and Science (1975).
3   Department of Education and Science, 'Statistics of Education', vol.2.
4   HM Inspectorate (1977).
5   'The Times', 22 January 1975, p.4.
6   See note 2, above.
7   See Ormerod (1975).
8   Kelly (1976).
9   Rosenthal and Jacobson (1968).
10 Curriculum Diffusion Research Project, supported by SSRC (1971-4) and based at the Centre for Science Education, Chelsea College, University of London, under the direction of Professor P.J. Kelly. See Harding (1975).
11 Harding (1975).
12 'Girls and Science Education Project', supported by the Nuffield Foundation and based at Chelsea College, 1974-5, under the supervision of Dr J. Harding.
13 Ferguson (1977).
14 Ferguson and Wood (1974).
15 Dale (1974).
16 Rauta and Hunt (1975).
17 Lavigeur (1976).
18 Delamont (1978).
19 The Newsom Report (1963).
20 Taylor (1978).
21 Douvan and Adelson (1966).
22 The influence that a prospective job has for a boy may be lessened at a time of heavy unemployment for the young school-leaver. R.E. Pahl ('New Society', 2 November 1978) has suggested that the girl may view work (often unskilled and part-time) as an escape from the isolation of the home, while the boy seeks personal satisfaction in the rewards of family life.

Chapter 8

Into work
Continuity and change

Teresa Keil and Peggy Newton

Any review of academic research about the social organization of
non-industrial societies will provide examples of well-documented
fieldwork where the relevance of sexual ascription, particularly in
relation to the division of labour, is recognized and analysed.(1)
In contrast, far from being an established theme in academic
research in industrial societies, the relevance of sex in the
division of labour has been relatively neglected. Until recently,
researchers were content to use all-male samples in their studies
of workers, and either to ignore female workers or to assume that
their experiences were, in every way, similar to those of males.(2)
Reappraisals have been prompted by challenges from the women's
movement, combined with contributions from economists and sociologists concerned to analyse the relevance of ethnicity in the
social processes which govern entry into work and experiences in
the labour market.(3)

The mid-1970s may be characterized as a period which saw the
publication of a wide range of new material which debated and
demonstrated the ways in which an understanding of the pattern of
sexual ascription continues to be relevant to understanding social
relationships both within the family and in the wider social structure. Attention was drawn to the ways in which the assumptions and
expectations which structure family relationships are reinforced by
experiences in the education system and set the framework for differential patterns of occupational experience. In Britain, for example,
girls are offered different subject choices within the curriculum
and take up the less 'powerful' subjects;(4) their early standard
of achievement compared with boys declines to the point where a
smaller proportion achieves 'A' levels in GCE examinations;(5) once
in the labour market they are less likely to enter skilled work, and
they have less frequent access to day-release from employment.(6)

An important feature of this differential structuring of educational and occupational opportunity by sex is the articulation of
assumptions and expectations about women's family relationships with
employers' perspectives on the recruitment and selection of their
employees. This results in strategies for recruitment, selection,
training and promotion which rest upon the conventional wisdoms that
women have, or will have, two roles, domestic and occupational, and

that they will give priority to the domestic.(7)   As a consequence,
it is 'natural' to assume that women, whether married or unmarried,
are not seriously committed to the labour market and need only be
regarded as temporary or relatively short-term workers who may be
seeking part-time rather than full-time work and who may, as likely
as not, be relegated to the secondary sector of the labour market
with lower pay and poorer conditions of service when compared with
their male counterparts.(8)   In such a context it is almost inevitable that opportunities for training, with the concommitant over-
tones of serious commitment and potential for promotion, are restricted.(9)

One of the most interesting aspects of this literature is the
suggestion that the assumptions about women's two roles and their
lack of commitment to the labour market have persisted in the face
of readily accessible and well-publicized demographic data about
the reduction in family size, the decreasing amount of time spent
caring for dependent children, and the data about the actual incid-
ence of women's employment, particularly the increasing rates of
employment of married women.(10)

The contradiction between changes in the pattern of women's
involvement in the labour market and the lack of change in the conventional wisdoms about it, raises many questions about the possible
barriers to change, not only in employers' perspectives but also
in the perspectives of others concerned with making or supporting
decisions relevant to the allocation of work.   In this chapter it
is hoped to identify some of the issues which need to be considered in the analysis of continuities and potential changes which
structure women's 'place' in the labour force.   To do this the
chapter draws upon two recent British research programmes.   Neither
was specifically designed to explore these issues in a systematic
way; but the emphasis of the first, the Leicestershire project,(11)
on established routes for entry into work and typical experiences
in the work situation, and the emphasis of the second, the EITB
project,(12) on an experimental programme to train girls as technicians in the engineering industry, provide useful and relevant
comparisons which it is hoped will provide a basis for further
discussion.   In the account of each project attention has been
drawn to employers' and employees' perspectives on the transition
from school, recruitment and selection, and experiences at work,
in an attempt to indicate the extent to which they throw light on
the ease with which conventional frameworks are accepted and the
difficulties involved in challenging them.

FOCUS ON CONTINUITIES: THE LEICESTERSHIRE PROJECT

The Leicestershire research project, completed at the end of 1976,
was undertaken in response to the initiative of the Working Party
on Education and Industry which was established by the county's
Education Committee in the early 1960s.   The Working Party was concerned to co-ordinate the knowledge available about education and
industry and the relationship between them and, where appropriate,
to provide for the collection of new data.   The main objective of
the research project was to gather information about the pattern of

induction practices in the kinds of work organizations entered by
young people in the county and to record their experiences of them.
With such an objective a sample of work organizations rather than
of school-leavers was indicated and, because relatively little was
known, a larger sample rather than intensive study of a smaller
number also offered the opportunity of reflecting the variety of
practices and experiences. Time and resources permitted a total
number of 93 work organizations to be considered, the selection
guided by the information available from the Youth Employment Service (now the careers Advisory Service) about the pattern of
employment entered by school-leavers in Leicestershire in the five
years prior to the survey.

The work organizations were drawn from the public sector (10
research sites covering central and local government and national-
ized industries), and the private sector (83 research sites,
including 19 in professional services such as banking, insurance
and building societies and 64 in a wide range of commercial and
industrial categories. In each of the 93 work organizations the
member of management responsible for the recruitment of school-
leavers was interviewed, and interviews were also carried out with
young workers who had entered that work organization during the
preceeding year. A total of 307 young workers (151 females, 156
males) was interviewed. The members of management were asked about
recruitment, selection, and induction policies and practices; the
young workers were interviewed about their recollections of knowledge and expectations about work before starting work as well as
their experiences since starting work.

As a consequence of the emphasis on the range and variety of
the normal pattern of employment in Leicestershire, the research
material may be used to point up the characteristics of typical
experiences and to draw attention to continuities in the process
of entering work. In addition, although the research was not
designed to analyse sex differences, comparisons between the data
from males and females may be used to highlight any differences
linked with sex.

Views on the transition: young workers

When asked to recollect their views about work before actually
starting work, the Leicestershire sample were no different from
respondents in other research surveys in looking forward to entering
work. Fewer than one in ten looked forward to nothing about work,
the others had a range of reasons: 'being a worker'; 'meeting
people'; 'earning money'; 'the job itself' and, inevitably, there
were some (20 per cent) who looked forward to work as a means of
getting away from school. The pattern of replies between the sexes
was very similar; the most significant difference was that 16 per
cent of the males, compared with 8 per cent of the females, looked
forward to going to work as an opportunity for meeting people.
Going to work was recollected as such a positive step that almost
one third said that they had no worries or concerns about the move.
Where there were worries, the highest proportion (about 20 per cent)
were focused on whether they could do the job.

The sample was also asked for their opinions as to whether the last year at school was a useful preparation for work, and the replies confirmed an impression in much of the literature that entering work relates to home experience rather than school, in that about 60 per cent of males and females expressed a negative view. Nonetheless, they were prepared to suggest ways in which schools should help to prepare young people for work with recommendations for more visits or experience of employment, more visits to schools of people from various employment situations, and more time for careers advice.

Entry into the labour market: recruitment and selection

Many studies, particularly those which concentrate on the individual characteristics of the job seeker, tend to overlook the fact that the demand for labour remains relatively stable in the short term, both in terms of the numbers recruited and the types of recruit desired. The variety of employment available in Leicestershire and the general prosperity of the area has normally guaranteed that the demand for labour will be high, and that the great majority of school-leavers will find themselves in employment within a relatively brief period after leaving school. The interviews took place against this background but during a period - between Summer 1974 and Autumn 1975 - when the market was much less buoyant and when the first delays in finding work were being reported. During the survey, those responsible for recruiting school-leavers maintained that they were continuing conventional policies about the numbers recruited and the skills needed. Their calculations were based on previous experience and the organizations' manpower development policies, although many acknowledged that their current market position gave them more choice in selection than previously.
    Although some members of management were careful to emphasize that they would consider male and female recruits for particular jobs, there was an acceptance of a conventional view of work for men and work for women. Typically, the members of management would mention that they were seeking 'suitably qualified lads to take up apprenticeships' or 'a young girl to work in the office'. The likelihood of sex being mentioned was also related to the emphasis placed on formal qualifications: the more important they were considered the more likely were employers to be recruiting 'people with at least four GCEs at "O" level'. It is interesting to note that, apart from employers in the public sector, the relative ease of recruitment did not express itself in demands for increased formal characteristics. Employers appeared to prefer the established means of selection but with a greater number from whom to select. Where formal qualifications were not emphasized, 'suitability' often meant a series of ascriptive characteristics relating to appearance and/or attitude, with the neat appearance and general willingness to be helpful being particularly emphasized in typically 'woman's work' such as that of shop assistants and office workers. However, it is important to note that the characteristics sought are linked to the skill level as well as to the sex of the recruit. As

well as the emphasis on the 'presentable' female worker with the
potential to project a 'secretarial image', there are some types of
semi- or unskilled work where for male and female recruits the
demand is for 'a bit of intelligence - not much in our trade! plus
punctuality and a willingness to learn'.

The ways in which vacancies were made known to potential
recruits varied. Newspaper advertisements were a frequently mentioned 'valuable way' of recruiting, particularly for semi-skilled
workers, both manual and non-manual. Formal contacts with schools
and the careers service were also useful ways of recruiting. Family
contacts were rarely used to recruit to non-manual work but were
used relatively often to recruit to apprenticeships.

Overall, there was no direct evidence of overt sexism but an
impression of employers working in a familiar market recruiting to
well-established categories of work which had long been recognized
as appropriate for men or women. Where there was 'open' recruitment, it was in the bureaucracies of local and central government,
and the achievement of formal educational qualifications rather than
traditional managerial practice which could be used to distinguish
between potential recruits. Only one work organization, in the
professional services category, maintained a 'double standard' by
recruiting both sexes according to the same formal qualifications
and allowing local managers to make the job offer to females but
insisting on head office confirmation of offers made to male
applicants.

In contrast with employers, young people have little or no
direct experience on which to draw when entering work, but move
into the labour market within a framework already structured by the
pattern of 'job horizons' indicated by their families, information
acquired at school, and knowledge about employers' requirements for
specific jobs in relation to their own formal academic qualifications achieved at school. In the sample of young people interviewed at work approximately 80 per cent held some academic qualifications by the time they left school. The overall pattern was
similar for males and females, though a slightly higher proportion
of females had no formal qualifications and a lower proportion had
left school with GCEs at 'A' level. The pattern of job seeking
complemented the pattern set out by the employers: the acknowledged
importance of newspaper advertisements, school and careers service
contacts, and, in some circumstances, family connections. In
addition one in ten of both males and females mentioned the importance of unprompted enquiries at the local firm, particularly in
order to obtain semi-skilled manual work. These similarities
between young men and women in their approach to work persisted in
their recollections of their reasons for wanting the job which they
held at the time of interview: replies such as 'the type of work';
'the training offered'; 'the prospects', appeared independent of
the sex of the respondent.

Such similarities, however, provide a marked contrast with the
actual placement of males and females in the occupational structure.
Table 8.1 indicates the differing skill 'profiles' by sex. Comparing all skill categories, the highest percentage of males (36 per
cent) appears in the skilled manual category, i.e. apprenticeships,
whereas the highest single percentage of females (40 per cent)

appears in the non-manual trainee category. Overall there is a
similar distribution of males and females between the public and
private sectors and, within the private sector, between the professional services and industrial and commercial sectors; but they are
employed in differing capacities: females are distributed more or
less equally between manual and non-manual work, whereas almost
two thirds of males are to be found in manual work. The pattern of
jobs entered throws some light on the structure of the local labour
market: semi-skilled or trainee work for the majority, with more
opportunities for males than for females to enter jobs in the
highest skill categories of both manual and non-manual work. Thus,
similarities in comments about entry into work conceal important
differences in allocation to work. Although the data do not support

TABLE 8.1 Distribution of young people interviewed by skill level

Skill category	Males	(%)	Females	(%)	All	(%)
Manual work						
1 Apprentics	56	(36)	26	(17)	82	(27)
2 Semi-skilled	48	(31)	46	(30)	94	(31)
3 Unskilled	1	(1)	4	(3)	5	(2)
Non-manual work						
4 Professional						
trainee	12	(8)	3	(2)	15	(5)
5 Trainee	32	(22)	61	(40)	96	(31)
6 Unskilled	4	(3)	11	(7)	15	(5)
Totals	153	(101)	151	(99)	307	(101)

any simple version of dual labour market analysis with females
excluded from the primary sector, the pattern in this local labour
market follows the characteristic pattern of the concentration of
females in those jobs which offer the least opportunity for access
to high levels of skill.

Experiences at work

The positive approach to entering the labour market described above
carried young workers through the sometimes bewildering and tiring
first days at work. Different job categories were associated with
differing networks of relationships which provided information about
the work situation in different ways. About half the sample (rather
more than half the females and less than half the males) were provided with a formal programme of induction, the provision of a programme being virtually guaranteed for those entering the public
sector and being more likely in large-scale organizations in the
private sector. Except for the public sector, where males and
females received identical induction programmes, an analysis of the
wide variety of programmes demonstrates that, for females, induction

programmes tended to be shorter than those for males (for example,
49 per cent of females compared with 23 per cent of males were
given programmes which lasted half a day or less, and 56 per cent
of females compared with 30 per cent of males received programmes
which lasted a day or less), and a higher proportion of males compared with females (25 per cent compared with 11 per cent) were
given induction programmes which were indistinguishable from the
first stages of training.

However, it is important to note that a lack of a formal induction programme was no bar to acquiring a wide range of knowledge
about the work situation. Other established workers and other new
workers figure strongly as informal sources of information, and both
sexes indicated the importance of the work group as a means of
establishing means of interpreting new experiences and learning the
appropriate responses and activities in the work situation. Indeed,
the major differences are not between the sexes but between the
public sector and the rest: young workers in the private sector
agreed that they were 'told all they wanted to know when they
wanted to know', whereas in the public sector there was more likely
to be dissatisfaction with the amount and content of information
given. It seems a reasonably hypothesis that it is the informal
network of work relationships which provides the information which
is most salient to 'settling in' relatively quickly.

These networks of established workers are characteristic of
certain kinds of work for both males and females. However, the
longer-term consequences differ for each sex. At the end of several
months at work, there are already marked differences in the replies
to the question 'What do you like most about working here?' when
analysed by sex. Comments were distributed into four main categories (and combinations of these): people; job; contract (i.e.,
relating to hours, pay, holidays, etc); and environment (i.e.,
relating to work conditions in terms of light, cleanliness, space,
etc.). Almost one third of the females commented favourably about
the people (compared with 16 per cent of the males), with the next
most frequent category being the people-job combination (26 per
cent). People, combined with some other comment, appeared in 67
per cent of the replies. The job alone accounted for 20 per cent
of replies.

When replying to questions about what was liked least about the
job, females were as likely as males to mention job issues, less
likely to mention people, and more likely to mention environment
characteristics. The pattern of relationships at work or the
characteristics of the jobs undertaken or some combination of the
two appear to be generating differences in the response to work
relatively quickly. Interestingly, however, the emphasis on people
as the most liked feature of work does not appear to influence
replies to questions about the most important things which young
people ought to be told when they first come to work. The emphasis
on the importance of information about the job itself is overwhelming, from males and females and, indeed, from management.

Views on the transition: management

Although members of management were not asked in any systematic way about sex differences in the rate of 'settling in' to work, several volunteered comments to the effect that girls adapted to the work environment more quickly, appeared less conscious of and embarrassed about status differences, and generally became more adult more quickly. Certainly within a year of starting work, at the point when the interviews took place, females were readier than males to reflect on their experiences and comment on the ways in which going to work had changed their lives. Almost half the females compared with a quarter of the males made some comment which indicated that they thought they had achieved greater maturity and they often emphasized some aspect of personal development such as a growth in confidence or less shyness in social relationships. Similar pro- portions of males and females, over one third, emphasized that the main change had been in other people's assessments of their status, particularly in terms of being treated as an 'equal' or as an 'adult'.

Summary

The general impression which emerges from the features of the Leicestershire project emphasized here is of a local labour market which operated relatively smoothly along traditional lines. Man- agement had clear ideas about the kinds of young people they wished to recruit and young people had sufficient guidance from the careers service, families and friends to be able to negotiate the appro- priate procedures, formal and informal, for obtaining jobs. The similarities of the sexes in the comments about reasons for seeking jobs had different meanings in terms of the sector of the job market applied for and entered, and the pattern of jobs held at the time of interview followed traditional lines. This is not to suggest that there is no opportunity for females to enter skilled work or indeed that no change could occur in such a labour market; it is to suggest that change is more likely in the public sector where meritocratic constraints rather than sexual ascriptions pre- dominate; or that changes will come relatively slowly in that there is no direct confrontation of the conventional division of labour.

FOCUS ON CHANGE: THE EITB PROJECT

Background of the research

In 1976 the Engineering Industry Training Board (EITB) began an experimental programme to train girls as technicians in two geo- graphical areas, the West Midlands and Surrey. The training initi- ative was designed to meet the problem of the increasing shortage of well qualified applicants to engineering at technician level, and to begin to redress the sex ratio in a strongly male-dominated industry. (Currently women hold approximately 2 per cent of engineering jobs at technician level and above.)
     In each of the years 1976, 1977, and 1978 and EITB has awarded

two-year scholarships to between 45 and 50 girls, and has sponsored them in their first two years of technician training. The programme, while generally successful, has raised a variety of issues concerning the recruitment and employment of women in a non-traditional field.

The findings presented below represent preliminary results from a large programme of research which has been funded by the EITB and the Social Science Research Council. The evidence on entrants to engineering is taken from individual interviews with 90 girls who began training under EITB sponsorship in 1977 and 1978, and 45 boys who began similar company-sponsored training in 1977. Information on commitment to engineering and plans for the future is based largely on comments made by 20 girls who were interviewed towards the end of their second year of training. The speculations on company policies towards women are based on interviews and informal conversations with employers who have been involved with the EITB girls' training.

The school context

One of the unexpected problems in recruiting girls for engineering was the opposition of many schools to the idea. In the first year of the programme a surprising number of schools refused to allow members of the training board to give careers talks to girls. Some headteachers responded to the scheme as 'preposterous', feeling that engineering was entirely unsuitable for girls.(13)

Individual interviews with girls who joined the EITB programme reveal that many of them had difficulty in taking courses that would prepare them for engineering. Over half (53 per cent) of the girls who began training in 1977 or 1978 reported that they had wanted to take technical subjects, such as woodwork or technical drawing, but had been unable to do so. Either the school did not allow them to do these subjects, they were treated less favourably than the boys, or the facilities were not available. Lack of appropriate courses was a particular problem in single-sex schools. Of the girls who did do one or more technical subjects at school (3o per cent of the 1977 group, 18 per cent of the 1978 group), a majority described having to 'put up a fight' to do so.

Most of the schools attended by the girls appeared to have very definite categorizations of 'girls' subjects' and 'boys' subjects' which are closely linked with notions of 'girls' jobs' and 'boys' jobs'. In the 1978 group of girls who came from mixed schools, 58 per cent described having careers lessons in which girls and boys were sometimes or always separated. This practice was justified by the idea that certain jobs were of interest only to members of one sex, thus reinforcing traditional sex-role boundaries.

Although girls were frequently dissatisfied with the careers advice they had received at school or from the Careers Advisory Service, they were most likely to hear about the EITB programme from these sources (see Table 8.2). If they are compared with a group of boys training at the same level in engineering, 51 per cent of the girls but only 31 per cent of the boys heard about their job through their school or the Careers Advisory Service. Girls

and boys were equally likely to hear about jobs in engineering
through advertisements in the newspaper or on the radio, with these
sources accounting for approximately one-third of each group. Boys
more frequently found jobs through parents, friends and other
'contacts' in the community; these sources of information were
reported by 27 per cent of the boys but only 9 per cent of the
girls.

TABLE 8.2   Sources of information about jobs and courses: comparisons of boys and girls in engineering

Source of information	Boys in engineering (N = 45)		Girls in engineering (N = 45)	
	No.	%	No.	%
Newspaper or radio**	14	31	31	34
Careers teachers from school or the Careers Advisory Service*	14	31	46	51
Friends, parents, 'contacts', etc.**	12	27	9	10
Self, i.e. wrote or phoned for information	2	4	0	0
A College of Further Education	2	4	2	2
Other	1	2	2	2

*   Differences between the groups significant (p < .02, χ^2 test)
**   Differences between the groups significant (p < .001, χ^2 test)

Parents did not usually suggest engineering as a career for their
daughters, but most girls reported that their parents were supportive of their choice. Fathers who were in engineering were somewhat
more likely to approve of engineering for their daughters than were
mothers, and many girls described having become closer and having
much more in common with their fathers since beginning the EITB
course. The experience of the EITB in recruiting girls for the
course suggests that parents are more liberal and willing to consider unconventional roles for their daughters than are schools.(14)
The reactions of the girls' classmates to the girls' choice of
engineering were mixed. Many of the girls who made the decision
during their final year of school reported that their friends (both
male and female) reacted with astonishment and disbelief. A
typical comment was: 'Once they got over the shock they were very
good about it'. Several girls in their second year of training
felt that their friends were envious of their jobs and their career
prospects. Many girls recounted experiences of meeting lads who
would not believe that they were trainee engineers, and who quizzed
them on technical terms until the girls were able to provide a convincing demonstration of their knowledge.

Selection and entry into work

Since schools and parents did not usually consider engineering as a
career choice for girls, it is interesting to note that 18 per cent
of the girls beginning the EITB course in 1978 had made a definite
commitment to engineering before or during their third year in
secondary school. These girls had chosen their subjects for examination with engineering in mind. Another 48 per cent of the girls
reported thinking seriously about engineering during their last two
years in school, but 34 per cent of the girls admitted that they had
not really considered engineering until they heard about the course.
Many of the girls making a late decision mentioned that they hadn't
know that the field was open to women.
     When asked their reasons for choosing engineering, most girls
mentioned the training and career opportunities that it offered.
Many girls said they wanted to be in a field that made use of their
scientific interests but that was also practical. Some girls were
initially attracted to the field because they wanted to do something
different and because they found the traditional female options -
secretarial work, shop work and nursing - unappealing.
     A problem faced by many of the girls and the panel who selected
them for the course was the girls' lack of knowledge of what engineering entailed. Girls who had not done technical subjects at
school were often unfamiliar with tools and with machinery on the
shop floor. Although they had attended an 'open day', when they
had been shown around a factory or a training centre, some girls
were uncertain about what they would be doing and whether they would
like it.
     The members of EITB staff who have been involved in selecting
girls for the course have found that the selection procedures used
for boys were inappropriate for girls. The norms for standard
batteries of tests for engineering apprentices have been developed
for males, and their relevance for females is unknown. In inter-
viewing boys, employers and training staff frequently ask questions
about engineering-related hobbies. Since few girls have such
hobbies, these questions are rarely useful. The selection panel is
forced to rely on girls' formal qualifications and their assessment
of motivation. They look for girls who are keen and who seem
likely to 'stick the course'. Although girls are not required to
have family in engineering, some members of selection panels regard
this as a 'plus factor', feeling that these girls are likely to
know more about engineering and be more realistic about the training
required.
     Many of the girls in their second year of training describe a
process of growing commitment to engineering. 'I didn't really know
what it was all about, but now I can't imagine doing anything else,'
commented one girl. The need to defend her choice constantly and
to prove her capability served to reinforce her dedication to engineering. Other girls talk about their growing interest in a particular aspect of engineering and their pride in products produced
by the company providing their training.
     When asked about their plans for the future, most of the girls
on the EITB programme mention that they would like to marry and
have children. A majority of these girls plan to take at least five

years off work to take care of young children and then hope to return to engineering. Many assume that companies will welcome them back and provide them with appropriate re-training.

Conversations with personnel officers in several engineering firms suggest that the girls are probably over-optimistic. Although some companies have made special arrangements to re-train women whom they regarded as outstanding employees, none of those sampled had specific re-training courses for men or women who had taken time out from engineering. If the numbers of women in the field increase and there continue to be shortages of appropriately qualified men, employers may find it necessary to make provisions for women and their children. At the present time, young women's chances for re-entry depend largely on market forces and the needs and circum-stances of individual employer and employee.

DISCUSSION

The comparisons and contrasts provided by the two studies raise a series of issues both about the processes of allocation to work and the problems of social change.

The contrast between the experiences of those following well-established procedures compared with those making 'unusual' choices is considerable. Where perspectives on employment are narrowed to those parts of the labour market considered appropriate by both potential workers and potential employers, young people quickly learn the 'rules of the game'. It is only in times of relatively high unemployment that the transition from full-time education to full-time employment proves difficult; and even then it is because jobs have to be taken which are considered below the appropriate skill level or status level rather than crossing sex lines. Where an 'unusual' choice is made new procedures must be established and explanations given at each stage. The new 'rules of the game' have to be discovered. The recruitment of females as technicians in the engineering industry provides a sharp challenge to male dominance in manual work and in skilled work and thus confronts both the ideologies and structures of the traditional division of labour.

The number of people involved in any reappraisal of the conven-tional allocation to work is considerable: parents, teachers, employers, supervisors, workmates. Each group has to be confronted with the unusual choice and persuaded that it is 'worth' the change in attitude, procedures, behaviour. This contrasts with the rela-tively straightforward and smooth transition for those who can rely on the support of parents, work friends and supervisors to 'settle in'. For them the social pressures are to conform to existing patterns of work speed, punctuality, social relationships; their right to be there is not under debate.

Linked with the point above is the general point that what appears to be a decision about job choice at a particular moment in time is revealed as a continuous process of affirming one's position in the labour market, either as an acceptable and supported member of an appropriate group, or as a person determined to follow an unusual path.

Thus sex remains relevant in the process of entering work,

guiding personnel selection, authority relationships, and relationships with fellow workers. The extent to which formal educational
qualification may modify the relevance of sex is yet to be fully
explored.

As a consequence of social processes which structure entry into
work and subsequent experience, social change is not easy to implement. Even in the context of 'liberal' legislation, conventional/
traditional procedures predominate because they reinforce employers'
recruitment strategies, do not 'upset' other workers and, to a
considerable extent, confirm the views of young people, their
parents and their teachers about what is appropriate work.

In addition, it will be clear that mere investment of resources
does not necessarily resolve problems. The sponsorship of change,
the impact on the status of other workers and employers' long-term
commitment also have to be taken into account.

Both the Leicestershire and EITB projects suggest that pragmatism
is an important strategy in young people's choice of work and in
employers' selection of workers. Decisions on both sides are taken
in the light of immediate factors and the implications of such
decisions (e.g., the desire of many young women to return to work
after child care) are rarely explored. The current pattern of
training for skills is relatively rigid, involving entry soon after
the statutory school-leaving age. It offers few opportunities for
those who wish to begin training after 17, or for those who wish to
change their field of work. Yet, if microprocessors bring about
the dramatic technological changes that are predicted,(15) training
opportunities and occupational structures for men and women will
need to be revised. A massive redistribution of labour will
involve new patterns of training and re-training for skills which
are, as yet, unplanned.

NOTES

1 Lewis (1976).
2 Brown (1976).
3 Doeringer and Piore (1971).
4 Shaw (1976).
5 Byrne (1978).
6 'Social Trends', Central Statistical Office, 9 (1979), p.79.
7 Myrdal and Klein (1968).
8 Barron and Norris (1976).
9 Mackie and Patullo (1977), ch.5.
10 Halsey (1972), ch.4, and 'Social Trends' 9 (1979), pp.83-6.
11 The Leicestershire Project was financed by the Leicestershire
    Working Party on Education and Industry and by the Training
    Services Agency of the Manpower Services Commission and carried
    out by J.A. Eldridge, J. Kelly and E.T. Keil of the Department
    of Social Sciences of Loughborough University. A concise
    report, 'Becoming a Worker' was published in 1976.
12 The research on the Engineering Industry Training Board pro-
    gramme has been supported by a Social Science Research Council
    Programme Grant to G.M. Stephenson and by an EITB research
    grant to G.M. Stephenson and P.D. Newton. A final report on

the work will be published by the EITB in 1981.
13   Wellens (1977).
14   Ibid.
15   Barron and Curnow (1979).

Chapter 9

Young women in the labour market
Stability and change

David Ashton and M. Maguire

INTRODUCTION

This chapter is concerned with the structure of job opportunities
that face women in general and young women in particular. In recent
years there have been a number of changes that have affected the
distribution of women in the labour force. In addition there have
been very significant changes in the participation of women in the
labour force. Against this general background we will attempt to
examine some of the factors that determine the distribution of
opportunities for women at the local level.

In recent years there has been a substantial shift in the distribution of occupations between the three sectors of the economy:
primary, secondary, and service. This is part of a longer-term
process of change that is characteristic of the more advanced
industrial societies of the West, in which employment in the primary sector and industry declines while the service sector expands.(1)
In Britain this decline of employment prospects in the manufacturing
sector has been more dramatic than in many other European societies; but what is of particular significance here is the effect
it has had on the structure of opportunities for women. In 1965,
3.14 per cent of women in employment were employed in manufacturing
industry, and within ten years this has fallen to 23.5 per cent.
The expansion of jobs for women has been in finance and insurance
and most dramatically in the field of community, social and personal service. This latter area accounted for 30.9 per cent of the
female labour force in 1965 rising to 39.3 per cent in 1975. The
overall effect of these changes, as Table 9.1 illustrates, has been
to create a situation in which almost three quarters of the women
at work are to be found in the service sector.

The last three decades have also witnessed a major change in the
social composition of the female labour force, caused by the influx
of married women. Table 9.2 provides some indication of the magnitude of this change. It shows how the activity rates of males and
non-married females have steadily declined, while that of married
women has increased substantially. Women in Britain have one of
the highest activity rates in the European Economic Community,
although there is reason to believe that it could increase still

TABLE 9.1 Sector breakdown of the labour force, 1965–75 (%)

Great Britain	1965			1970			1975		
	Total	Males	Females	Total	Males	Females	Total	Males	Females
Agriculture	3.8	4.9	1.9	3.2	4.1	1.7	2.7	3.5	1.4
Mining, quarrying	2.5	3.7	0.2	1.7	2.5	0.2	1.4	2.2	0.1
Manufacture	35.0	36.9	31.4	34.7	38.1	28.8	30.9	35.7	23.5
Electricity, gas, water	1.7	2.3	0.6	1.6	2.1	0.7	1.4	1.9	0.7
Construction	7.4	10.8	1.0	6.8	10.1	1.0	6.9	10.6	1.1
Industry, Total	46.6	53.7	33.2	44.8	52.8	30.6	40.7	50.4	25.4
Wholesale, retail, hotels, restaurants	17.1	12.6	25.5	16.4	12.2	23.7	16.9	12.6	23.6
Transport, communication	6.8	9.0	2.8	6.7	8.9	2.9	6.5	8.8	2.8
Finance, insurance	4.2	3.4	5.7	5.0	4.0	6.8	5.7	4.6	7.4
Community, social, personal	21.5	16.5	30.9	23.9	18.0	34.3	27.5	20.0	39.3
Service, Total	49.6	41.5	65.0	52.0	43.1	67.7	56.6	46.0	73.2

Sources: OECD Labour Force Statistics 1965–76, pp.432–7; OECD Basic Statistics, Paris, 1978.

TABLE 9.2   Economic activity rates by sex, 1951-76

	1951	1961	1971	1975	1976
Males	87.6	86.0	81.4	80.6	80.6
Married females	21.7	29.7	42.2	47.9	49.0
Non-married females	55.0	50.6	43.7	41.8	41.6

Source: 'Social Trends' No.9, 1979, Central Statistical Office,
        HMSO, 1978.

further.(2) One of the reasons for the decline in the activity
rate for the non-married is that more young women are staying on
at school and delaying their entry into the labour market. The
implication of all this for young female school-leavers is that
when they enter the labour market they face stiff competition from
married women, whom, for reasons to be detailed later, many
employers prefer.

On the national level the type of manual jobs that women tend to
be concentrated in are catering, cleaning, hairdressing and other
personal services, which account for 52 per cent of female manual
workers, and painting, assembling, inspecting and packing in manufacturing industry that account for a further 18.7 per cent. In
non-manual work 55.2 per cent are to be found in professional
occupations in education, welfare and health.(3) If current trends
continue these then are the areas where young female school-leavers
are destined to find work.

THE RESEARCH PROJECT

If it can be established that employment opportunities for females
are located largely in a limited range of industrial and occupational sectors, it follows that there will be considerable regional
and local differences in these opportunities, dependent upon the
characteristics of local labour markets. This is highlighted by
the variations in industrial and occupational structure in the
three labour markets we are studying in our current research project, into the structure of opportunities that face young people
in their early years in the labour force. The three local labour
markets are characterized by differing industrial structures and
levels of unemployment. Local labour market A has an industrial
structure skewed in the direction of general and mechanical engineering, textiles and footwear, and an unemployment rate slightly
below the national average. Local labour market B is dominated by
traditional heavy engineering industries and has an unemployment
rate two and a half times as great as the national average. Local
labour market C has a relatively low level of unemployment and an
industrial structure over-represented in the chemical, instrument
engineering and aerospace equipment manufacturing industries.

The distribution of employment opportunities in the three local
labour markets is represented by Figure 9.1. The textiles,

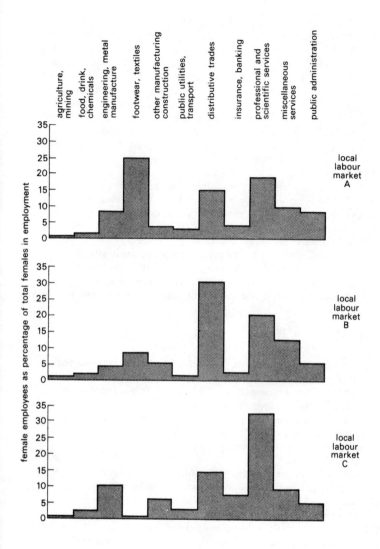

Figure 9.1 Employment opportunities for women in three local
labour markets

Source: Department of Employment Statistics 1975. Categories based
on the Standard Industrial Classification.

clothing, and footwear industries in local labour market A account
for 16.8 per cent of all employment and 24.5 per cent of female
employment, whereas the figures for local labour market B are 3.6
per cent and 7.2 per cent, and for local labour market C, 0.8 per
cent and 1.4 per cent. The distributive trades account for 30 per
cent of female employment in B, but for only 15.6 per cent in A,
and 14.9 per cent in C. In C, with its predominance of white-
collar employment, 33 per cent of females work in professional and
scientific services, compared with 19.4 per cent in A and 21.3 per
cent in B. These differences indicate the effect which the industrial structure of the local labour market can have on employment
opportunities for women.

The analysis in this account is based on the preliminary findings of the research project, derived from 120 interviews with
employers in the three areas. Of these 80 were conducted in local
labour market A, and consist of a representative sample of employers by size of establishment in the food, engineering, textiles,
clothing and footwear and metal manufacture industries, supplemented by additional interviews with employers in distribution and
public administration. The remainder are drawn from a variety of
industrial orders and are predominantly from local labour market B.

MALE AND FEMALE WORK

Just what determines the distribution of occupations between the
sexes? When asking individual employers whether they would consider females for such jobs as engineer, knitter and warehouseman,
we are frequently given the answer that these are 'traditionally'
male jobs. Similarly, when we ask why it is that only women are
recruited into the making-up side of the knitting industry,
packing in the food processing industry, typing and secretarial
work in administration and sales work in certain retail organizations, the response is sometimes stark amazement that one should be
so naive as to ask such a question; or alternatively surprise,
because that kind of question is not often asked. In either case
the answer one frequently receives is that these are 'traditionally' women's jobs or jobs that are more suited to women. However,
many of these jobs have not always been the exclusive preserve of
women, neither have all the 'traditionally' male jobs always been
the exclusive preserve of men.

During the nineteenth century, women and children were exten-
sively employed in heavy and dirty work in mining and the manufacture of iron, some of which required considerable physical strength
such as that involved in filling the iron furnaces and pulling
coal trucks. It was the morality of the Victorian aristocracy as
embodied in the Factories Act that forced women out of these and
other jobs in manufacturing. The conditions under which women may
sell their labour are still subject to the control of the state
through the Factories Act and the Health and Safety at Work etc.
Act, and an exemption has to be obtained from the authorities
before they can work shifts. The fact that women are not allowed
to work shifts is still given as a reason by some employers for not
employing them. It should be pointed out that many employers do

obtain exemptions from some of the provisions of the Act, especially when employing women for repetitive work in process production.

In the service sector, many of the jobs that are now predominantly filled by women in sales and clerical work were traditionally male occupations. In both of these areas, which have expanded substantially in this century, women have gradually displaced men as the major source of labour.(4) The reasons for this may well lie in the lower cost of female labour that became available once these occupations were rationalized within the context of modern bureaucratic organizations; office work, for example, became routine and specialized. In addition, the growth of adult literacy meant that the employers could recruit from a larger market in which female labour could compete. The result has been a decline in the relative earnings of clerical workers and the growing predominance of women within their ranks. A similar trend has been observed in the retail and distribution trade. Thus, while the picture we present here may appear static as we investigate it at one point in time, it is merely a snapshot of a broader series of changes that are affecting the distribution of occupational opportunities.

It is against this background of longer-term changes that the following comments from employers need to be viewed. Generally speaking, they will not consider employing women when the job makes heavy physical demands on the employee;(5) perhaps this reflects the extent to which the morality embodied in the early Factory Acts has become generalized and accepted as a self-evident truth. Another similar reason for excluding women from consideration for certain jobs is employers' belief that women would not be able to cope with the behaviour, attitudes and language of the male work group within which the jobs were located; especially where the women employed would constitute a small minority. This does not mean that we have not come across a number of smaller employers in the engineering industry that employ small numbers of women in what are predominantly male work groups. In these cases the women are recruited as they provide low-cost labour for repetitive assembly work. In such circumstances a great deal depends on the attitude of the individual employer.

In some work female labour is preferred to the total exclusion of males. The larger employers have frequently remarked to us that women are far better at coping with boring, repetitive assembly work than males. For this reason many employers in the food processing and light engineering trades employ large numbers of women. Such labour is considerably cheaper than that of males, a fact that managers are clearly aware of, yet some still maintain that even if this cost advantage of female labour was removed they would still recruit females for this type of work. This may be a measure of the strength of their belief in the superior ability of women in coping with these situations.

A similar belief is used to explain the preference for female labour in the textile industry; namely, that women are far better at jobs that require dexterity, turning out neat work at high speeds. Here again employers are clearly aware of the cost advantage of female labour, but maintain that it is not just the cost that makes women preferable as employees. We are not aware of any research that would either confirm or dispute the validity of these beliefs, but they are widely held among employers.

One further advantage that many employers perceive in female labour is its flexibility. This is particularly the case in certain types of office work and in the labour-intensive but seasonal trades such as textiles, where extensive part-time labour is employed. The working hours fit in with domestic commitments, but can be expanded and adjusted within those limitations to meet the requirements of the employer. For example, if there is an increase in orders, part-time workers may be persuaded to work a few more hours per week, and extra homeworkers may be recruited.

In the managerial, professional and administrative occupations it is very difficult to generalize about employers' beliefs concerning the suitability of female as opposed to male labour. Apart from the obvious case of nursing, where it is generally regarded as a female profession, the situation varies enormously. In the public services such as local government, the health service and education authority, it appears that women are more likely to compete on equal terms with men, at least at the point of entry. In private industry we have some evidence that men are preferred for managerial positions because of the old belief that women between the ages of 25 and 40 are likely to leave the job for the purpose of child-rearing. For example, in a large electronics firm there were 58 male managers and no females.

This belief has been reinforced in some cases by the maternity provision included in the Employment Protection Act, for now employers are obliged to keep jobs open for women while on maternity leave. Some employers believe that while it may be relatively easy to find a temporary replacement for someone on an assembly line, or to keep the line moving with one person absent, it is much more difficult to find a suitable replacement for someone in a key managerial position where the disruption caused is likely to be that much greater. Here again we must express caution, as some organizations in the private sector do employ women in managerial positions, especially in retail and distribution and certain functions in the manufacturing firms, such as personnel, design and buying. Obviously this belief about the possibility of women taking pregnancy leave does affect the opportunities that are open to them in the private sector and, one suspects, in the higher echelons of the public sector.

These are some of the reasons that employers advance for either excluding or preferring female labour: the demand side of the equation. As our research is concerned primarily with the provision of opportunities we can only offer some tentative suggestions about the supply side. One is that, as married women frequently place their domestic responsibilities above their commitment to work, their orientation to work tends to differ from that of many men and non-married females. They seek work that will fit in with their commitments, often preferring part-time work. For similar reasons many women are less instrumental in their attitude to work, placing greater importance on the significance of friendships formed at work.(6) In addition, notions of femininity acquired during the primary socialization of the young person tend

to steer young girls away from certain types of factory, in the
same way that notions of masculinity function to steer young males
away from certain types of office work.

In this respect we have some tentative evidence to suggest that
there may be more opportunities for girls to enter the engineering
trades than are reflected in the actual numbers employed. Many of
the larger firms have individual young women in their craft and
technician training programmes and are willing to take more. One
of the reasons the number remains small is that few young women
apply. As an alternative to office work or nursing it does not
appear to be very attractive. The fact that girls are now entering
these traditional male preserves does indicate that there has been
some shift in attitudes on both the young person's and employer's
part, although we would stress that it is the larger employers that
are taking the initiative and employing young women. As yet we
have had no sign of a comparable shift in attitude among the
smaller employers.

We have discussed some of the factors that determine the structure of opportunities for women. For the young female school-
leaver employment opportunities are further restricted by two
additional factors: age restrictions on entry and, more importantly, competition from married women. The age restrictions on
entry may be a product of the requirements of the Factories Act,
and the provisions of them incorporated into the Health and Safety
at Work, etc. Act, that prevent young women under 18 working nights,
or the stipulation that a driving licence is necessary for the job.
In practice it means that once a young person is 18 a new range of
opportunities opens up. Yet even these opportunities may still be
restricted in situations where the young person faces the competition of married women.

In general employers tend to believe that married women are
more stable and reliable as employees, and, given a choice, many
opt for married women; young school-leavers, they believe, are
more likely to be irregular in their attendance and more likely to
quit the job. When the job requires the company to make a substantial investment in training this belief may be further reinforced. The company may be afraid that a school-leaver who takes
a year to be trained may only stay with them for a short time
before starting her own family or moving to another job. In such
a case their investment in the training would be costly when compared to that made in the training of a married women who had
completed her family and who would be more likely to stay with the
firm for a number of years. Once again, it must be stressed that
not all employers hold this belief, but it does play a part in
restricting employment opportunities for young female school-
leavers.

One other belief that functions to restrict opportunities for
young women is that concerning the morality of employing them in
part-time work. A number of employers refuse to consider young
people for part-time work on the grounds that it is wrong to
recruit them for such jobs on leaving school, when they should be
entering full-time employment. It must also be said that many of
these same employers engage two shifts of part-time females per
day, and that they need not necessarily be regarded as part-time
jobs.

TRAINING

It has been established that, among school-leavers, a great many
more boys than girls enter employment involving some lengthy
planned training period.(7) This is certainly borne out by the
early findings of our research.

On the clerical side, for secretarial and typing jobs employers
expect new recruits to be proficient in the appropriate skills
before they take them on. Typists may be recruited straight from
school if they have attained a reasonable standard of typing at
school. For more advanced jobs requiring shorthand and secretarial skills, however, applicants will have undertaken college
courses in these skills. Many employers further reduce the
element of risk involved in engaging new personnel for clerical
posts by using a private employment agency to recruit girls as
temporary workers, and then offering permanent positions to any
who are considered satisfactory. In effect they are using temporary employment as a screening device, involving no commitment to
further training.

We have encountered only a very few organizations, one notably
in the public sector, which have recruited girl school-leavers as
supernumerary office juniors to be trained in various clerical
skills. Our feeling is that this practice has declined, due to
increased employment costs.

While girls entering clerical jobs are expected to possess
certain skills, many employers, mainly larger ones, are prepared
to give them day release to gain skills at college, in addition
to their own firm-specific on-the-job office training. It is often
claimed that only half of those to whom this facility is offered
actually take up the offer, and that even then there is sometimes
a noticeable lack of commitment to the day-release course, as
reflected in poor attendance. For this reason, employers are
inclined to stipulate that before they, the employers, are prepared to foot the bill for any further training, in terms of
payment of college fees and time off work, there must be some
evidence of commitment on the part of the employee. Thus they are
prepared to offer day-release provision after the employee has
spent a year studying in her own time, at evening classes.

It was interesting to find that one of the largest employers of
female clerical workers in the public sector undertook no training
whatsoever, but was content to 'buy in' experienced labour, relying on its favourable salary levels and structure to attract
sufficient suitably qualified candidates. Finally, it should be
noted that we did find firms which were undertaking the training
of girls in commercial occupations, such as accountancy, although
this does not appear to be widespread.

As far as training on the manual side is concerned, our research
information is primarily restricted to the manufacturing sector.
As mentioned previously, we have come across isolated incidences
of girls undertaking craft or technical apprenticeships in the
engineering and printing industries, but the only industries we
have found with widespread training provisions for young female
manual workers are the food-processing, textile and footwear
industries. The demand is for machinists and packers.

In the textile industry the larger firms have their own training schools, where the girls are paid a training rate until such
time as they are able to earn more through piecework on production.
Girls are expected to be able to 'hold their own' on production
after about six weeks, but employers find that there are difficulties, not in the initial transition from school to work but in the
transition from the training school to the production section.
Apparently girls are often content to continue working for the
training rate, as this still represents a considerable increase in
their weekly spending power. Among smaller firms in the textile
industry, the training period is of about the same length, but the
content is not as planned, and training usually consists of
'sitting with Nellie'. Some smaller firms form training groups,
which offer similar training at local colleges to that carried out
within employers' own training schools. The training lasts six
weeks, but girls are taught a variety of skills and are therefore
more versatile than those trained in specialist operations
within firms.

Similarly, in the footwear industry the larger firms have their
own training schools for young girls entering machining occupations;
but, apart from that, training is given on the job or occasionally
through day release. Once again, employers are reluctant to allow
day release because of the cost and the poor attendance by young-
sters. Overall, training for girls in manual occupations is of
very short duration.

CHANGES AT THE LOCAL LEVEL

At the local level it is difficult to establish with any precision
the extent to which the changes that are taking place nationally
are extending the opportunities for young female school-leavers.
The decline in the number of opportunities for females in manufacturing varies in its impact from one local labour market to
another. Changes in employers' perceptions of what is suitable
work for young females and the effect of legislation appear to
have a more uniform impact at the local level, although there may
still be some variation. The decline in manufacture has been in
textiles, footwear and clothing, and engineering industries that
have traditionally supplied a large number of semi-skilled, careerless opportunities for young women. The loss of these jobs will
affect only those local labour markets where these industries
dominate. On the other hand, the expansion of service sector jobs
that took place in the health service, local government and education was likely to have a more uniform impact at the local level,
except for commercial and central government services that are
more variable in their regional location.

We have not discovered any instance in which legislation has
had any dramatic impact on broadening the scope of opportunities
for women, for the pressures at work maintaining the existing
pattern of opportunities appear to be very strong. Certainly we
have little evidence of any marked change in employers' attitudes
in this respect. Where the legislation may have made an impact is
in raising the employers' consciousness about the possibility of

employing women in traditional male occupations. This is particularly the case in the large firms with a personnel department in which the members tend to be fully aware of the implications of legislation and who may create a pressure for change within the organization. In the smaller firms that do not have a separate personnel function the employers are not necessarily as fully informed about the contents or implications of legislation. Consequently it is larger, more prestigious firms that have been the first to introduce young female school-leavers into traditionally male occupations such as engineering.

Among the smaller employers, legislation has at least raised the question of employing women in male jobs. For example, one employer in the printing trade spoke of the possibility of training young female school-leavers in typesetting in the future, as this particular skill he saw as one appropriate for women: it was clean work, slightly monotonous, but required attention to detail. The other skills in the trade he saw as more appropriate for men. In the construction industry there is a belief that young women would not be able to cope with the physical demands that the construction trades make on apprentices. These examples illustrate some of the success and the limitation of legislation in influencing attitudes, although it is often the case that the unions as well as the employers have to change their attitude. In general we suspect that changes in opportunities for women are more likely to take place first in those areas where labour is scarce. However, in such areas there is less need for the young women to create pressure for change through applying for 'male' jobs, as there are substantial alternative opportunities.

So far in this discussion we have focused on the changes that are taking place at the point of entry to the organization; but in order to provide a more adequate analysis of the structure of opportunities it is also necessary to examine the workings of the internal labour market. The following two case studies of 'progressive' organizations provide an insight into the impact of the forces for 'stability' and 'change' on the structure of opportunities that face young women once they enter work.

Both organizations had recently introduced changes in the organization of work, and both provided an opportunity to compare the progress of young males and young females within the firm. They are also alike in that they recruit predominantly female labour, firm A in manufacture and firm B in the service sector.

Firm A recruited school-leavers and married women for semi-skilled careerless manual work, and male workers for skilled maintenance work, machine minding and management. It had recently rationalized its wage payment system, which meant that it had a uniform system of grading all wages; on the basis of this it was possible to compare the progress of all employees. The fact that it did have a uniform system of grading meant that elements of career progression had been introduced into what had hitherto been semi-skilled careerless occupations. The number of steps were limited to four, but nevertheless they provided a clearly defined hierarchy up which the unqualified female school-leaver could move. The firm had an active personnel department which, together with the union, had instituted the grading system and was fully aware of the implications of legislation in the field of employment and equal opportunities.

The young women are located primarily in the middle and lower grades, two and three, with older longer-service women employed in jobs in the higher grades and as supervisors and chargehands. There is a relatively high turnover of female employees, typical for the industry; and to combat this the firm recruit female school-leavers and married women, who after training enter the lowest grade in the job hierarchy. The number of school-leavers they recruit is restricted to a certain extent by constraints stemming from the shift system operated at this establishment, as the firm does not like to use young women on the night shift. By their early twenties a number of women employees are in the second grade. Males are employed in certain departments as trainees, in maintenance and in distribution. They tend to be more highly qualified than the females on entering the firm and are more often found in the higher grades, one and two, by the time they are in their twenties.

Firm B, in the service sector, is concerned primarily with clerical and administrative work; it also employs predominantly female labour. It operates a complex wage grading system that provides a career progression of five or six steps from trainee to junior management. Once again, there is an active personnel department in which the members are fully conversant with recent legislation. By contemporary standards there is a sophisticated system of internal promotion, which, together with the grading system, has been used to introduce an elaborate career structure into what had previously been routine clerical work with few prospects. As for the distribution of male and female labour, the ratio of young women to men is about 8:1, although in this case the males are not in separate departments but competing directly with females. Although they are distributed throughout all the grades they tend to move rapidly through them, and form 50 per cent of the younger employees in more senior positions at the fourth point on the scale.

What these two firms illustrate vividly is the potential flexibility that management or employers have in the way in which they structure work, for both introduced career structures into 'women's' jobs with which they are not usually associated. In the case of firm B, when this happened they also changed their recruitment policy and started to take large numbers of unqualified school-leavers in preference to married women, who were difficult to attract locally.

The other point they illustrate is the limit to which changes in the legal system have been able to produce changes in the distribution of opportunities. There are still jobs that are generally thought of by both employers and employees as women's or men's work. Few young men apply either at firm A for manual jobs or at firm B for clerical work, a comment no doubt on the all-pervasive efforts of gender identity. Similarly, the differences in the rates of job advancement between males and females may be in part a reflection of the different orientations to work of the unqualified female school-leavers as opposed to that of the more highly qualified male leavers.

CONCLUSION

It must be emphasized that the findings on which much of this
chapter are based are preliminary and tentative. They have been
taken from the responses of a sample of employers biased towards
one particular local labour market and to the manufacturing side
of industry. We would also readily admit that, in approaching the
whole question of employment opportunities, there are additional
factors at work which have not been covered. However, we believe
that we have provided some indication of the limits to change in
the structure of occupations. There does not appear to be in
process any appreciable broadening of scope of employment opportunities for women. In terms of legislation, some employers have
cited the Factories Act, and the Health and Safety at Work etc.
Act, as imposing restrictions on the employment of women for shift
work and of young people for working with certain machinery.
Others have expressed a reluctance to employ women because of the
maternity rights provisions of the Employment Protection Act.

There continues to be widespread acceptance of differentiations
between men's and women's work. This is partly attributable to
established and traditional attitudes and perceptions adopted by
employers. From our interviews this is especially significant in
jobs at managerial level.

Lack of representation in certain occupations does not necessarily stem from employer resistance. Some of it can be traced
back to the socialization process, which creates a gender identity
whereby girls do not consider attempting to enter traditionally
male occupations. This self-exemption results in some employers
complaining that they do not get any young girls applying for jobs
such as craft or technician apprenticeships.

It remains true that the actual employment opportunities available will largely be determined by the economic, industrial and
occupational structure of the local labour market.(8)

NOTES

1   The general pattern of change from primary to secondary to
    tertiary occupations is well established. For a recent debate
    over the determination and significance of the change see
    Payne (1977) and Garnsey (1975).
2   The UK has one of the highest female activity rates in the EEC,
    but the comparison with Sweden suggests that it could move
    higher.
3   The figures are drawn from the Equal Opportunities Commission,
    Second Annual Report, 1977. For a more detailed discussion
    see Pettman (1979).
4   The growth of female employment in clerical occupations is
    discussed in Lockwood (1958).
5   Many of the reasons that managers give for excluding women
    from manual work and managerial occupations have been thor-
    oughly documented in Hunt (1975).
6   For a discussion of some of the differences between men and
    women in their perceptions of work see Beynon and Blackburn
    (1972).

7 See Pettman (1977), and also Mackie and Patullo (1977), p.97.
8 We wish to acknowledge the invaluable help of Gill Wallis in
   the preparation of material that has been used as a basis for
   this chapter. The project referred to throughout is funded by
   the Department of Employment.

Chapter 10

Women in higher education
A case study of the Open University

Moira Griffiths

INTRODUCTION

This chapter is concerned with describing the contribution that the
Open University is making to higher educational opportunities for
women in this country. It argues that this is a significant contribution, with illustration from University statistics and survey
findings. It begins, though, by outlining the background against
which these statistics must be assessed: the early learning experiences of boys and girls and their achievements in school; and the
differential opportunities of men and women in post-school education.

EARLY LEARNING EXPERIENCES: ROLE EXPECTATIONS

The current stereotypes of girls' and boys' and also women's and
men's roles in society do little to encourage aspirations for high
educational achievement in girls.
    The male stereotype is 'instrumental, active, skilled, technic-
ally competent, directive and exploitative', while the female stereotype is 'expressive, passive, decorative, manipulative, non combat-
ant and non competent outside domestic and nurturing situations'
(Weinreich, 1978, p.20). These stereotypes are continually reinforced; for example, through dress and toys. Comics and books
portray the role of the girl as helping her mother with cooking and
cleaning, while the boy is with his father involved in some outdoor
or energetic pursuit. The media also present women in such a way
that 'teachers, parents and pupils themselves have notions of
"femininity" which affect the treatment and expectations of girl
pupils' (Marks, 1976, p.197).
    The chief role that girls are expected to fulfil in adult life is
that of wife and mother. Jobs are of secondary importance, and long-
term careers, especially those which cannot readily be seen as an
extension of the wife-mother role (such as careers in science,
engineering and management) are seen as being exceptional, even
aberrant. Fogarty et al., analysing the status society gives to
'women's jobs', conclude that they are generally low.(1) Further,
they point to a process where such jobs are then seen as unsuitable

for ambitious men: men will only enter female occupations in a supervisory or leadership role. For example they found that in primary schools women teachers outnumbered men as assistant teachers in the basic grades by a ratio of three to one, but had considerably less representation at the level of headteacher. Similarly they mentioned that, while women accounted for 25 per cent of hospital doctors in England and Wales, they only represented 7 per cent of consultants.

EARLY LEARNING EXPERIENCES: SCHOOL AS A PREPARATION FOR POST-SCHOOL EDUCATION

Schools are involved in the process of 'role conditioning' (Byrne, 1975a), and, moreoever, in a way that tends to put girls wanting to go on to further and higher education at a disadvantage compared with boys. This involvement is at two levels: the official curriculum and the hidden curriculum. The former deals with the overt selection of subjects taught and general activities within schools. The latter looks at the covert way in which teachers have different attitudes towards and different expectations of certain groups of children and these, in turn, affect the expectations and aspirations of the children themselves.(2)

Glenys Lobban (1978) looks specifically at the effects of the official and hidden curricula as they relate to children of different sex. In terms of the official curriculum she argues that secondary schools are more effective than primary schools in segregating boys and girls into different study areas. At the secondary level boys are encouraged to work at such subjects as maths, 'hard' science and mechanics, while girls traditionally study the arts, and, as a gesture towards a science subject, biology. This separation also extends to vocational subjects like woodwork and metalwork for boys, with the girls studying domestic science and needlework. An example of overt discrimination against girls in certain subject areas is noted by Byrne in her study of attitudes and practices in 88 secondary schools in England. She found that, when there was insufficient laboratory space to serve all students wishing to take science, in all but four cases the laboratory space available was used by the boys while the girls had to make do with converted classrooms in which there was a minimal amount of scientific equipment.(3)

Even where no apparent discrimination exists within the official curriculum, Lobban suggests that 'messages about which is "correct" behaviour for the sexes are being communicated nonetheless via the content of textbooks, the teacher's interactions and prohibitions, and the pupils' observations of female and male teachers and the staff hierarchy' (Lobban, 1978, p.51). But it is not only 'correct behaviour' that is learnt through the unofficial curriculum. Lobban further argues that teachers communicate to children different standards for boys and girls, so much so that boys continue to strive for success while girls lose confidence in their own ability and exhibit 'fear of success'.(4) Another message conveyed through the unofficial curriculum is mentioned by Walum (1977), when looking at the disproportionate number of positions of responsibility

and authority occupied by men in schools: 'this pyramidical staffing
teaches the teacher and the female students to limit their aspirations: there is no room at the top for women' (Walum, 1977, p.57).
Attention is given to boys' careers and their destiny as breadwinners,
while Byrne (1975) argues that for girls there is an implicit assumption that they will ultimately follow the occupation of wife and
mother to the exclusion of any other.(5)

The determination of educational futures is strongly bound up with
results gained in national 'O' and 'A' level examinations. The
qualifications with which girls leave school tell their own story.
Taking the year 1975 as an example, DES statistics indicate that at
'O' level girls were meeting with considerable success. Rather more
girls than boys took the examination and their results were just as
good: only 7 per cent failed to gain any 'O' levels compared with 9
per cent of the boys, and for both sexes the proportion gaining
passes in five or more subjects was almost half. 'A' level results
for the same year show that many girls are failing to realize their
full potential whilst at school: fewer girls took the examination
than boys, and the ones who did so did less well. The proportions
failing in all their exams again differed, little but 73 per cent of
boys compared with 65 per cent of girls gained two or more 'A'
levels and 51 per cent of boys passed in three or more subjects compared with 40 per cent of girls. This latter difference is crucial
for chances of going on to the most prestigious form of higher
education - degree-level courses - for which three 'A' levels are
often the effective entry requirement. It means that girls who
wish to enter further education must be filtered into other areas of
post-school study.

The 'A' level results highlight a further important difference
between girls' and boys' school qualifications. Girls' qualifications tend to be in the arts and languages rather than in science
and other 'hard' subjects such as maths and economics. For example,
34 per cent of boys who left school in 1975 gained a pass in 'A'
level physics compared with 9 per cent of the girls, while the
figure for English 'A' levels were 21 per cent and 46 per cent
respectively.

This concentration on arts subjects further restricts the possibilities that girls have for going on to university. Arts and
social science courses, for which girls tend to be qualified, are
oversubscribed, and only the girls with good 'A' levels have a high
change of being accepted. It also means that girls who are being
channelled into or are choosing arts subjects when they have
abilities in science and maths are effectively restricting the
possibilities of other girls' gaining university places. Marginally qualified girls have a less good chance of higher education
than their male counterparts, who are likely to be qualified in
science where less competition exists for degree places.

In sum, the failure of girls to progress is a combination of
subjective and objective factors in which expectations from the
school and the family, peer-group pressure and, increasingly, all
forms of the media play a part. Allocations of resouces are different for the schooling of children of each sex, and clearly different
routes through their future lives are intimated throughout their
schooling. The potential of girls to progress from school into

further or higher education and successful careers will not be
realized 'so long as decisions about their education are taken in
the light of restrictive social definitions about their future role
in society' (Blackstone, 1976, p.200).

WOMEN IN POST-SCHOOL EDUCATION

Full time

'In institutions of higher education, a girl's career is a downhill
struggle, a denial of her potentialities. The system is one of
progressively contracting opportunities' (Mitchell, 1971, p.133).
If they go on to further education at all, girls tend to be filtered
into teacher education and non-advanced courses. Figures for 1974-5
demonstrate this clearly. Women occupied only 33 per cent of university places and 31 per cent of those in further education
(advanced courses), but took up 72 per cent of places in colleges
of education. The domination of girls in colleges of education is
related to their lack of 'A' levels and general expectations of a
woman's career, such that 'girls are more likely to be found following what are considered lower-status courses in lower-status
institutions' (Blackstone, 1976, p.206).
     The implications of declining numbers of places and changes in
policy concerning teacher education are serious for girls. First,
the closing of many colleges of education must obviously affect the
majority group of students (i.e. girls), especially if, as suggested by Keith Scribbens, 'the signs are that the colleges which are
to cease training are those which admitted more women in the past
than the surviving colleges' (Scribbens, 1977, p.194). Apart from
being the most popular among all girls, in the past teaching has
been the only form of higher education in which girls could engage
with qualifications of less than two 'A' levels. The very fact that
teaching is to become a graduate profession is likely to exclude
more girls than boys. Second, the replacement places in higher
education are being made available mainly through the Diploma in
Higher Education, a development which at least in the short term is
likely to disadvantage girls, since it is a qualification with a
two 'A' level entry requirement. The third factor affecting girls'
opportunities in higher education is the country's requirement for
more graduates in science and technology, traditionally non-female
areas, rather than in the arts and social sciences. These three
factors could bring the education of girls to a crossroad of decision.
     The choice is either to continue in the traditional way and
simply exclude more girls from higher education because of the 'lack
of motivation', nurtured by school and the study of the wrong
subjects, or to push for equal education for the two sexes.
Genuine availability of all school subjects, equal allocation of
resources, and also positive encouragement of girls to take three
'A' levels would leave open the option to girls of entering
teaching or other degree programmes.
     As well as the girls continuing to higher education, a large
number took full-time non-advanced courses. It is in this area in
particular that the boundaries of sex-related study topics persist.

DES statistics show that in 1975 an overwhelming proportion (ii per
cent) of the places on nursing and secretarial courses were occupied
by girls, who also accounted for 67 per cent of the courses in
catering. (6)   Boys on the other hand occupied 67 per cent of the
places on HNC/D courses and 65 per cent of those on ONC/D courses.
The disparities go even further than can be explored here, extending
even within subject areas.   Sue Sharpe commented that 'the main
courses that girls are found in at further education colleges are
business and commerce, which include a disproportionate amount of
shorthand and typing', while for boys these same disciplines 'are
oriented towards management, and they don't learn the "feminine"
skills of typing and shorthand' (Sharpe, 1976, p.180).

Part-time day release

The provision of part-time education for girls is something of a
scarce resource.   The picture overall is biased towards the education of boys rather than girls, so much so that of those receiving
day release in 1975 82 per cent were boys and 18 per cent girls. (7)
    In terms of different age-groups, girls form a larger proportion
of the population receiving day release at 16 and 17 than they do
amongst the 18- to 20-year-olds.   For the younger girls, much of
their day release is in the category of 'miscellaneous services'
which is likely to include small industrial concerns sending them
to shorthand or typing classes one day a week.
    A closer look at the employers releasing students for part-time
study (DES, Statistics of Education) reveals that the main areas
for girls are in the professional and scientific services (20 per
cent) and in the public administration and defence (30 per cent).
The area releasing most boys is that of manufacturing industries
(43 per cent).   Within the grouping there are 11 per cent of boys
employed in mecahnical engineering and 6 per cent in electrical
engineering.   In contrast with the generous treatment of boys, the
manufacturing industries - the largest single sponsors of all
release students (38 per cent) - sponsor only 19 per cent of the
girl students.
    The provision of day-release training had in the past to be won
as a right by trades unions in industry.   The majority of these
opportunities are likely to continue to be available only for boys,
bearing in mind that girl school-leavers tend to go into 'unorgan-
ized' training.   It seems, therefore, that girls leaving school
and not carrying on with full-time education will have relatively
few chances to gain further qualifications unless they are prepared
to commit themselves socially and economically to the rigours of
part-time study in the evenings and at weekends.

Evening classes

A variety of courses are offered on a part-time evening basis by
polytechnics and other further education institutes.   DES statistics
for 1975 show that in that year 270,978 people enrolled for courses
leading to a non-advanced certificate and 37,731 for advanced
courses. (8)

It comes as no surprise that women comprised only 15 per cent of
those doing advanced work. However, they made up almost half (47
per cent) of the group registered for non-advanced work, and it is
notable that 84 per cent of them were registered for 'O' and 'A'
level courses compared with 60 per cent of men. Women comprised 56
per cent of those doing 'O' levels and 59 per cent of those taking
non-maths or science 'A' levels. Men, on the other hand, made up
80 per cent of the group doing ONC courses, 75 per cent of those
taking City and Guilds, and 69 per cent of those working towards a
non-advanced professional qualification.

The statistics provide convincing evidence that women are interested in going on to post-school education: they volunteer for it in
their own free time in large numbers. Unfortunately, there are no
statistics that throw light on their motivations, in particular how
many are trying to make up for missed opportunities or lack of
opportunities at school, perhaps with the aim of going on to more
advanced studies, and how many are just doing it for fun.

The advanced courses that most part-time students (64,101) are
taking are those leading to professional qualifications. Both men
and women are attracted to such courses: 66 per cent of the men and
55 per cent of the women. However, women comprise only 13 per cent
of all students taking this type of course. The areas in which
women are best represented are university first degree courses (28
per cent), CNAA first degrees (25 per cent) and college diplomas
and certificates. Fourteen per cent are doing such courses compared
with 6 per cent of men. This suggests that many women who did not
go on to degree-level work on leaving school, or who had not the
qualifications to do so, are nevertheless interested in studying
for a degree.

This inference is supported by the fact that women are becoming
involved in full-time undergraduate studies at universities and
other educational institutions in increasing numbers. In 1975
mature women students comprised 6 per cent of women in universities
and 12 per cent of all those in polytechnics and maintained
colleges.(9) The proportions were identical to those for mature
men. It is interesting to note that the polytechnic sector, especially since the introduction of the CNAA programmes with their more
flexible entry requirements, are attracting so many mature students.
Both they and the part-time degree courses offer, to some extent,
the flexibility which is the outstanding characteristic of Open
University studies.

THE OPEN UNIVERSITY

The Open University was set up to provide education at degree level
for 'all those who, for any reasons, have been or are being pre-
cluded from achieving their aim through an existing institution of
higher education' (Report of the Planning Committee to the Secre-
tary of State for Education and Science, 1969). The first section
of this chapter clearly illustrated that fewer women than men are
involved in other forms of higher and further education, and that
those who are so involved tend to take lower-status and non-
advanced studies. It is safe to assume, therefore, that a very

large number of women fall into the category of potential OU
students.

The Open University deliberately broke away from the traditional
'A' level requirements of other institutions of higher education:
there are no entry requirements other than that students be adults
of 21 or over. Entry is on a 'first-come, first-served basis'.
The number of new places offered each year is large - in the tens
of thousands, so that it is potentially able to take in large numbers of 'unqualified' students.

The University also sets out to give its students maximum choice
in what they study and the pace at which they study. Its degree is
a modular one, with the students choosing their own course combination and choosing the number of courses they wish to study in a
given year.

The multi-media distance-learning system that has been devised
paces students through each course, but allows them to fit their
studies into their lives as they are best able. They can study
the course materials in their own homes, at the times they wish,
but have access to local tutors and to study centres.(10)

The University seems ideally suited for women who wish to undertake degree-level studies in adult life. It has no educational
prerequisites, so lack of the magic three 'A' levels does not count
against them, and its flexible part-time study requirements (12
hours per week per full-credit course) allows all students to
devise study timetables that fit in with their other duties and
responsibilities.

Are women coming forward to take advantage of this new educational opportunity? University statistics indicate that they are.
Initially, in 1970, women applied in relatively small numbers compared with men, but their applications have gradually increased
and now seem to have found their level at around 20,000 each year.
The proportions of women applying for places has risen from 30 per
cent in 1970 to 44 per cent of 1977 applicants.(11)

However, the women who are applying are not dramatically breaking away from their earlier conditioning. They tend to apply for
the traditional 'girls' subjects' like the arts and social sciences
as opposed to 'boys' subjects', which are 'scientific and technical,
involving mathematical problem-solving and analysis' (Sharpe, 1976,
pp.147-8). In 1977, for example, 59 per cent of the applications
for the arts foundation course and 46 per cent of those for the
social science foundation course were made by women, though women
comprised only 39 per cent of applications for all foundation
courses. Nevertheless, significant minorities are taking the
opportunity to study other subjects: 28 per cent of the applicants
for science were women, and women comprised 19 per cent of those
applying for mathematics. Looking at trends in applications over
the period 1971 to 1977 it is encouraging that the proportion of
women applying for science courses has been maintained and the
number of women applicants has increased. Further, the proportion
of women applicants for the mathematics course has risen from 11.7
per cent to 18.9 per cent, an increase of 7.2 per cent compared
with the overall increase of 6.2 per cent.

THE 1977 STUDENTS

What kind of women are studying with the Open University? Where
do they live? What age groups are they drawn from? What previous
educational qualifications have they? How many are housewives and
in what sorts of occupation are the working women involved? And
how successful are their Open University studies? The rest of this
chapter will describe some of the characteristics and achievements
of women who were studying with the Open University in 1977 to
demonstrate the extent to which it is making a contribution to
opportunities for women to participate in higher education at
degree level.

In the description, attention will be focused on two groups of
women (housewives and women in employment for over 20 hours a week),
who are dealt with separately because their daily order of living
is different. Ann Oakley points out in her book 'Housewife' that
'the housewife's isolation emphasizes her difference from other
workers. She lacks the sociability of a workgroup; informal
associations of workers engaged on the same job are an important
source of standards of performance in employment work' (Oakley,
1976, p.8). It would seem likely that OU studies could provide
the possibility of informal study groups and discussion groups
which would lessen the isolation for housewife-students.

TABLE 10.1 Finally registered students in 1977 by work and
marital status

	All students	Women	Men
All finally registered	55,563	22,573	32,990
	%	%	%
Work status			
Working	82	60	96
Housewives	15	38	*
Retired	3	2	3
Marital status			
Single	19	20	19
Married	74	69	76
Widowed	1	2	*
Divorced	2	3	1
Unknown	4	6	3

* Denotes less than 1%
Source: OU Statistics, 1978.

Table 10.1 gives an overall picture of the population under discussion in the rest of this chapter. As well as analysing students by their work status, their marital status is also presented.
The composition in terms of marital status is not very different
between men and women students, but marginally fewer of the women
(69 per cent) are married than the men (76 per cent). Not surpris-
ingly, a much higher proportion of women are housewives.

Region of study

The University draws its students from over the whole of the United Kingdom, and tries to make special provision (e.g., telephone tutorials) for those who are in really remote areas away from study centres. Women in all 13 Open University regions are making use of the opportunity it offers. There are some regional differences.

The lower take-up of higher education by women in general is reflected by the fact that women represent 41 per cent of the OU population compared to 51 per cent of the UK population (Office of Population Censuses and Surveys, 1978). Taking England and Wales as a group, the proportions of women in the OU and the UK are similarly related to their totals (41 per cent to 51 per cent). This is also true for Scotland (43 per cent to 52 per cent) but not for Northern Ireland, where OU women students represent a significantly smaller proportion (34 per cent) than their UK counterparts (51 per cent). Of all the women studying with the OU, the largest population is in the London region (15 per cent) which accounts for their high relation to all women in London: 47 per cent compared to 52 per cent.

This may, in part, be due to the nature of the OU system of allocating students to their regional centres: students are classified in terms of the study centre which they choose to attend. Thus the very high figure for London may reflect in part the fact that some women students who work in London choose to go for their tutorials to a study centre near their work rather than one close to their home outside the region. The London region also stands out in ways that reflect the city's position as a large centre for employment, with special opportunities available there in certain types of employment. Of the women registered there 69 per cent are working women; it has the largest proportions in the professions and arts (16 per cent) and clerical and office occupational categories (20 per cent) and also the second largest proportion of single women; 31 per cent of women students in the region.

The highest proportions of housewives are found in East Anglia and in OU regions covering the south of England. The proportion of working women employed in the teaching area is fairly large in all regions, which is what one would expect bearing in mind that 'over twice as many girls as boys go to colleges of education rather than to universities ... their reliance on teaching is increased by industry's reluctance to regard qualifications from colleges of education as anything other than a preparation for teaching' (Davies, 1975, p.133).

Age of the students

Women of all ages are registering for Open University degree level courses. In 1977 the distribution was as follows:

30 and below	32%
30-39 years	35%
40-49 years	20%
50 and over	13%

Studying in order 'to widen my knowledge' is a very widespread
motive: it was given spontaneously by 40 per cent of all women in
the first entry cohort of 1971, but was especially strong among
those aged 45 and over (51 per cent).(12)

Rather more women than men were in the youngest and oldest of
the above age-groups. Studying with the University is proving
particularly attractive to younger women in full-time employment:
36 per cent of working women students were 30 or under compared
with 29 per cent of their male counterparts and 26 per cent of
housewives. The 1971 survey showed that over a third of these
younger working women, a similar proportion to their male counterparts, were studying with the aim of gaining higher educational
qualifications. This aim was given by only one in four of housewives of the same age. Interestingly, fewer of the younger women
(25 per cent) than men (34 per cent) were studying with the
explicit aim of helping them in their job or changing their job.
This suggests that there is a great deal of unsatisfied demand for
higher education per se that is not being catered for by conventional universities, even though there has been an increase in
the proportions of women in universities from 26 per cent in 1965
to 33 per cent in 1975.

Housewives are taking up OU studies at a rather later age than
working women. The modal age group in 1977 was 31-35 years, with
28 per cent in this group. Over two-thirds of the housewives
were between 25 and 40.

These statistics suggest that many housewives are waiting until
their children are at school before contemplating studying for a
degree. Their earlier priorities were full-time care of their
pre-school children and home. Hannah Gavron's study 'The Captive
Wife' showed quite clearly that mothers both from the working and
middle classes felt a pressure to stay at home and devote themselves to their children; 'in both cases, however, the impression
given was that the return to work was to some extent an automatic
process' (Gavron, 1966, p.143).

They can now extend their horizons outside the home, and the
Open University allows them to do this while remaining home-based.
In Naomi McIntosh's 1971 survey over one in four of the housewives
gave 'convenience' as a reason for studying with the University.
The same survey also pointed to another motive: 23 per cent of
those aged under 45 were hoping their studies would help them to
change jobs. In contrast with younger housewives, 'convenience'
(12 per cent), 'job change' (9 per cent) and also 'gaining higher
educational qualifications' (13 per cent) mattered relatively
little for housewives aged 45 and over.

Finally on the subject of age, it is worth noting that in 1971
many more older students than younger ones spontaneously mentioned
'no previous opportunity' as a reason for choosing to study with
the Open University; and the older women gave this reason more
often than the men, (the figures being 28 per cent for housewives,
22 per cent for women in employment, and 16 per cent for men). The
fact that so many older women explicitly mentioned lack of opportunity in the past underlines the fact that the University has
opened up a totally new avenue for pursuing degree-level studies
for those who had no chance earlier in their lives.

Previous education

Housewives are starting off on their Open University degree studies
with far less in the way of educational qualifications than
working women, and the latter contrast sharply with men in the
type of further education they have previously undertaken.   It is
interesting to look first at how housewives differ from other
students.

Though fewer housewives (7 per cent) than men (9 per cent) had
no educational qualifications at all, more had finished their education by the 'O' level/CSE/RSA stage: 37 per cent compared with
30 per cent.   As many as 19 per cent of them had gained five or
more 'O' levels then stopped their studies, while only 10 per cent
of the men ended their education with a similar 'O' level performance.   The position is just the same with respect to two or more
'A' levels: 20 per cent of housewives had failed to build on this
achievement through post-school education compared with 10 per cent
of men.   Overall, 47 per cent of housewives had gained between five
'O' levels and two-plus 'A' levels and had not proceeded further,
while only 24 per cent of men fell into this category.   It is clear
that many of the housewife students had done well at school but had
not fulfilled their potential to continue studying.

In contrast with housewives, but more like men, the working
women in the 1977 student population tended to have built on their
school qualifications.   Only 5 per cent had no formal educational
qualifications at all.   Compared with the men students, a slightly
higher proportion (28 per cent to 24 per cent) failed to proceed
past school qualifications of five 'O' levels or more, but 59
per cent studied and succeeded at some level after leaving school
compared to 57 per cent of the men.   Predictably, bearing in mind
the evidence of the first part of this chapter, the women and men
had gone on to different types of education.   Forty-three per cent
of the working women had teaching certificates compared with 22
per cent of the men who were similarly qualified.   The figures for
ONC/OND/HNC/HND are reversed: 3 per cent compared with 21 per cent.
Housewives follow the same pattern as working women, in that a
teachers' certificate is by far the most common type of post-school
qualification gained (22 per cent).   It is interesting also to
note that as many as 10 per cent of the working women are taking
the opportunity to upgrade their university diplomas to degree
level.

The statistics point to two numerically large groups of women
in the University: those for whom the University is providing a
first taste of post-school education leading to a qualification,
many of these being housewives who did not proceed to such education earlier although qualified to do so; and women who had already
undertaken post-school studies below degree level.

A further important group is comprised of those with less than
five 'O' levels.   In 1977 there were just under 3,500 such women
students.   Though they represent a small proportion of all the
women students in the University, they point to the fact that aspirations for degree-level studies are by no means restricted to
those who have done well in school.

Occupation

Sixty per cent of the women students in 1977 were working women, a majority (60 per cent) being married and a further 5 per cent widowed, separated or divorced. Thirty-eight per cent were house-wives and 2 per cent were retired. Comparing men-women ratios in the Open University with those recorded in the 1970 census, it seems that OU women are overrepresented in non-working groups. While women comprise 80 per cent of those not in employment in the country as a whole, they comprise 89 per cent of the 'housewives' and 'retired' group in the University.

One group that is notably underrepresented in the OU is women employed in the sales and personal services area. They comprise 59 per cent of those in this type of employment in the general population, but only 16 per cent of such OU students. The position is a little better in the case of skilled trades and other manual workers; they comprise 5 per cent of workers in this category in the University compared to 17 per cent in the general population.

The distribution of occupations amongst the women students in full-time employment shows that they fall into three main areas: education (47 per cent), clerical and office staff (22 per cent), and the professions and arts (19 per cent). Proportions in other occupations are small. Working men, in contrast, are spread more widely across the occupational groups. The best represented occupations are education (30 per cent) and technicians and related workers (39 per cent).

In terms of their marital status there is a greater bias towards employment in education among the married women in employ-ment (50 per cent) than the single working women (43 per cent). In other words, they are in an occupation where they have rela-tively long holidays, which make more feasible the combining of study with looking after a home and family. Single women were no more spread out across the full occupational range than their married counterparts. However, a greater proportion of them were in the professions and arts: 24 per cent compared with 17 per cent in the married group.

The nature of the occupations included in this latter category gives some clue as to why so many single women from it had decided to register for Open University studies. The category includes a wide range of occupations: medicine, medical social auxiliary working, nursing, social work of all kinds, librarianship, journal-ism, etc. Many are occupations where good school educational qualifications are a prerequisite, but where there is a diversity in the level of post-school education. Some, such as nursing, are filled by people who have had extensive training but not always a broad higher education. The fact that almost one in four of the single working women are drawn from this group suggests that professional women have been quick to recognize the opportunity that the University offers. They can acquire a degree - a qualifi-cation that is higher than their present ones and also one that has general currency rather than being a qualification (e.g., SRN) that is recognized only within one profession - while continuing in full-time work.

Interestingly, the small group of 834 widowed and divorced

women who were in full-time employment contained a relatively high
proportion of clerical and office workers: 30 per cent compared
with 25 per cent of working married women and 22 per cent of those
who were single. It may well be that they represent a group of
women who are turning to the University as a way of starting afresh
on a new basis, developing new interests and a broader perspective
and at the same time acquiring a qualification. The latter may not
be the main reason for their studies but it could well allow them
to move into a more satisfying and a better-paid job.

At the beginning of this section it was reported that women in
occupations such as sales and personal services were not registering in such large proportions as men. But to expect them to do so
would be over-idealistic; after all, they work in occupations
where there is not a career structure closely linked with educational qualifications. Nevertheless, in 1977 2,898 women in
clerical and office jobs and 314 in sales and services were finally
registered OU students. A further 626 women were employed as
technical personnel (e.g., laboratory workers and technicians),
who typically undertake occupation-specific training but have
relatively little in the way of broad-based further education.
Though they comprise only 18 per cent of the women in the University, they are very important standard bearers, indicating both
the fact that women in non-professional occupations are interested
in education for themselves and also that they can succeed at
degree level.

PERFORMANCE IN THE UNIVERSITY

Open University students can register for up to two credit equivalents (made up of whole or half credits) in any one academic
year. Women tend to be rather less ambitious, or perhaps more
realistic, than men in terms of the number they register for: 79
per cent of the women were registered for only one course in 1977,
while only 67 per cent of the men came into this category; 19 per
cent of men had registered for two half-credit courses - a rather
more demanding undertaking than a single whole-credit course -
compared with 11 per cent of women. More men (14 per cent) than
women (11 per cent) had taken on courses adding up to one-and-a-
half or two credit equivalents, and involving a time commitment
of at least 20 hours' study a week.

One explanation for these sex differences may be that women are
rather lacking in confidence, doubting their own ability to do
degree-level courses. Women have less money available to finance
their studies than men: fewer are in employment and able to ask
employers to support their studies. Working women tend to get
lower salaries than men, and housewives may well be dependent on
money saved from the housekeeping or a subsidy from their husband.
Many women just do not have uncommitted monies for private use.

Another important factor is time for study, particularly time
for summer schools. For housewives and married women particularly,
the weekly study time requirement of 12 or so hours a week for
each whole-credit course may involve a novel agreement or understanding about the need for personal time for self-fulfilment and

development. Courses with a summer school component involve, of
course, a further extension of the 'private' time that is required:
the married woman actually goes away, handing over to her husband
or others the care of home and family.

Though the large numbers of women who are registered indicates
that it is possible to find some time for study and some money to
finance these studies, it may well be impossible or unrealistic
for many of them to undertake the commitments implied by studying
for more courses in a given year.

TABLE 10.2 Percentage of finally registered students gaining
credits, by faculty and sex, 1977

Faculty	All students	Men	Women	Difference (women – men)
	%	%	%	%
Arts	72.7	69.0	75.4	6.4
Social Sciences	69.3	67.8	71.4	3.6
Educational Studies	68.1	66.2	70.2	4.0
Science	68.0	65.5	73.2	7.7
Technology	62.7	61.9	70.3	8.4
Mathematics	61.6	60.0	69.2	9.2

Source: OU Statistics, 1978.

How well are women performing in the University? The unequi-
vocable answer is 'Very well'. Their success rates on the courses
they finally register for is high; indeed, they do rather better
than men in all faculties, as Table 10.2 indicates.

Interestingly, the women who finally register for courses in
all the traditionally male strongholds of science, technology and
mathematics are doing particularly well relative to the men. It
could be argued that these women did well because they were
specially motivated or particularly interested, while some of the
men taking courses in these faculties were not so concerned with
proving they could pass the courses. But if this were so, we
should find that men did especially well in arts, traditionally
the faculty that women tend to apply for. We find, however, that
women do better than men in this faculty too; 75 per cent of the
women registered gained credits compared with 69 per cent of the
men. Indeed, there are few courses at all in which women have a
lower success rate than men. One should not imply from this,
however, that women are superior - to do so would be making
invidious comparisons. Rather, women take on rather fewer courses
and do rather better in those they register for.

The University's first graduates, 898 in all, gained their
degrees in 1972. By December 1977, 27,204 students had graduated,
including over 9,000 women. As one would predict from the facts
that fewer women can claim credit exemptions and that women tend
to opt to undertake fewer courses in any one year, women tend to
graduate more slowly than men. However, a higher proportion of
women than men from each entry cohort are becoming graduates, as

McIntosh (1978) has pointed out. For example, by 1977 57 per cent
of the first year's intake of women had graduated compared with
51 per cent of the men. Figures for 1972's students at that point
were 45 per cent and 42 per cent respectively. The crossover point
at which more women than men graduate is not reached, however,
until students have been registered with the University for five
years or so. The statistics underline both the high degree of
motivation among its women students, as well as the fact that so
many women who had no chance of degree-level studies earlier have
shown their ability to complete a highly exacting degree course.

Graduates gain much more than a qualification, as a survey of
students who graduated by December 1975 demonstrates. The vast
majority report personal changes of the type normally attributed
to full-time study at a conventional university: for instance, more
self-confidence, greater ability to communicate with others, being
more balanced and mature people, having new horizons and new goals
and also a new way of looking at things, a different perspective
on life (Swift, 1979). Women tend to report these changes even
more than men, and housewives more than women who were in full-
time work on entry. The experience of studying with the University
has proved so stimulating that a majority are keen to continue with
some form of post-graduate work or training, and one in six have
already begun such studies.

Significantly, many graduates are finding their degrees of use
in the occupational field. Twenty nine per cent of all the women
and 20 per cent of the men in the survey reported having 'developed
a new career' as a consequence of their studies, and yet others
expected to do so. (The figure for housewives was 36 per cent).
Almost a third of the women graduates reported having already
gained a promotion or having improved their promotion prospects.
These results are striking because, as reported earlier, this was
not their main reason for studying.

SUMMARY AND CONCLUSIONS

This chapter first outlined the achievements of women in the educational system in this country and the social and other constraints
on high achievement. It then went on to describe the number and
characteristics of Open University women students and also their
progress in the University. It is clear that the Open University
is playing an increasingly large part in the provision of higher
education for women in the UK. Its appeal is gradually spreading
to women from many different walks of life and different educational backgrounds. The majority of women students are studying
in the traditional areas of arts and social sciences, but a highly
successful minority is taking courses in science and technology
subjects. The number of women graduates, over 9,000 by 1977, is
impressive by any standards.

Evidence of the impact of their studies on the women's lives is
gradually being accumulated and analysed, but it is already clear
that the University is having an enormous - and in most respects
beneficial - effect. A majority, and especially the housewives,
find it has satisfied one of their important aims, that of bringing

new stimulation into their lives. It appears, too, to be stimulating new ambitions: for example, in the educational area and the
occupation field. Already many women with Open University degrees
are proving that they can achieve one or both of these ambitions.

The effect of studying with the OU for many of the women graduates is succinctly expressed in this comment: 'It has meant that I
have started to find myself as a person, and has opened up the
world.'(13)

NOTES

1 See Fogarty et al. (1971).
2 Rosenthal and Jacobson (1968).
3 Byrne (1975).
4 See Horner (1970) for a discussion of girls' 'fear of success'.
5 At no other time is the role of husband and father ever considered an 'occupation' by boys, their teachers or their
   families.
6 Department of Education and Science, (1975), Statistics.
7 Ibid.
8 Idem, vol.3.
9 Idem, vols 3 and 5.
10 See McIntosh, Calder and Swift (1976) for a fuller account of
    the teaching system.
11 Open University Annual Digest of Statistics (1978).
12 McIntosh et al. (1976).
13 An earlier draft of this chapter was given to the BERA Seminar,
    'Women, Education and Research', University of Loughborough,
    14-16 April 1978. Thanks are due to Naomi McIntosh and Jack
    Field for their comments on earlier drafts of this chapter but
    in particular to Betty Swift for all the time and effort she
    has put into helping me to revise it. Finally, I would like
    to thank Margaret Marchant and Pam Berry for typing the numer-
    ous drafts.

Chapter 11

How many women academics 1912-76?

Margherita Rendel

There is nothing new about women scholars. Hermione Grammatike,
whose mummy rests at Girton College, Cambridge,(1) was probably a
woman of letters in Egypt in the first or second century AD. In
the eighth century, Abbess Hild at Whitby and Leoba at Tauber-
bischofsheim drew students from far and wild (Stenton, 1957,
pp.13-15). From the eighth to the eleventh centuries, women
lectured in law (and served as judges) in Cordoba, Granada and
Seville (Wallach, 1975, p.91, quoting Pettus). Throughout the
late Middle Ages, women studied and graduated from Italian universities; Novella D'Andrea was in 1335 well known as a professor of
canon law, and Cassandra Felice was probably dean or professor of
jurisprudence at Padua in the fifteenth century. Other women
studied and taught at Bologna and other Italian universities, and
in Spanish, German and Dutch universities. Nor did women have
such opportunities only in the Middle Ages: in 1678, Elena
Lucrezia Piscopia Cornaro held a chair at the University of Padua
(Jex Blake v. Senatus of University of Edinburgh, XI Macph. 784
at 789).

These were exceptional women and their circumstances may have
been unusually favourable. Isotta Nogarola's experience in the
fifteenth century is closer to that of modern women. A scholarly
and learned humanist, Isotta was forced to retire from the culti-
vated, humanist and worldly society of Venice by false and luridly
obscene accusations. She was driven to self-deprecating apologies
on account of her sex and to a choice between abandoning either
her literary studies or the satisfactions of friendship, comfort
and sexuality. She chose her literary studies. She won fame and
encouragement as a scholar, but only after becoming an ascetic
recluse. She was denied her own authenticity, her own personhood,
and was compelled to conform and comply with a role defined by
men. King (1978: 811) concludes that this period was even more
unhappy than the period when, living as a secular scholar, she
was calumniated.

In Britain women were excluded from all universities until they
were admitted to all scientific courses at the newly-created
University of Durham College of Science in Newcastle in 1871.
This reflected not intellectual inferiority in British women in

comparison with those of other countries, but, as Sophia, a Person of Quality, wrote in 1739 (p.40):

If we are not seen in *university chairs*, it cannot be attributed to our want of capacity to fill them, but to that violence with which *men* support their unjust intrusion into our places; or, if not, at least to our greater modesty and less degree of ambition.

A woman was first appointed to an academic post in 1893 and to a chair in 1894 (Sommerkorn, 1967, p.15). The proportion of women academics now is virtually the same as in the 1920s, and the proportion holding senior posts virtually the same as in the 1930s. Since the proportion of women nearly doubled in ten years and of women in senior posts slightly more than doubled in twenty years, want of capacity is no explanation. The feminist, then, sees no improvement during more than half a century. And individual women have learnt it is not enough to be better than men. Like Isotta, they are not perceived as scholars, but either as women or as acting outside their proper role as women, and accordingly to be punished. Thus they are excluded from the meritocracy which is said to govern university appointments.

There are now some 38,000 university teachers in Great Britain. If half were women, there would be some 15,000 more women academics than there are: 0.02 per cent of the female population. Is it possible to justify spending time and effort on so few? Of course any group, however small, is entitled to have its rights considered. But university teachers as a whole constitute only 0.07 per cent of the total population, and it is not suggested that universities, higher education or university teachers are an unworthy topic. So the smallness of the numbers is not a reason for disregarding women academics. Furthermore, in addition to women's right to participate in an important profession, some seven other reasons can be found for studying the role of women in higher education. There is space here only to summarize them. First, if the nation and society has to live on its brains, then we cannot afford to ignore the brains in women's heads. Second, sex-stereotyping has the effect of specializing men and women in different qualities. If both masculine and feminine qualities are valuable - and both supporters and opponents of sex-stereotyping claim they are - then both men and women are needed to bring these qualities to bear in teaching and research. These are both general reasons which also underline those which follow.

Universities perform certain powerful functions in society. The democratization of society means allowing women their equal share in these functions. Third, then, universities act as licensing, selecting and gate-keeping institutions. They determine, directly through their own examinations and indirectly through parallel examinations such as CNAA, and subordinate examinations such as GCE, who shall and who shall not be allowed to proceed to professional and most of the higher administrative and managerial posts. Fourth, in a broadly similar way, universities greatly control and influence what constitutes received and accepted knowledge, and on what topics research shall be undertaken. Influence is also exercised by individuals when acting as publishers' readers as well as in determining syllabuses and courses. Fifth,

the educational system, through which all individuals pass, is
largely subordinated to the control of universities and wholly subordinated to those who have directly or indirectly been licensed
by universities. Thus, sixth, universities control directly or
indirectly, much, though not all, of the ideological machinery of
the state and of society.

Finally, seventh, it has been pointed out that 'where the women
are, there power is not' (Novotny quoted by Stacey and Price); by
finding where the women are missing, some clues may be afforded to
the location of power in society.

At the end of the nineteenth century in England, the relevance
of higher education to professions and occupations other than the
church became apparent. In the last third of the century new university colleges were founded, the developing sciences required
expensive laboratories, departments began to develop, and professors outside Oxford and Cambridge began to obtain a share in the
government of their universities (Morrell, 1976, p.39; Moodie and
Eustace, 1974, p.29). The academic profession emerged, and universities assumed their modern function as the producers of new knowledge and as the producers and reproducers of highly-trained
workers who were increasingly to be employed rather than self-
employed.

In spite of or, more likely, because of these changes, women
managed to force their way into universities, although with much
difficulty. As activities and occupations became professionalized
as well as industrialized, women found themselves excluded from
providing for themselves except by marriage, domestic service or
prostitution, a choice between lifelong dependency, low status or
degradation. The professionalization of long-standing occupations,
such as medicine, and the development of new professions in
science, engineering and teaching meant that women had to find
the means of entering these professions, access to many of which
was guarded directly or indirectly by the universities.

How did these women fare? The story of the admission of women
to universities as students has been told elsewhere (2), and
accounts of some of the more colourful incidents enjoyed with an
unjustified feeling of moral superiority. But I am aware of little
or no work on the obtaining by women of academic posts and of
their progress in them. One explanation of this is clear: there
are no easily available statistics. The statistics of the University Grants Committee give some quite detailed analyses of the
numbers of men and women students, home and overseas, by university,
subject, financial assistance, degrees awarded and residence from
1919 onwards. The numbers of academic staff are given from 1923
onwards by grade and university, but with no indication of sex or
subject. In their Report for 1923-4 (p.21) the UGC wrote:

> Finally, we may repeat what we said in our previous Report on
> the subject of women teachers. We would especially emphasize
> the importance of adequate status as well as emoluments for
> women teachers. The numbers as well as the duties of women
> teachers are steadily increasing, and we believe that this
> development is generally regarded as satisfactory and success-
> ful. It is clearly of the first importance that women of the
> highest ability should be attracted to this work, and we think

that a more ample recognition of their claim is due from certain
of the Authorities!

But the UGC did not ensure that it had the means to check whether
the 'Authorities' were taking their advice.

In spite of the omissions of the University Grants Committee and
the lack of readily available sources, it is possible to establish
approximately how many women held university posts at different
periods, where they held them, in what subjects and at what levels,
by the tedious process of counting the names of staff in the
Commonwealth Universities Yearbook.(3)   This chapter sets out the
results of such a count, and suggests possible interpretations.
The results show that the position of women academics has not
changed much in half a century.   Indeed, in some universities, it
seems to have deteriorated.   The tables show the wide divergence
between the proportions of women in different types of university,
and in the numbers of women in different subjects.   It is imprac-
ticable to indicate the proportion of women in each subject as the
only way of finding this information is by counting all the names.

Several of the women at all periods were married, but it is
impossible to tell how many.   The academic profession as a whole,
unlike schoolteaching, did not operate a marriage-bar in the inter-
war period, although it is possible that some universities may have
done so.   Blackstone and Fulton (1976) have shown that marriage
cannot account for all the discrepancies between the salaries and
ranks of men and women.   They conclude that 'sex discrimination is
the villain'.   However, a relatively high proportion of academic
women do not marry.   Williams et al. (1973, p.376) found that 80
per cent of the men but only 42 per cent of the women were married,
and that of these women nearly one-third had no children.

I will discuss first the distribution of women between types of
university, then the ranks they held, and finally the subjects
they taught.

It will be seen from Tables 11.1-11.4 that in all periods the
number of women holding university posts at Oxford and Cambridge
was far below the national average, whereas it was twice the
national average at the young civic universities.(4)   Wales was
also consistently above average and Scotland consistently below.
However, Williams et al. in their survey undertaken in 1968 found
that 15 per cent of these in Scottish universities were women
(1973, p.25),(5) which was substantially above the national
average.

London tended to have more women than the average, but women
there were clearly helped by the presence of women's colleges.
The explanation of the small number of women at Oxford and
Cambridge lies in the long refusal of those two universities to
admit women to membership or full membership.   It is not clear
why women did so well at the young civic universities and in Wales,
but it is unlikely that personal choice by itself is the explanation; after all women did not choose not to have posts at Oxford
and Cambridge.   The young civic universities and the Welsh colleges
had three things in common: they were small, new, and often in
relatively small and out-of-the-way places.   They would have been
less attractive to candidates for university posts likely to
succeed elsewhere.   Until after the Second World War, the pay of

TABLE 11.1 Numbers, ranks and types of universities of women academics, 1912-13

University	Profs	R/SL, etc.	% of women holding senior posts	L	AL	Other	Total women	Total staff	% of women staff
All universities	4	5	5.9		152		161	3,135	5.1
excluding Oxbridge	4	5	5.9		152		161	2,791	5.8
Oxbridge	Note: No women held university posts at Oxford or Cambridge								
London	2	5	13.2		46		53	696	7.6
Old civic					60		60	1,190	5.0
University colleges: Exeter, Reading, N'ttm, Southampton	1		4.3		22		23	193	11.9
Wales	1		7.1		13		14	156	9.0
Scotland					11		11	556	2.0

Source: Commonwealth Universities Yearbook, 1914.

TABLE 11.2 Numbers, ranks and types of universities of women academics in Great Britain, 1921-2

University	Profs	R/SL, etc.	% of women holding senior posts	L ⎰ AL	Other	Total women	Total staff	% of women staff
All universities	13	14	6.9	326	35	390	4,037	9.7
excluding Oxbridge	13	14	7.0	325	34	388	3,653	10.6
Oxbridge	Note: No women held university posts at Oxford or Cambridge			1	1	2	384	0.5
London	9	11	24.1	63		83	874	9.5
Old Civic	2	3	3.4	114	26	145	1,486	9.8
University colleges: Exeter, Reading, Nott'm, Southampton				49	4	53	244	21.7
Wales	2		4.5	38	4	44	25	16.6
Scotland				63		63	784	8.0

Source: Commonwealth Universities Yearbook, 1922.

TABLE 11.3 Numbers, ranks and types of universities of women academics in Great Britain, 1930-1

University	Profs	R/SL, etc.	% of women holding senior posts	L	AL	Other	Total women	Total staff	% of women staff
All universities	17	39	10.9	279	118	61	514	5,196	9.9
excluding Oxbridge	17	38	11.4	258	117	54	484	4,503	10.7
Oxbridge		1	3.3	21	1	7	30	693	4.3
London	11	32	28.7	84	16	7	150	1,283	11.7
Old civic	2	6	5.0	89	38	25	160	1,566	10.2
University colleges: Exeter, Reading, N'ttm, Southampton and Young civics	1		1.6	42	8	10	61	315	19.4
Wales	3		7.3	17	12	9	41	342	12.0
Scotland				26	43	3	72	997	7.2

Source: Commonwealth Universities Yearbook, 1931.

TABLE 11.4 Numbers and ranks of academic women in Great Britain, 1951

University	Profs	Rdrs	SL	% of women holding senior posts	L	AL/D	Other	Total women	Total staff	% of women staff
All universities	23	54	73	11.4	719	305	145	1,320	10,861	12.2
excluding Oxbridge	20	47	73	11.5	637	296	143	1,216	9,541	12.7
Oxbridge	3	7	*	9.6	82	9	3	104	1,320	7.9
London	14	38	35	21.9	201	73	35	397	2,422	16.4
Old civic	3	8	19	7.1	221	92	81	424	3,685	11.5
University colleges: Exeter, Reading, N'ttm, Southampton and Young civics			2	1.4	105	22	15	144	816	17.6
Wales (incl. Lampeter)	2		12	20.6	35	12	7	68	641	10.6
Scotland	1	1	5	3.8	75	97	4	183	1,977	9.3

Source: Commonwealth Universities Yearbook, 1952.

* No rank of Senior Lecturer at these universities.

university teachers, outside Oxford and Cambridge and including
that of some professors, was low and was a matter of some concern
to the University Grants Committee.(6)

Halsey and Trow (1971, p.153) show the proportion of academics
holding senior posts (that is Senior Lecturer and above) for all
universities except Oxford and Cambridge as being consistently
around 30 per cent from 1910-11 to 1968-9. The UGC statistics show
the average as being around 27 per cent to 28 per cent in the late
1960s, and as 31.5 per cent in 1975-6. Thus, it is only at London
in 1930-1 that the proportion of women in senior posts corresponds
at all to the national average. But at London the proportion of
women holding senior posts was consistently above the national
average for women. Table 11.5 gives the details. When the women's

TABLE 11.5 Women academics at London and in Great Britain, 1912-51

Year	London		All universities		% of women at London	
	Senior women	All women	Senior women	All women	Senior Women	All women
1912	7	53	9	161	77.8	32.9
1921	20	83	27	390	74.1	21.3
1930	43	150	56	514	76.8	29.2
1951	87	397	150	1320	58.0	30.1

Source: Commonwealth Universities Yearbooks, 1914, 1922, 1931, 1952.

colleges and the mixed colleges are considered separately, it
becomes clear that the number of women holding senior posts as a
proportion of the total number of women holding posts was the same
in both the women's colleges and the mixed colleges; that is, about
29 per cent. However, as a proportion of all staff, senior women
were 19 per cent in the women's colleges compared with 2 per cent
in the mixed collages. Women's colleges seem therefore to have
been important in providing posts for academic women. It is as if
men and women constituted two different populations for promotion
and that in the mixed colleges only a fixed proportion, under one-
third, or women could receive promotion and that in mixed institutions only about 10 per cent of staff could be women. By putting
it so boldly, I might appear to be advancing a conspiracy theory.
But such a theory is unnecessary. People do not react in the same
way to men and to women. Many feel they do not want to be
'swamped' by women or subjected to 'petticoat government'. Women
are a visible minority and much more visible than their numbers
warrant, the so-called 'halo' effect. It might be thought from
this that women would tend to benefit from the existence of women's
colleges; however, comparable prospects for women did not exist at
Oxford or Cambridge, nor at London by 1951. The truth is that at
London in 1930, the women were concentrated in the women's
colleges: 60 per cent of women staff were to be found in 9.1 per

cent of all the posts in the University of London (that is the proportion of women in the women's colleges and the proportion of posts in women's colleges), and only 6.3 per cent of the posts in the mixed schools and colleges were held by women.(7) This latter figure is a little better than for Oxford and Cambridge and a little worse than that for Scotland.

By 1951 the proportion of women academics had risen slightly, the increase being attributable largely to the increase in the proportion of women at London, Oxford and Cambridge. At London, women constituted half or more of the academic staff of each of the women's colleges (62 per cent altogether) and 15.3 per cent of the staff of the mixed schools and colleges, excluding medical schools. There were women in all institutions, including the very small ones, the only exceptions being 7 of the 17 medical schools. The academic staff (including the clinical teachers) of the medical schools constituted 30.7 per cent of the academic staff of the university, but women numbered only 5.7 per cent. Within the medical schools, women were concentrated at Royal Free, with 30 of the 42 women, so that 12 were spread in ones or occasionally twos among the other 9 medical schools.

As regards rank, the proportion of women in senior posts did not increase in two decades, but the distribution changed. Women's position improved at Oxford, Cambridge, Wales and the Scottish universities, but deteriorated at London. It looks as though at Oxford, Cambridge and Wales women already in the system were being recognized, but that in England generally women's opportunities were not improving. After 1951 the proportions (both representation and distribution) of women in senior posts in Scotland continued to improve, but in 1975 were still below the national average, whereas in Wales they declined markedly. The UGC statistics do not permit comparisons for any other categories of university. Between 1966 and 1975 in Great Britain the distribution of women holding senior posts increased by 0.3 per cent, from 12.7 per cent of all women to 13.0 per cent of all women, a gain of 2.49 per cent, whereas the distribution of men increased from 29.1 per cent to 33.9 per cent of all men, a gain of 16.5 per cent. In other words, women's chances of gaining promotion are deteriorating, as proportionately more of the promotions available are going to men.

Women have held senior posts in the full range of subjects. The four chairs they held in 1913 were in botany, education and two in English, and at least one woman held a chair in each of these subjects in each of the three later years. In 1922, women were holding chairs in languages, history and medical subjects; and in 1930 in zoology and social sciences. At the level of reader/senior lecturer, the range is wider, and from 1913 included sciences and social sciences, but only in 1951 did women hold senior posts in engineering, mathematics and dentistry. No woman held a senior post in law in any of the four years.

Tables 11.6, 11.7 and 11.8 show the distribution of women by subject at various periods. In Table 11.6, the figures for 1912-13 and 1930-1 are drawn from the Commonwealth Universities Yearbooks, whereas those for 1966 and 1975 (which also include the representation of women in subject groups) are drawn from the University

TABLE 11.6 Numbers, distribution and representation of women and men academics in subject groups in selected years

Subject Groups	Distribution								Representation			
	1912 Women		1930 Women		1966		1975		1966 Women		1975 Women	
	N	%	N	%	%W	%M	%W	%M	N	%	N	%
Education	44	27.3	81	15.9	8.1	4.3	6.7	4.4	236	19.9	295	17.6
Medicine	9	5.6	48	9.4	20.1	15.6	23.6	16.8	585	13.7	1,035	16.2
Engineering, Vocational	1	0.6	10	2.0	1.6	12.5	3.9	14.7	47	1.4	171	3.1
Agriculture	2	1.2	5	1.0	3.5	4.1	2.7	2.7	102	9.0	118	11.6
Science	38	23.6	133	26.1	21.6	32.4	17.4	28.0	627	7.1	764	7.2
Social, Administration	9	5.6	39	7.7	17.6	13.9	21.3	17.1	511	13.4	933	14.3
Humanities, Languages	58	36.0	193	37.9	27.4	17.2	24.3	16.3	797	16.9	1,065	17.1
Total %	99.9		100		99.9	100	99.9	100				
N	161		509		2,905	27,404	4,381	38,067	2,905	10.6	4,381	11.5
Education	44	27.3	81	15.9	8.1	4.3	6.7	4.4	236	19.9	295	17.6
Sciences	50	31.0	196	38.5	46.8	64.6	47.6	62.2	1,361	7.7	2,088	8.8
Humanities, etc.	67	41.6	232	45.6	45.0	31.1	45.6	33.4	1,308	15.3	1,998	16.7

Source: Commonwealth Universities Yearbooks 1914 and 1931; Statistics of Education, Universities 1966 and 1975.

TABLE 11.7   Number of universities with at least one woman academic in a subject within the subject group, 1912-51

Subject group	1912		1921		1930		1950	
	No. of Univs. w. women subject	No. of Univs. w. subject	No. of Univs. w. women subject	No. of Univs. w. subject	No. of Univs. w. women subject	No. of Univs. w. subject	No. of Univs. w. women subject	No. of Univs. w. subject
Education	14	22	16	23	16	23	23	26
Medicine	4	16	12	17	15	17	16	16
Engineering, Vocational, etc.	1	18	4	20	4	20	7	20
Agriculture	1	14	3	14	3	13	12	13
Science	13	22	21	24	22	25	26	28
Social Administration, etc.	5	22	13	23	16	23	24	27
Humanities	15	22	22	23	23	24	25	27
Total of universities	19	22	23	24	24	25	28	29

Note: Owing to the way in which the Commonwealth Universities Yearbook is compiled, London is counted as one university throughout; Dundee is counted as part of St Andrews throughout; Newcastle is counted as a separate university throughout. When they are listed, St David's Lampeter, the Welsh School of Medicine and the Royal Technical College, Glasgow, are included as separate institutions.

Source: Commonwealth Universities Yearbooks, 1914, 1922, 1931, 1952.

TABLE 11.8 Women academics in selected subjects, 1912-51

Subject	Number of women		Number of universities with at least one woman in the subject			
	1912	1930	1912	1921	1930	1951
Biology		6		3	4	2
Botany (inc. Agric. Botany)	14	31	8	14	15	18
Physiology/Anatomy	4	15	3	8	10	11
Zoology (inc. Natural History)	7	21	6	10	13	16
Maths	6	19	3	7	8	20
Chemistry (inc. Tech. Chemistry)	5	23	3	13	10	17
Physics	1	4	1	9	2	8
English	16	37	10	18	16	19
French	10	48	4	7	17	25
German	4	17	3	10	11	17
History	9	27	6	13	14	22
Philosophy	3	9	1	5	6	8

Source: Commonwealth Universities Yearbooks, 1914, 1922, 1931, 1952.

Grants Committee returns. They are not therefore exactly comparable because the UGC figures do not include part-time staff, whereas the Yearbook figures do include some part-time staff.(3) The
figures give an order of magnitude as between different subjects
and as between men and women, and can be compared on this basis
with caution.
   The decline in the distribution and representation of women in
education has been compensated for by an increase in medicine. It
seems probable that women held a much higher proportion of posts in
education in 1912 and probably in 1930 than they do now, but the
data are not available. Also, education seems in some universities
to have been a more important subject in the past than it is now.
Women have always held a proportion of posts in medicine, and in
1975 held 16.2 per cent of such posts. Nearly one third of women
in 1912 and almost a half from 1966 onwards have been in science
and science-based subjects. This is rather different from the view
expressed by Halsey and Trow (1971, p.158) that women were concentrated in arts and social sciences.(8) It is true that the representation of women in the science-based subjects is under 10 per
cent, but only about 10 per cent of academics are women in any
case. For women, the distribution between sciences and social
sciences reversed between 1966 and 1975, but for men the shift
away from science towards social science was less marked. Women

continue to make very slow progress in engineering and slightly faster progress in medicine.

Another and slightly less laborious way of obtaining an indication of the representation of women in different subjects is to count the number of universities where women held posts in the various subjects. Table 11.7 presents this information by subject groups. The first column for each year shows the number of universities where there was at least one woman in at least one of the subjects within the subject group; the second, the number of universities teaching at least one of the subjects in that group. It is apparent from the numbers of women shown in Table 11.6 and the numbers of departments shown in Table 11.7 that women were to be found on average in ones or twos in each department. The only exception to this is education, where there were a considerable number of women in a few universities. The small number of women in engineering and other vocational faculties is in accordance with common expectation. What is more surprising is the small number of university departments with women in the social sciences subject group. This group comprises business and management studies, economics, geography, accountancy, government and public administration, law, psychology, sociology and social anthropology. These subjects tended to be 'late developers' in British universities, with the exception of geography and law, which is also a predominantly male subject where no women were to be found in 1912 or 1921, two in 1930 and only four in 1951.

There are important differences within subject groups, both in the numbers of women and the date at which they penetrated the subject. Table 11.8 gives the details. In 1912, there were more women in botany than in any other subject except education or English. The absence or the small number of biologists is surprising. Among the humanities, French is a 'late developer' but had considerably more women than English in 1930. Women were, however, to be found in less expected and less common subjects, such as glass technology, mineralogy, astronomy, Egyptology and Asian and African languages. By 1951 women were represented within most subject groups in nearly all universities and in particular had made gains in agriculture and in the social and administrative group of subjects. The increase in the latter group is attributable to expansion in economics and geography as well as in social studies, social work and sociology. French was the subject which most universities were likely to have at least one woman teaching, with education the runner-up. History and mathematics departments were much more likely than before the Second World War to have women members. Women had begun to obtain more posts in engineering, technological and other vocational subjects, including architecture. Thus, the total proportions and levels of women had not changed much, but their distribution between subjects had. In particular, they had entered more subjects, but they still had not made much progress in law or engineering.

It is impossible without knowing more about the size and scope of subjects at university level at different periods to attempt an explanation of these differences. It is, however, possible to put forward hypotheses for the differences as well as for the distribution of women between universities and their lack of promotion.

HYPOTHESES AND EXPLANATIONS

The data, incomplete though they are, raise many questions. These
questions can be divided into three groups: those concerning the
rank of women, and those concerning their distribution among subjects. The first group of questions has been briefly discussed and
it is not proposed to say more here. The second and third groups
of questions raise issues concerning social-psychological pressures
and access to power.

It will have been noted that the proportion of women reached a
certain level, about 10 per cent unevenly distributed between subjects, and in senior posts about 5 per cent, and then seems to have
got stuck. The data themselves and published work (BSA, 1974;
Blackstone and Fulton, 1975, 1976) cast doubt on the notion that
women 'choose' to participate in the academic profession in the
particular ways in which they do. And if they do, the meaning of
their 'choice' would itself be problematical. Most people have
little choice about their first job, least of all members of disadvantaged and visible minorities; and that first job disproportionately influences subsequent opportunities.

The data throw no light on when women were recruited or whether
they were recruited when few men were available or at periods of
expansion. Some outstandingly able women obtained their posts only
at a time or in a place where no suitable man could be found
(British Sociological Association, 1973). The proportion and
influence of women may be limited by not appointing them, and by
terminating temporary and un-tenured appointments regardless of
merit. However, women's abilities may be made use of by appointing them to those temporary research posts where they will do the
work which will make men's reputations. Wives also often perform
this role (Glastonbury, 1978).

Once in tenured posts, neither men nor women can be sacked
without considerable trouble and expense. Advancement is said to
depend on publication, research, performance of administrative
duties and teaching, in that order. Recent work in this country
and some other countries (9) suggests that male sex is also a major
advantage. Women have reason to feel that, no matter how able or
how intellectually productive, they are likely to be denied both
posts and promotion.

Some women can be discouraged; and their working lives can be
made disagreeable, with the intention of encouraging them to
resign. Academic women may be especially vulnerable to such
pressures because they are acting contrary to the assumptions of
society: they are exceptional, possibly 'abnormal'. They can be
isolated from such intellectual and scholarly life as goes on
within the academic community, so that their intellectual development is impaired and they thus become less eligible for promotion
(Epstein, 1970, pp.173ff; Hochschild, 1975; Deem, 1978, p.96).
Some women feel that their work is not taken seriously or as
seriously as that of their male colleagues (BSA, 1975; Sommerkorn,
1967, pp.158ff.). Joking is used in common rooms, as elsewhere
(Whitehead, 1976, p.169) as a means of belittling, punishing or
expressing antagonism to women acting in a professional capacity
or outside the sex-role stereotypes.

For the consistent pursuit of scholarly research many people need a supportive environment. Teaching, administration, external interests such as public and voluntary work, the day-to-day pressures of ordinary living and of keeping friendships in repair: all demand time and energy. But research requires continuous time and an ability to postpone immediate demands. Women academics, who are often in a position of having always to prove themselves, must necessarily find it difficult to postpone immediate demands for long-term ends of uncertain outcome - for the outcome of research cannot be known. Furthermore, sex-role stereotypes and conventions require women to pay attention to immediate demands and to be conscientious about routine work. A woman may find herself having to choose between meeting these demands by conforming to men's definition of women as junior academics, not assertive, doing useful and necessary teaching and not involved with the shape and direction of her department, discipline or university, and enjoying agreeable collegial relationships on the one hand; or of pursuing fully her professional career and research interests, but in isolation and in conflict with her environment. 'The men in this institution expect women to be seen (if they are pretty) but not heard. I am not pretty, I am heard and I am heard of - and they don't like me', one woman remarked. In substance, women academics face a dilemma similar to that of Isotta Nogarola.

It is perhaps understandable if an unmarried woman with intellectual interests in a provincial town opts for good relations with colleagues; otherwise, whom is she able to talk to? She does not have the companionship of husband and children. Her colleagues are likely to be members of the non-university organizations - civic, political, religious, voluntary, intellectual - where she might otherwise seek congenial companionship. Such factors may lessen the productivity of single women and help to explain the finding of Williams et al. (1973, p.399) that married women had published more than single women. Doing research is a venture into the unknown, and inevitably is seldom carried out from the beginning in the most economical way. But much can be learnt from trying out ideas on sympathetic colleagues. Great commitment is needed to carry through a research project largely in isolation, as all work on PhD students shows (for example, Rudd and Hatch, 1968; Rudd, 1975).

It is possible, even probable, that women overestimate the extent and depth of scholarly talk among men. It is understandable that such a mistake should be made. The women have had to be very committed to their work and scholarly interests to have undertaken research and to have overcome all the barriers to holding a university post. Naturally, such women wish to discuss their work; they know that at least some men do. But are the majority of male academics cast in the same mould as the women? For some men, obtaining a university post may be the culmination of a natural progress of being good at school-work and of being delivered successively from good school to university, to post-graduate work and so on to a permanent position and at least some promotion. It is seen as natural that a man who is good at academic pursuits should follow such a course. But for a woman, such a course is problematic at all stages. Sommerkorn (1967, pp.101,104) found

that women needed encouragement to take up an academic career.
Furthermore, able men have a much wider effective choice of
careers than do able women, and many of these careers offer
greater rewards of pay, power and prestige for hard work than
does university teaching. University teaching appears as one of
the more open careers for women. Nonetheless, the refusal to take
a woman's work seriously, joking and outright hostility can all be
used to keep down those few women who get in, and so to keep down
the numbers in senior posts, and the numbers who apply for posts at
all.

The distribution of women between subjects raises other issues.
Unfortunately, there are no data available showing the distribution
of men and women staff for individual subjects as opposed to
subject-groups. The data do not show, for example, whether the
large number of women botanists reflects large botany departments,
although subjective impressions suggest that it does not. It is
not possible in the space of this chapter to examine the relationship between the numbers of undergraduate and post-graduate students and the academic staff in the various subjects. It seems
unlikely, however, that small numbers of students can wholly
account for the extraordinarily small numbers of staff in some
subjects, if only because academic careers last so much longer
than student careers.

The decline in the proportion of women in education is very
striking. It has been suggested that this decline reflects the
increasingly academic development of the subject, but it is not
certain that it is so. The academic side of education departments
seems to have grown faster than the methods side, and women seem
not to have maintained their proportion of new posts. However, a
count of staff, excluding research staff, at one major education
department suggested that women's share of methods posts declined
both proportionately and in absolute numbers, but their share of
academic posts increased slightly in both ways.(10) If such a
development has occurred generally (and further work needs to be
done to establish this), then the following hypothesis might
explain it. Methods lecturers are recruited from schoolteachers,
and for schoolteachers the education departments of universities
have high status and prestige. For academics, education departments, rightly or wrongly, tend to have low status and therefore
are less attractive for this and no doubt other reasons to those
who could expect to obtain appointments in mainstream departments.
(11) Able women have more difficulty in obtaining appointments
than men and may therefore be more likely to apply for and to
accept appointments in education departments.(12)

There is no study of the sex-stereotyping of subjects in
Britain such as Feldman (1974, p.43) has done for the USA. But it
is clear from Table 11.8 that sex-stereotyping is not a sufficient
explanation of the different proportions of men and women. Similarly, concern with people (Bernard, 1964, p.83; Epstein, 1970,
p.154) will not do. Bernard also suggests that women have made
their major contributions in areas and at levels where there are
definitive bodies of knowledge, and relatively little controversy;
the great social critics had been academic men (p.124), but if
women's work is not taken seriously, women will not be perceived

as great social critics. Riesman, in his introduction, suggests that women have been poorly represented in political science because it emphasizes power (Bernard, 1964, p.xx).

Subjects may be related to power in various ways. They can be those which, within the university, involve the expenditure of large sums of money or the deployment of large staffs; for example, engineering and medicine. They can be concerned with the study of power and with instruments of power; for example, politics, economics and law. They can involve teaching those who will later exercise power; for example, businessmen and lawyers. Within a wider context, powerful subjects can be those which influence the ideological climate of society; for example, theology in the past and, perhaps, education at the present time. But control over the content and development of a subject, which includes its ideological content, rests in large measure with those in senior positions, especially those in professorial and head of department posts. Promotion to such posts depends both on an ability to do the job and on an ability to please, in a professional capacity, those in positions of power. Such posts confer power, status and prestige on the individual and on her or his subject and activities. Conversely, the refusal of recognition devalues the individual and her work. D.E. Smith (1978) tellingly explores some of these relationships and finds 'power and authority in the educational process are the prerogatives of men' (p.289).

The subjects in which the proportions of women are low tend to be those which are powerful in one or more of the ways already referred to. A technological society makes this true of education. As Touraine (1974) has shown, access to many positions of power requires ability and a high degree of technological knowledge of the sort obtained in higher education. Furthermore, access to higher education, especially in Britain, requires good schooling. Hence the training of teachers becomes increasingly important. Again following Touraine, it is inevitable that universities should reproduce the social hierarchy. It is therefore not surprising that the proportion of women in university posts and in senior posts should not have increased over half a century. It seems as though the struggles at the turn of the century were necessary to obtain for women a 10 per cent token share. The Women's Liberation Movement needs both to safeguard this share and to increase it.

The Women's Movement and the development of women's studies now provide help that was largely lacking in earlier centuries, although women's religious houses in the Middle Ages and women's colleges from the late nineteenth century did provide support for women scholars. The Women's Movement goes much further. It provides sisterly solidarity and a political base, for which there were clear precedents in the nineteenth century. The development of women's studies provides a forum for intellectual discussion. More than that, women's studies is concerned with the ideological climate of society.

APPENDIX: NOTE ON METHODOLOGY

The first issue of the Commonwealth Universities Yearbook appeared
in 1914, and included for each university a report for the year
1912-13 and a staff list. The Yearbook has since appeared annually
except during the two world wars. The staff lists normally show
names of staff with their rank or status under departments or with
an indication of subject. Part-time and temporary staff are often
included. The Yearbook has generally followed the usual convention
of listing men with initials and women with first names. In the
earlier years, some male first names and the titles Mrs or Miss
were sometimes included.

The Yearbooks I selected for examination were 1914, 1922, 1931
and 1952. To bring the analysis up to date, I also examined the
UGC statistics for 1966, 1969, 1972 and 1975. Only the data for
1966 and 1975 are reported, as there was no change in direction in
the intervening years. I chose all the dates to accord as far as
possible with the conventional 10-year intervals, but to take
account also of events which I believe to be relevant to the proportion of women in universities during this period: the two wars
and the slump.

I counted the number of women by university and rank, and listed
each department and subject in which they appeared for each of the
four years. For the women holding senior posts, I noted the subject for each woman. I counted the number of men in each university for each of the four years. For both men and women, I
counted every name, regardless of status and whether part-time or
temporary, but excluded any names listed twice wherever possible.
Where the list showed, for example, 8 research assistance without
any names, the 8 were entirely omitted, as there was no means of
knowing how many were men and how many women.

I compared the figures resulting from my count with some UGC
statistics for one year for some universities, but the differences
were so great for some of these universities and were clearly not
attributable to the inclusion of part-time staff (as the UGC
return gave separate figures for these) that I could see no purpose
in attempting to reconcile the two. My figures are consistently
higher than those of the UGC.

The UGC returns show that the numbers of university teachers
rose from 2,606 in 1923-4 to 3,907 in 1937-8. There has also been
a rise from 6,536 in 1947-8 to more than 38,000 in 1975.

The figures I have compiled offer an order of magnitude, a
basis for further work, and an indication of what might be fruit-
ful questions to ask.

NOTES

1 Girton College was the first of the women's colleges to be
   established at either of the ancient universities, but Cambridge was the last university in Britain to exclude women
   from full membership - which it did until 1948.
2 See, for example, Kamm (1965), McWilliams-Tullberg (1975).
3 See Appendix for a note on the methodology.

4 The term Young Civic is taken from Williams et al. (1973, p.433).

London: 41 colleges, excluding Chelsea.
Scotland: Aberdeen, Dundee, Edinburgh, Glasgow, St Andrews.
Wales: 6 colleges.
Old civic: Birmingham, Bristol, Durham, Leeds, Liverpool, Manchester, Manchester Institute of Technology, Newcastle, Sheffield.
Young civic: Exeter, Hull, Keele, Leicester, Nottingham, Reading, Southampton.

5 Williams et al. (1973, p.442) chose their sample from Dundee, Edinburgh and St Andrews, which, according to my data, had a rather better proportion of women than Aberdeen, Glasgow and the Royal Technical College, Glasgow (later Strathclyde); but their data is 17 years later and the position of women could have changed in the interval.

6 Salaries ranged as follows, according to the Report for 1923-4, HMSO (1925), p.30:

Professors   £550-£2,000, av. £977
Readers, etc.   £350-£1,000
Lecturers   £250-£800
Asst. Lecturers and
Demonstrators   £150-£500, av. £307

7 The proportion rises to 8.6 per cent if the theological, medical and dental schools are excluded.

8 Halsey and Trow (1971, p.158) were relying on the figures quoted by Ingrid Sommerkorn in her thesis (1967, p.111). Her figures do not entirely support their view. The first figures showing the subject distribution of men and women academics appear in 'Statistics of Education' for the year 1965-6 which was published in 1968, and would therefore have been available by the time Halsey and Trow were writing.

9 In Britain surveys have been done in several universities, but have not been published, and have been or are being done in the British Sociological Association, British Psychological Society and the Political Studies Association. Numerous university and discipline studies have been undertaken in the USA and many have been published. Surveys have also been undertaken in Canada, Australia, New Zealand and Norway.

10 In that institution, and excluding all research staff, in 1966 about one-third of the methods staff were women, and in 1975 about one-quarter. Of the women staff, in 1966 about one-sixth were on the academic side and in 1975 about one-quarter. The numbers are small and the classification difficult, so these figures must be treated with caution.

11 For example, a senior lecturer might decline an invitation to apply for a relevant chair in an education department (personal communication).

12 Several women in this position are known to the author.

Chapter 12

The experiences of women graduates in the labour market

Lynne Chisholm and Diana Woodward

'And we were told there were five things a woman graduate could
do: teach, the Civil Service, the armed forces, secretarial
work - I can't remember what the fifth was ... and you didn't
know yourself if you were capable of going into something which
seemed a very male preserve' (1960 woman graduate respondent)
Out of date? Over a decade later (in 1974) the Working Party on
Equal Opportunities for Women of the Standing Conference of University Appointments Services reported as follows:
Legislation making it compulsory for posts to be advertised to
both sexes does not mean that women are more likely to be
appointed to the posts offered (response of one engineering
company to working party enquiries).

One gets the impression that a considerable number of women
graduates have limited career ambitions, do not want to find
themselves in highly-competitive situations.... I am sure these
attitudes develop at a very early age. (University Appointments
Officer's report)

There is discrimination right through the education system....
University and polytechnic careers advisors often get involved
in remedial work, or find themselves advising women students
whose prospects have been blunted by poor advice at school ...
which has narrowed their field of choice to the traditional ...
women's occupations. (Working party proposals)
This report concluded that women graduates who are actively and
consciously challenging discrimination are in the minority; most
accept the barriers or give up after rejection from one or two non-
traditional job applications. Where they did choose and succeed
in entering untypical fields, they appeared to do well - but such
women are probably a self-selected group with characteristics not
shared by the majority of their peers.
Material focusing on the interaction between higher education
and the labour market specifically for women is scarce on both
sides of the Atlantic. This shortage of useful work in the fields
of occupational choice, labour market structure (especially occupational segregation) and career development results essentially

from the traditional stance adopted by occupational sociology:
women are either ignored, assumed to fall within the terms of a
general analysis which on closer inspection proves to be predic-
ated upon purely male experience, or are treated as second-class
citizens with 'special problems' (Claude-Mathieu, 1977; BSA, 1975.).
(1)   On an empirical level, the majority of the research originates
from the USA and deals largely with the aspirations and expectations of college women: in effect, orientated towards the 'homework dilemma' as opposed to studying graduate women as workers
(e.g., Angrist and Almquist, 1975; Baruch, 1972; Ginzberg et al.,
1966; Wolfson, 1976).

Educational channelling and sex-role socialization at home and
school result in girls and women entering a narrow range of occu-
pations with lower aspirations and expectations for progress
therein (Byrne, 1978; Levy, 1972; Marini and Greenberger, 1978;
Mathews and Tiedeman, 1964; McKeefery-Reynolds, 1977; Oxford
University Department of Educational Studies, 1971; Rosen and
Aneshensel, 1978; Wait and Dye, 1977; and chapters in this volume).
Further, the existence of a sexually-segregated dual labour market
(Barron and Norris, 1976) is an important structural factor in the
explanation of women's employment patterns: most work at a narrow
range of tasks within a narrow range of occupations, in low-status
badly-paid positions offering little opportunity for career progress (Hunt, 1968; Epstein, 1970; Robinson, 1978).   Women suffer
both overt and covert discrimination in recruitment, promotion,
salary and day-to-day interaction at work (Epstein, 1970, 1976;
Hunt, 1975; Hartnett, 1978; Wolff, 1976; Valentich and Gripton,
1978; Chiplin and Sloane, 1976; Hagan and Kahn, 1975; and others).

Graduate women are no exception: most enter teaching or public
service occupations traditionally dominated by women; they achieve
less in purely career terms; they are discriminated against; and
they appear to manage their careers less well than their male
peers because of a complex of structural and situational constraints, together with the effects of socio-psychological barriers
which are reflected in women's typical lack of self-confidence in
their abilities (Chisholm, 1978).

The following examination of the progress and experiences of
1960 British women graduates expands upon the issues raised above.
The extent and patterning of their career development over fifteen
years not only demonstrates sharp disparities between women and
men graduates, but also illuminates the radically different con-
texts in which the two groups approach and experience the labour
market.

The material presented arises from successive phases of the
longitudinal DES/SSRC-financed 'National Survey of 1960 Graduates':
questionnaires distributed in 1966 and 1973, and in-depth interview data collected from a sub-sample of the cohort in 1975.(2)

OCCUPATIONAL DISTRIBUTION OF THE COHORT

In that 70 per cent of the women respondents graduated with an
arts or social science degree, whereas only 45 per cent of the men
did not (Kelsall, et al., 1970, table 2.1), the broad occupational

destinations of the two groups were bound to diverge. Many women
graduates, by virtue of the subject of their degree, were automatically excluded from a wide range of technical and scientific jobs,
especially within industry. Yet even those women who did graduate
in science or technology were unlikely to enter such occupations:
only 17 per cent were first employed in industry, whilst 59 per
cent went into the education sector. Almost half of their
similarly-qualified male peers entered industry - a sharp contrast
(Kelsall, et al., table 4.5).

The vast majority of both women and men graduates (86 and 80 per
cent respectively) first took posts in three sectors: public administration, education and industry. Public administration drew 15
per cent of the women and 12 per cent of the men. But whereas the
remaining 68 per cent of the men were split equally between education and industry, all save 9 per cent of the remaining women fell
within the education sector. In other words, over three-fifths of
1960 women graduates went into schoolteaching (the majority) or
lecturing.

By 1966 there had been some movement between sectors, in favour
of education, which now employed 71 per cent of women and 41 per
cent of men graduates in the sample. Industry was the loser in
this process. The men graduates, however, were more likely than
the women to have remained in the same employment sector over the
period between their first job and that in 1966. In particular,
women were likely to have moved out of industry, commerce and
private practice. Whilst clearly a sizeable proportion shifted
to education, some also transferred to the public administration
sector (Kelsall et al. pp.52-6).

Such changes continued in the same vein between 1966 and 1973,
but the extent of the net movement between sectors was of a lesser
order. As people gradually 'settle down' the desire and opportunity to 'change horses' diminish. The proportions of women and
men graduates employed in education increased slightly (to 73 and
43 per cent respectively); industry continued to lose its recruits
(by 1973 employing only 22 per cent of the men and 4 per cent of
the women respondents); public administration remained virtually
stable.(3)

Whilst all graduates tend to be concentrated in a few sectors
of the economy, then, women are even more so confined. Given
earlier educational and general socialization experiences, which
led 60 per cent of the women to graduate in an arts discipline,
such occupational segregation was largely predictable. More
interesting is the process of retreat over the years: the data
suggest (supported by the interview material discussed below) that
a significant proportion of those women who initiated careers in
fields other than teaching encountered difficulties which led them
to return to the traditionally 'feminine' and female-dominated
sphere of education.

'The finer the distinctions, the more segregation one will
"catch"' (Gross, 1971, p.48). Occupational segregation by sex is
observable using the broad classification of employment sector;
the distribution of the women and men graduates within these sectors achieves a sharper focus.

Women graduates are almost always numerically fewer than men graduates in any occupational group; there are fewer of them, employed or not. Proportionately their representation in various occupational branches varies widely. For example, of those employed in public administration in 1973, 42 per cent were in local government and 20 per cent in hospital services. Together with those employed in museums and libraries, these three are the only within-sector occupational categories where women graduates are disproportionately overrepresented in comparison with those of their male peers employed in public administration. Within the civil service - to refine the classifications still further - graduate women proportionately exceed their male fellows only in the lower-status executive grades (which offer fewer opportunities for high-flying careers).

Most economically active women graduates were and are employed in the education sector: but they predictably predominate in the less prestigious and less well-paid categories. Almost two-fifths of the men employed in this sector in 1973 were in the universities, but only 16 per cent of the women were. Where men graduates are in higher education employment, again they are far more likely to be found in the universities. In the less prestigious polytechnics and other FE/HE institutions were to be found 15 per cent of the women graduates employed in education overall in 1973, and 17 per cent of the men. At the other end of the spectrum, 8 per cent of the women employed in the sector in 1973 held state primary teaching posts, compared with 1 per cent of the men.(4)

Outside public administration and education, the numbers of 1960 women graduates economically active in 1973 were so small as to be swamped by their male peers. In the engineering industry, 99 per cent of the 1960 graduates employed are men, although the branch accounted for less than a third of the male respondents employed in the industrial sector. Those few women in industry are to be found in those categories including big combines like ICI, Unilever, the breweries, Kodak and Beecham. The very scale and diversified character of these undertakings mean that women graduates can be absorbed into more 'acceptable' areas: research,(5) personnel, etc.

In the commercial sector, minute numbers of 1960 women graduates are employed in banking, insurance and finance, market research, advertising, and PR work. (There may well have been some change during the 1960s in the latter three groups, due to expansion both of these branches themselves and of social science courses at degree level. But if subsequent cohorts follow the pattern of the 1960 cohort, it seems likely that women graduates initially employed in these fields will retreat from them after marriage and children. The structural demands of, for example, the occupation of advertising executive are such that require 'the sale of one's soul' (and time) to a degree typically unacceptable and impossible for married women with children.) For this cohort, women proportionately exceed their male peers only in the traditional fields of wholesale/retail distribution and in the service trades.

In 1973, there were no 1960 women graduate respondents who were practising architects, accountants, surveyors, or consultant engineers. There were seven practising women solicitors (100 men), and three women barristers (18 men).

The graduate labour market structure is as strictly sexually-

segregated as the general labour market is. The situation does not
appear to have altered over the years since this cohort left
university (Standing Conference of University Appointments Services,
1974). Our data also suggest a retrenchment over time: 1960 women
graduates have withdrawn ever more solidly into traditional fields
of employment. This has not been the case for men graduates: if
anything, by relinquishing industry and moving into education, they
are accomplishing the reverse. This conforms with Gross's (1971)
findings for the USA: occupational segregation by sex has remained
high through this century. Traditionally male-dominated occupations have apparently become more resistant to female entry, whereas
traditionally female-dominated occupations have become less resistant to male entry.(6)

SINGLE GRADUATE WOMEN'S CAREER DEVELOPMENT

Career achievement

Throughout the period 1960-75, single women have been less likely
than married women to be employed in the education sector, though
the difference is not great.(7) As early as 1966 women whose
first posts had been in the minority sectors of communications,
private professional practice, the armed forces or the churches
were less likely to have married since graduation (Kelsall et al.,
1970, p.81). Initially this suggests a quality of 'innovation'
amongst some of these women: remaining single and not entering
education. The 1975 interview material collected from single
graduate women did not substantiate this notion; but we did not
select specifically for those in non-traditional fields (although
in practice, those employed in such fields are likely to be found
in a small number of 'female' branches).
     Of these 33 interviewees 13 (40 per cent) were employed in
education: fewer than we would expect, but the small size of the
sample can account for such imbalances.(8) Their occupations were
as follows:

Schoolteaching	(N = 6)	Lecturing: universities	(N = 5)
Civil service	(N = 3)	other FE/HE	(N = 2)
Social work	(N = 3)	Research: universities/govt.	(N = 3)
Librarianship	(N = 2)	industry	(N = 3)
Publishing	(N = 2)	Transport engineering	(N = 1)
Admin. (govt.)	(N = 3)		

In comparison with a group of their male peers (N = 50, all
married) also interviewed in 1975, the single women had achieved
markedly less in both status and salary terms. Only four of the
women could be termed high achievers,(9) whilst two-fifths of the
men were. The 1973 median income for these married men was
£3,550 p.a.; for the single women, £3,000 p.a.(10) The lesser
achievement of the women is partially due to the restricted and
stereotyped range of occupations they chose to enter. They did
not enter industry, which, for this sample of graduate men at
least, patently offers high rewards in both salary and status.
Why they do not do so is well known (see Mattfield and Van Aken,
1965; Acker and Van Houten, 1974). Their preference for the

education sector does not compensate: teaching and lecturing in Britain structurally provide few opportunities for high achievement (Hilsum and Start, 1974; Williams et al., 1974).

Yet those single women employed outside the education sector are prone to have suffered, both in terms of risking career blockage and the diminution of earning potential (contrary to the impressions formed by university appointments officers noted earlier.(11) So whereas schoolteaching in particular is a secure but relatively badly-paid occupation for men graduates, for women graduates it is an equally secure but relatively well-paid option. If women are to stand a good chance of approximating to the earning potential of even the lowest-paid of their male peers in professional occupations, they should enter teaching or another of the public service professions. In having done precisely that, they are exhibiting a pragmatic rationality (Chisholm, 1978, p.329).

The single women's social class backgrounds were as high as the married men's, in fact, higher. (This is not surprising; as any edition of UCCA statistics will reveal, it has been known for some time that social class inequalities in university entrance are more marked amongst female undergraduates.) Overall, 78 per cent of the married men in the interview sample came from at least routine non-manual families, whereas this was the case for almost all the single women (92 per cent).(12) The single women were also awarded equally good degrees. In that both of these factors - social class background and degree class - could be argued perhaps to influence (in differing ways) the likelihood of career success, we can conclude that since the single women were not 'inferior' in either aspect their lesser career achievements cannot be attributed to such factors. Interestingly, the data suggest that social class background does not function to aid career development for women in the same manner as it does for men. As Epstein (1973) postulates, sex acts as an overriding dominant variable.

The single women also held as many extra qualifications on top of their degree as did the married men. Such qualifications are of most use when specifically related to the occupations held; in this, the single women tended to fall down. We suspect this reflects a higher level of ambivalence at graduation over future career plans. American college women graduating in 1968 were reported by Angrist and Almquist (1975, p.80) to display precisely this quality:

> The study class reflects the cumulative effects of a college education. They feel and express the push towards the work-world, picking a field, etc.... But they have to mesh these multiple interests in terms of the larger societal expectations for women. Thus they adopt a contingency orientation: they are indecisive, vague, weighing out alternatives, stalling for time.

The authors regarded this as the cornerstone of their findings.

Our single women tended to take up academic diplomas leading to no professional qualification or specific vocation. Otherwise they pursued secretarial diplomas. Their motivations to do so are telling:

> 'My parents were very insistent that I did it.... I needed something practical to add a vocational edge to a non-vocational degree.... I didn't want to do it but I could see it was a sensible thing to do.'

'Girls usually get into publishing with the aid of shorthand
and typing.... My first job wasn't in any way a secretarial
post, but ... I wouldn't have got the job if I hadn't had it.'

'My first employers said, "Fine ... you must do a secretarial
course before you come here." So I told them I didn't want to
do secretarial work, so they said, "Oh, no, this isn't secretarial work but you've got to have it".... So off I went.'

One final point about the effects of degree class and extra
qualifications upon career progress: it is frequently said that
women need to show themselves to be positively better than male
competitors to achieve similar rank; Hunt (1975, p.85) evidences
this. Whilst for the married men in this sample neither factor
appeared to be related to career success,(13) the four high-
achieving single women all had good degrees (first/upper second),
and all possessed more than one extra qualification, each of which
was vocationally related.

Discrimination against women

A fuller exposition is detailed elsewhere (Chisholm, 1978); it
suffices to say that a considerable proportion of the interviewees
had been affected by discriminatory practices, directly or indirectly. Occupations (university administration) and posts central
to the work of an organization (broadcasts from the Meteorological
Office) were reported by respondents as having been closed to
women in 1960. Lower pay than that given to male graduate recruits
to similar posts was common; publishing was particularly bad here.
Women graduates were not given the same training as men graduates,
and were thus irremediably excluded from promotion (industrial
research). Others were simply not promoted anyway (government
training board; publishing; industry; librarianship; civil service;
teaching; social work; university lecturing) for a variety of well-
worn 'reasons'. These experiences were by no means confined to
the period preceding equal opportunities legislation (which has
merely driven discriminatory practices underground). The problem
is in any event crucially and deeply rooted in the attitudes of
those individuals in the workplace in a position to make personnel
and promotion decisions: Epstein's (1976) gatekeepers. Several
respondents talked about bosses who simply did not like working as
equals with women and who would not promote them. Reports from
Hunt (1975), the Standing Conference of University Appointments
Services (1974) and INSEAD (1977) have confirmed these attitudes
as prevalent in industry, amongst management in general, and for
a wide range of employers who recruit graduates.

It is disturbing to note that these women were noticeably reti-
cent to state categorically that discrimination occurs, whether
against themselves or others. They frequently made contradictory
statements in this connection. They displayed a truly remarkable
propensity to fail - or positively to refuse - to recognize discrimination; to play down its significance; and to conform to
traditional sex-role ideology in finding justifications for its
practice (e.g., 'You see basically women aren't mechanically-minded';

'Very many women are married, for whom the earning is not the main
consideration ... and they are not career-oriented'; 'Women are
difficult to work with on the whole'). Women have collaborated in
the discriminatory process by concurring with the traditional conception of women as workers. They they do so is largely predictable, given the persistence of sex-role stereotyping which remains
an integral part of girls' school experience (e.g., Belotti, 1975;
Lobban, 1978; Wolpe, 1977). In addition, as Shaw (1976) points out,
the functioning of the education system is orientated to the
requirements of the wider social and economic system, in which
women as a group are tied in a characteristic manner to the systems
of production and reproduction. The channelling of self-conceptions
based on membership of one sex as opposed to another parallels and
reinforces the maintenance of a sexual division of labour fundamental to contemporary western social and economic organization.
In reality, women have little choice but to conform to traditional
expectations, whether in terms of their ideas about themselves or
in the actual patterning of their lives.

Career management

An abundant literature attests to the generally deleterious effects
of sex-role socialization upon women's participation and performance in the work-world (see Fransella and Frost, 1977, 5 and 6).
Others have shown how organizations do not respond rationally to
women because of cultural norms and beliefs about their role and
abilities (Jeghelian, 1976; Hagan and Kahn, 1975; Epstein, 1970,
1976; Miller et al., 1975; Wolff, 1976).
    The single women in this sample experienced far less promotion
than their married male peers; discrimination accounts for part of
this. In addition, they themselves may not have been as strictly
rational as the men in terms of career management. First, two-
thirds of the promotions they did receive were internal (i.e.
within the same employing organization); the majority of the
married men's promotions were external. The impression is that
women have not sought promotion so actively: probably because of
women's typical lack of self-confidence, an outcome of their sex-
role socialization. For example:
    'I suppose in another way a reason I'm nervous about applying
    for higher posts is that sometimes I lack confidence in myself
    ... and I feel happier at something I know I can manage.'
    Second, from a study of the reasons they gave for changing jobs
over the years, the single women emerged as having more often
found themselves in variously-defined unsatisfactory (14) job
situations, for both personal and career reasons. In other words,
then tended to be 'pushed out' of jobs as opposed to being 'pulled
out' (which was more typical of the married men). True, single
women without a family financially dependent upon them and settled
in residence, schools, etc., can more readily extricate themselves
from unsatisfactory jobs. Nevertheless we can conclude that
'push' factors are more likely to result in moves bad for career
prospects (e.g., the timing may be wrong).
    Finally, these single women continued to display the low

aspirations typical of women as a disadvantage social group, in spite of their status as graduates firmly established as single and working women.(15)   One-third had no career aspirations beyond their present level; but this was so for only one-sixth of the married men.   The men were also far less ambivalent about future promotion, and were clearer about the directions in which they wished to proceed.   Perhaps by this time the women had become resigned to their lesser chances of success?   Certainly; but their responses echo once more the characteristic ambivalence and lack of self-confidence:

'When I'm completely confident in what I'm doing, and feel that I've learnt it all, I may want to move on.'

'I don't know what I intend to do ... you know I don't plan any definite objective ... I think I wait and see how it turns out.'

'I have no pattern, no career ambitions ... each job is enough for the time, until suddenly it isn't and then I move.'

MARRIED WOMEN GRADUATES' CAREER DEVELOPMENT

These are full-time workers reflecting on their situation:

'I can remember when I was at university, if I had to make a choice between having a job or having a husband and family I'd rather have a husband and family.'

'I think a lot of my friends who did equally well at school were frustrated at home, or didn't bring up their family, or went without a family in order to achieve career satisfaction; and I really think I've been very lucky.'

Like the first respondent above, 1960 women graduates in general approached the labour market with the traditional dichotomy between home and work firmly established in their minds.   Very few of those who married have been as lucky as the second respondent, who has managed to keep up almost continuous career involvement since graduation (self-employed and working largely from home).   Higher education clearly raises possibilities and aspirations to combine work, career and family in some way: we know that highly-educated women are more likely to remain in or return to the labour force after marriage (Kelsall et al., 1970; Woodhall, 1973).   It does not broaden women's occupational horizons or teach them to question the taken-for-granted in this sphere of their lives.   Our married women graduates were even more heavily concentrated in the education sector (whether currently or in terms of former employment) than the female sample as a whole: this was clear in 1966 (Kelsall et al., table 7.3) and the trend has since intensified.

The education sector counted as the main occupational field for 77 per cent of the 1975 interview sample (N = 57) of married graduate women with children.   Of those currently employed in 1975 83 per cent were in education (three-quarters of them in school-teaching).   The range of occupations in which the interviewees were ever engaged was predictably narrow:

High frequency   Schoolteaching (incl. playgroup work)
                  FE/HE lecturing, tutoring, research
                  Social services (administration and practice)
                  Librarianship, archiving, curatorship
                  Professional services in industry (economic
                      forecasting, computing, personnel work)
                  Communications (public relations, advertising)
                  Secretarial work and related
                  Industrial research
                  Psychotherapy
Low frequency   Shopwork

Virtually all the interviewees had followed the 'in-out-in'
pattern of labour force participation; hardly any questioned a
social structure and cultural ideology which automatically limited
their career involvement in scope and significance. Amongst the
1960 female graduate cohort as a whole, labour force participation patterns closely follow those of marriage and family-building.
In 1966 only one-fifth of married women with children were economically active; by this date three-quarters of the cohort were
married and three-fifths of them had begun families (Kelsall et
al., table 2.8). The bulk of first births to these women occurred
during the period 1963-7; by 1973, when their children were growing
older, 55 per cent were employed. Amongst the 1975 interview
sample, 62 per cent had jobs of some kind, almost all part-time.

Had large numbers of the women decided to challenge ideology
and praxis, could they have been accommodated? In other words,
had they not accepted traditional definitions of the hierarchical
ordering of the home v. work priorities in the lives of married
women with children, and had they attempted to secure a viable
career for themselves in spite of the very real practical problems
entailed in combining work and family for women in our society
(unless they restrict themselves to intermittent involvement in
a small range of relatively flexible occupations), would they have
found jobs and careers anyway? Structural and situational factors
are the determinants of the extend and patterning of married
women's participation in the labour force, regardless of their own
preferences (Perrucci and Targ, 1978; Barron and Norris, 1976;
Hudis, 1976; Brosenschaft, 1978; Ginzberg et al., 1966). The
inherent conflicts and dilemmas at a socio-psychological level
which accompany such a context service the existing system via
the revocability of their status as working women (i.e., being a
housewife is a constant alternative). They also have negative
consequences for career development itself, typically characterized by irrationality of career decision-making and discontinuity
because of life-cycle changes (Bailyn, 1964).(16)

The study of labour market structure per se has grown in extent
in recent years, emphasizing its segmental character and in particular focusing upon the idea of a dual labour market. In this
model, 'primary' and 'secondary' sector jobs can be readily distinguished from each other. The former are characterized by
higher pay and fringe benefits, greater security and stability,
and wider opportunities for career progress; the latter display
the opposite attributes. Employers benefit from this arrangement
and may positively promote it: on the one hand, they retain groups

of valuable skilled employees by offering good wages and conditions; on the other hand, they have access to a supplementary labour force as required, at low cost and under little obligation to such employees in the long term. Barron and Norris have demonstrated how in Britain the secondary labour force is chiefly composed of women, on the basis of wage levels; and they point to various factors which promote the relegation of women workers as a group to the secondary sector (dispensability, clearly visible social difference, little interest in acquiring training, low economism, and lack of solidarity).

These factors apply even more forcibly to married women workers. Garnsey (1978) emphasizes on one side the changing character of advanced industrial economies' occupational structure (the shift to service sector employment with the opportunities for low-cost labour-intensive work paralleled by reduced opportunities in traditional male-dominated industrial jobs) together with the increasing availability of married women workers as a function both of demographic change and the increasing need for wives' wages to maintain household income. On the other, she stresses (p.230, pp.235-6) how

Internal forces within the family facilitate the distinction between primary and secondary employment as it applied to men and women's work.... Limitations are placed on women's employment opportunities and their bargaining power in the labour market is weakened as a result of the division of labour in the household.

Barron and Norris contend that a dual labour market can apply not simply over the whole economy but also within a particular firm, industry, or sector of the economy. Most of our sample of graduate women are employed in the education sector. The frequency with which the married women have taken not just part-time teaching or research jobs since returning to the labour force but also temporary non-established posts suggests that education itself contains a dual labour market structure. In recent years the sector has been under pressure from restricted public expenditure, combined with a threatened drop in pupil and an actual drop in student numbers. This situation has been controlled by the increasing creation of part-time temporary posts which commit the employer to little in terms of guaranteed salary scales and job security: an easily-shed load if necessary, a cheap source of labour in the meantime. Our respondents have typically held several such jobs in succession in an attempt to manoeuvre themselves into a more favourable position: they move for permanent jobs, more hours, and hence better pay and conditions. It is not simply a question of gradually increasing work involvement as domestic responsibilities allow: they have had to take what was available. These married women graduates are filling the secondary sector of a dual labour market for professionals. Their situation as re-entering married women workers poses for them distinct problems, as Garnsey (p.236) highlights: 'For women, bargaining capacity is likely to change over the life cycle, and this in itself will influence the occupational positions that they are able to take up and the market situations in which they are thereby placed.'

The women interviewed in 1975 have displayed a remarkable

resilience as workers within this contrained framework, though their approach has been one of conservative adaptation rather than radical change.

Typically, a married woman graduate worked for two or three years before interrupting her career (?) to have children. After this point, job moves or interruptions of employment were frequently occasioned by their husbands' job moves; this was at least one factor in a quarter of the women's labour force movements since graduation. One respondent gave up a promising career as a personnel manager after five years to go abroad with her husband; since then her only employment has been part-time teaching. Another, offered a traineeship as a television producer on graduation, turned it down for similar reasons. She has since re-trained as a primary teacher (though freely admitting she does not enjoy it), but hankers after her original choice. She has attempted to get into broadcasting but since she has no experience has met with no success. In fact there is a distinct trend for the women to retreat further into the female ghetto over the years. A quarter of the sample had changed fields at some point: half of them into schoolteaching. Of those who were always teachers, those who had changed the level at which they teach had almost uniformly transferred from the secondary to the primary teaching sector.

Their discontinuous work-histories (typically between five and eight years out of the labour force), involving much part-time employment, make their career achievements difficult to assess. Most do not see themselves as having had careers anyway; they do not look at their work in this way precisely because they continue to adhere both practically and ideologically to the traditional priorities (have they any choice?). Only eight of the 57 women interviewed were employed full-time; of these, only three accorded their work equal status and priority with their family. None could be termed high achievers in strictly career terms, and as one of them pointed out:

> 'I see my past jobs as a series of jobs that just happened....
> I don't feel that my current job is the full potential of the
> job that I might otherwise have done.... One feels that one's
> not doing intellectually a truly competent job because one has
> to break off to get the children's tea ... or something like
> that.'

Most of those interviewed had held one or two full-time posts since graduation, but had held several part-time posts since having children. Between them they have approximately 354 years of work experience (not including periods of further full-time study), about six years each on average (more or less half of that of their married men and single women peers also interviewed). They have had very few promotions between them, but in relation to the number of jobs they have held, they have performed as well as the single women in this respect. Both groups of women, in achieving little more than 'standing still' in terms of career (on average), have done far less well than the men. Partly this similarity arises because the married women are even more concentrated in the 'safer' fields of employment. But it also suggests that graduate women's career development is hampered first and foremost by their sex, via discriminatory attitudes about their actual and potential abilities and long-term usefulness as employees. Only secondarily

(without wishing to underestimate this, however) are the actual
constraints imposed by marriage and family upon women a hindrance
to career development. These problems are then compounded by
'barriers preventing women from succeeding which often exist at a
socio-psychological level' (Prather, 1971, p.173).

CONCLUSIONS

The experience of higher education clearly does nothing to mitigate
or reverse the effects of home, and particularly school, labelling
and channelling processes which direct women into traditional
fields of study and employment, typically ill-equipped to compete
successfully with men. Our women graduates, married and single,
have not in general achieved a similar measure of career success
as have their male peers, despite starting out at graduation with
similar qualifications and equally-distributed background advantages.

Discrimination at work has certainly played a part, as have
the practical difficulties inevitably experienced by married
women with children in our society in keeping up a measure of
career involvement. In addition, the stereotyped and restricted
range of occupations 'chosen' and aspects of career management
clearly evidence the consequences of sex-role socialization and
educational channelling. In the light of these factors one can
reasonably suggest that the concept of occupational choice has
little relevance or meaning for women in our society. Certainly,
by the time they reach university entrance it is extremely difficult, if not impossible (given the organization of degree study in
this country), to reverse this channelling which commits women to
traditional fields of employment and reinforces the discriminatory
character of the labour market structure - not to mention lending
a spurious justification to the same.

We know that the socio-psychological foundations of sex-role
prescriptive attitudes and behaviour are established much earlier
(see Belotti, 1975), but it is at secondary school that these do
irreparable damage by determining (far too early) subject specialization, and reinforcing its effects. Study choices which are
only partly based upon real (perhaps unrecognized) preferences and
aptitudes irreversibly affect and restrict later options, whether
in terms of higher education or occupation choice.

Such channelling is doubly deceptive, since the education
system superficially subscribes to an ideology of equal academic
competition between the sexes. This applies with especial force
in higher education: whilst on one level women entering university
are expected to compete as equals with their male peers, when they
finally enter the 'real world' they find their educational
achievements to be no protection against, first, the operation of
a dual labour market; second, prevailing ideologies about women's
abilities and characteristics which deny them career advancement;
and, finally, their own hesitancy and lack of confidence, outcomes
of the 'double bind' to which they have been relentlessly exposed.

The education system cannot change the labour market structure
directly; this requires social change of a radical and differing

order. But what is currently most disturbing, for this cohort of graduates and others, is that the education system has established the pre-conditions for the production of a doubly exploited group of workers, many of whom have become employees of the education sector itself. This cannot be healthy for anyone concerned.(17)

NOTES

1 Bibliographic research in preparation for this article turned up a review of four recently published American monographs specifically directed to the topic of the interaction between higher education and the labour market (Dreijmanis, 1978). Assuming that reviews address themselves to the core content of the publications at hand, one wonders how four sets of researchers centrally concerned with the problems of decreased demand, underemployment and restricted opportunities for gradu- ates over the last decade were able to ignore completely their undoubtedly different consequences for women and men.

2 Further details of the sample and methods of investigation are available in Kelsall et al. (1970, 1972) and Chisholm et al. (1977).

3 Other sectors (commerce, private practice, churches, the armed forces, communications) drew an increasing proportion of men graduates over the period of the project, though none of the sectors accounted for more than 8 per cent of the cohort at any one point. For women graduates (whose representation in any of these sectors never exceeded 5 per cent) the reverse was the case.

4 This process applies within sector too: see later.

5 Three of the four single graduate women (discussed below in text) employed in the industrial sector in 1973 were in research labs or departments. These are well known to occupy uncomfortable positions in the organizational structure and hierarchy (Dalton, 1950). Neither do they offer the career opportunities available in line management: the promotional pyramid is flat and the ceiling low. Some of the men graduate managers interviewed had faced precisely this situation. All had moved out of research and had benefited thereby. None of the three single women similarly employed had reached a stage where such a decline had to be made, and they did not envisage ever doing so.

6 In 1900, 70.3 per cent of US employed women (or men) would have had to change their occupation on order for a non- segregated labour force to exist. By 1961 this figure had dropped - but only to 62.2 per cent. These percentages were adjusted to allow for the fact that highly segregated occupa- tions (e.g., junior white-collar jobs) have grown much faster during this century than those which segregate less. Otherwise the figures would have hardly altered. Gross concludes that this slight reduction in occupational segregation has been effected by men entering 'female' occupations rather than the reverse.

7 67 per cent in 1973.

8   The interview sample was restricted to random selection from three geographical areas. The inclusion of Greater London means that, because it undoubtedly offers the widest range of posts in 'minority' sectors, a random sample will be naturally weighted towards those employed in such sectors.

9   I.e., above average for their occupational group. For further details see Chisholm (1978).

10 The women's salaries also occupied a far narrower range than did the men's, in conformity with Suter and Miller's (1973) findings for the US.

11 An exception are public service occupations, also 'protected' (= equal pay and superficially at least equal opportunities, and/or a high proportion of women employed). The highest earner by far in this group was in the civil service.

12 Social class origin was determined by already-collected evidence from earlier phases of the project on the basis of the respondent's father's main paid occupation. The one-sided basis of such a measure is appreciated; but in 1965, at the time of the project's design, social stratification theory and methodology had not adapted to conform to the new perspectives now emerging from critical feminist analysis.

13 Except for those in university lecturing; but here a good degree is an entrance qualification rather than anything else, and it applies equally - if not more so - to women applicants.

14 It may be that single women had not planned their careers so effectively in the crucial early years. Angrist and Almquist's (1975) findings support this; most of our sample said they had originally expected to marry at some point, and this is likely to have affected their planning in some way.

15 Very few continued to entertain the possibility or likelihood of marriage in 1975.

16 Bell and Bodden (1971) found these constraints still to apply ten years later for a sample of married women graduate US students.

17 An earlier draft of this chapter was given as a paper to the BERA Seminar, 'Women, Education and Research', 14-16 April 1978.

Chapter 13

Women, school and work
Some conclusions

Rosemary Deem

The chapters in this collection not only tell us about the current
fate of most women during their schooling, and subsequently in the
labour market or within the family; they also point to enormous
gaps in our knowledge about the processes, ideologies and mechanisms whereby women are schooled for their work in a quite different
way from the manner in which men are schooled for their work. In
addition some of the chapters make definite policy or strategy
recommendations for overcoming at least the most extreme forms of
discrimination against women. It would, of course, be foolish to
assume that changes in education alone can bring about radical
changes in the life-chances and power position of women, given the
all-pervasive nature of patriarchal relationships and the central
importance of the sexual division of labour to the organization of
capitalist societies. But this need not prevent us from trying to
alter the schooling of women so that they are less disadvantaged
in relation to men than they are at the present time.
   A number of chapters in the volume imply either directly or
indirectly that a major potential area of change lies in the training of teachers to be much more aware both of the processes of
gender-typing and gender categorization going on in schools, and
also in showing new recruits to teaching ways in which they may
deliberately try to overcome some of the worst effects of gender-
typing on their pupils. This could also be extended to existing
teachers as well, but, as Clarricoates and Llewellyn demonstrate
in their ethnographies of schools, such a task may prove difficult
to achieve if most teachers not only encourage the transmission of
a gender-code but also believe in its legitimacy. Although the
Women's Liberation movement may be able to provide psychological
and other support for those teachers who are prepared to challenge
the processes of gender-typing, reproduction of the sexual division
of labour and maintenance of patriarchal relations of dominance,
what the movement can offer is unlikely to appeal to those who do
not even perceive the validity of its aims. For example, Chisholm
and Woodward found that not only does the education system establish many of the preconditions for the double exploitation of women
at work and in the home, but that the same educational system
frequently forms a major market for the employment of women; yet

few of the women in their sample were even prepared to admit that
they might have been disadvantaged or discriminated against because
of their sex. It is apparent, then, that teacher training does not
very often, or indeed in some cases not at all, raise questions
about sexism and sexual divisions in education, nor point out the
effects of gender on schooling.

Although teachers are now much more likely during their training
to have pointed out to them the effects of ethnic minority group
membership on educational experiences and performance, if this is
not combined with an appreciation of the fact that, as Fuller's
chapter 4 notes, ethnicity does not have the same impact on girls
as it does on boys, then strategies which might help male pupils
from ethnic minorities will not necessarily help female pupils.

And it need not be imagined that all this applies only to female
teachers. The levels of gender-consciousness possessed by male
teachers are likely to be even lower than those of female teachers,
for, as Tolson notes, gender identity is often taken for granted
by men and not seen in terms of the problems that it may present to
men, as well as to women.(1) The teaching strategies developed by
male teachers may be especially critical in subjects which are
rarely taught by women, in encouraging patterns of curricular
differentiation between the sexes, and in bringing about particular
patterns of interaction between male and female pupils.

At the same time, it seems to me that we need to find out very
much more about both women and men teachers, rather than assuming,
as much past research on teachers has, that male teachers are the
norm, and female teachers less committed, problematic deviants from
this norm.(2) In other words, we need to discover whether, and in
what ways, women do approach teaching from a different perspective
than that held by men, and further, need to understand how such a
state of affairs, if found to exist, comes about.

Are women teachers separated from their male colleagues by contrasting conceptions of their occupation and occupational tasks?
Do women have dissimilar classroom practices, discipline procedures,
control over pupils, teaching methods, to those of male teachers?(3)
Is it the case that women can only successfully teach (and, more
importantly, see themselves as teaching successfully) young children, or is this a myth used to rationalize the monopoly of senior
teaching posts in secondary education by men? And how much does
the actual training of women as teachers reinforce the gender-
appropriate behaviour already transmitted to them by their earlier
schooling? Unless we know the answers to some of these questions,
we are not really in a position to suggest how teacher training may
be altered so that teachers become aware of, and able to combat,
the impact of gender on schooling. Nor can we hope that many
teachers of either sex will adopt the kind of positive strategies
towards female pupils which Weiner suggests might improve the
mathematical ability and potential of girls.

But it is not only teachers who need sensitizing to the ways in
which gender is made relevant in the schooling of both girls and
boys; it is also the case that parents need to be sensitized too.
And in a world where gender stereotypes are perpetuated not only
by the very existence of a sexual division of labour and a system
of patriarchal relations but also by the media,(4) by the state, by

culture itself as well as by education, we need not be surprised
that many parents never question the gender identities into which
they socialize their children.(5) And parents must be made to
realize (and teachers, as well as women's groups of all kinds, could
help with this process of sensitization if their own training had
already alerted them to its importance) that gender-typing adversely
affects not only girls but also boys.(6) As Tolson has demonstrated,
despite their patriarchal dominance, men are as imprisoned, albeit
in different ways, by their gender identities as are women.(7)

Within the school itself, there are also many possible changes
which might reduce the patterns of sexual discrimination to which
girls are subjected. Shaw indeed suggests that a return to single-
sex secondary schooling might be one way of overcoming some of the
problems created by sexual divisions in mixed education, although
she argues that it should be seen as a way of increasing parental
choice over schooling rather than as a process of putting the clock
back, and as a positive step towards affirmative action in the
education of girls. It may be the case that the possibilities of
achieving any large-scale return to single-sex schooling are fairly
limited, although this should not necessarily deter feminists from
trying to achieve such an objective. If, however, we assume that
in the foreseeable future at least, most girls will continue to be
educated in mixed schools, then the eradication of sexism in school
books of all kinds is an important step which must be striven hard
for, as Weiner notes in her discussion of girls and mathematics.
As well as encouraging women to be vigilant, both as parents and
as teachers, in looking for indications of sexism in texts and in
refusing to use them or allow children and adolescents to read
them, such a strategy must ultimately also involve publishers and
writers too. The latter is a much more difficult task, if only
because so many of those involved represent exactly those relationships of patriarchal dominance which women are fighting against.

But it is insufficient simply to fight against sexism in school
books (or indeed in any other kind of books) without finding out
more about just what kind of impact sexism in books has on those
who read them. Otherwise we are in danger of overestimating the
importance of books and the images and ideas they portray, and
underestimating the impact of other factors in schooling. Furthermore, we may fail to understand how such ideas and images fit into
the other processes of gender-typing and symbolic segregation of
the sexes which are occurring both inside and outside education.

It is also vitally important that we begin, through research,
to see to what extent gender-stereotyping and patriarchal relationships, as well as the sexual division of labour, are present in the
actual subjects which comprise the school curriculum. The 'hidden'
curriculum is clearly relevant here too, because as well as subject
matter reflecting predominantly the interests of one sex rather
than another, all kinds of subtle processes may be going on which
increase the degree of curricular differentiation between yoys and
girls.(8) For, as Clarricoates demonstrates in her study of primary
schooling, where there is usually little overt curricular differentiation, all kinds of other varieties of segregation between the
sexes are going on, which prepare the way for secondary schooling.
Just as Weiner in her analysis of mathematics teaching notes that

many examples are taken from the cultural world of the male rather
than the female, so in many school subjects the content falsely
assumed to be neutral is not so at all, and may well have a definite
sex as well as class bias.(9) So we cannot understand why girls
'prefer' biology to physics, or why boys 'choose' chemistry rather
than history or French without a more thorough examination of what
it is that they are choosing or rejecting. If science as currently
taught in many schools reflects in its content and emphases precisely patriarchal relations, then is it necessarily advisable for
us to recommend pushing girls into this area of the curriculum
without also trying to alter the form of what is being taught?

I have myself advocated elsewhere the adoption of a core curriculum in secondary schools, despite the many problems which surround
the interpretation and implementation of this, as at least a preliminary stage in reducing curricular differentiation patterns between
boys and girls.(10) But if such a move is to be effective, then we
have to be very clear about what subjects are to comprise a core
curriculum. We must ensure that the content of what we include
does not produce a pattern of competence at, liking for and interest
in subjects which differs only from the present system of allowing
pupils to 'choose' their subjects in the later years of secondary
schooling (11) in forcing all children to take subjects which they
may not like or be good at, but still retaining intact notions of
subject-gender appropriateness.

Harding's chapter 5 on Nuffield science and the relative performances of girls and boys in Nuffield science examinations points
also to another important area of research and potential strategy:
that of learning theories and assessment techniques. Despite the
work of people like Maccoby on sex differences in ability (12) we
still know relatively little about why those differences exist, and
are thus in no position to begin to remedy those areas of learning
in which girls frequently appear to be deficient. Learning theory
has tended to ignore gender and to talk about school pupils as
though they all learn in similar ways, regardless of whether they
are male or female, but if the transmission of the gender code
means anything at all, it is likely to have consequences for the
ways in which girls learn differently from boys.

Research on assessment and evaluation has also consistently
failed to take gender into account as a significant variable; as
Harding shows, this may be a serious shortcoming, since her evidence indicates that girls may perform better on essay-type answers
and boys better on multiple-choice answers. Hence, before we
embark upon new types of assessment or consider moving towards a
common 16-plus school examination (13) it is critical that more
research is carried out on the differential effects of different
modes of assessment on girls and on boys. Or further educational
innovations which look as though they increase the range of equal
educational opportunites may not do so at all, as far as girls are
concerned. Clearly the need to examine learning theories and
methods of assessment applies as much to further and higher education as it does to schools.

If we consider research on women's education as a whole, it is
evident that we need not only much more research on specific areas,
but also more ethnographic material of the kind presented in this

collection by Clarricoates, Llewellyn and Fuller, focusing not just
on schools but also on female youth cultures and extending to
further and higher educational establishments also. The sexual
division of labour and curricular differentiation between the sexes
may actually be much greater in further education colleges than it
is in schools,(14) with a majority of male teachers except in a few
areas like catering, hairdressing and secretarial skills; and with
female students following courses which will lead to boring, low-
paid occupations with few prospects, whilst male students are mainly
engaged in learning skills which will give access to much more
highly paid jobs with much greater prospects of promotion. Rendel's
chapter 11 on women academics suggests that higher education is
dominated by a male patriarchal culture which either excludes women
altogether or welcomes them as 'token men'(15), and it is likely
that this culture is also operant in colleges of further education.
But unless research is carried out in such colleges we do not and
cannot know how the patriarchal culture works in such a setting, or
what effects it has on female students and teachers.

We also need to be able to relate the culture of patriarchal
relations operating within schooling to the cultures of girls and
women outside educational settings. Llewellyn's work offers a
pioneering approach to this, and also makes evident our present
state of ignorance about the youth cultures surrounding girls as
opposed to boys. It is interesting that in the plethora of work on
youth culture very little has been said about girls, who are seen
as either peripheral or irrelevant to male cultures.(16) Yet if
the cultures of girls outside school reflect no less strongly than
their schooling does, the importance to their lives of domesticity
and marriage, then it is not surprising that so few women become
academics or that, as Griffiths points out in chapter 10, so many
women subsequently turn to the Open University as their only chance
of post-school education, having discovered either the limits of
domesticity or the problems faced by poorly qualified women in the
labour market.

The final area in which changes are essential and more research
urgently needed is that of entry into, and experience of the labour
market by women and girls. Chapter 8 by Keil and Newton and
chapter 9 by Ashton and Maguire display all too well the limitations of liberal legislation on equal opportunities in bringing
about changes in the typical employment patterns of girls and
women, and also dispel the notion of meaningful job 'choice' by
most female school-leavers. Newton argues that where girls intend
to enter 'unusual' jobs, it is not just their attitudes which must
change but also those of parents, schools, employers, supervisors
and workmates; the investment of resources does not necessarily
remove these problems. This is especially true where both employers
and a majority of employees retain traditional ideas about patterns
of male and female employment.

As Keil and Newton suggest, one way forward is a less rigid
pattern of skill training for jobs, one which can accommodate
individuals at any stage in their lives and not only on leaving
school or college; but equally important is acceptance by employers
of the domestic responsibilities of their employees, whether these
be male or female, and provision for dealing with these within the

context of paid work. Much more vigilance and monitoring of the
impact of legislation such as the Equal Pay Act (1970) and the Sex
Discrimination Act (1975) and the Employment Protection Act (1976)
is also called for.

But none of these strategies will actually change the labour
market; that is still left to the state, consumer demand, the state
of the economy, changes in technology, sources of raw materials and
many other factors which are outside the scope of attitude changes
or piecemeal reforms. The election in May 1979 of a Conservative
government, rapidly followed by cuts in public expenditure (which
is affecting both education and the availability of jobs in the
public sector, as well as the provision of job experience schemes
under the auspices of the Manpower Services Commission) is likely
to continue to reduce still further the extent to which school-
leavers (and especially girls, for whom paid employment may not
even be seen as a priority) have any degree of job choice at all.
This development, together with projected changes in technology
(the silicon chip and microprocessors), may merely serve to
increase the extent to which girls turn away from both school life
and work towards marriage and domesticity. It is of no help to
encourage girls to enter new fields of employment, areas traditionally dominiated by men, if such opportunities are only to be
available to a tiny minority of school-leavers. Equally, it is
almost irrelevant to talk merely of remedying girls' 'under-
achievement' whilst seeking to do nothing to alter the sexual
division of labour and the relations of patriarchy which dominate
our processes of production, and which ensure that most women are
forced to choose 'fulfilment' in domesticity.

The outlook then, both for girls who are currently at school
and for women who have already been schooled into accepting a
patriarchal class society, is not a particularly optimistic one.
It will be a complex and difficult task to overcome the structures
of patriarchy both inside and outside schooling in such a way that
they are not replaced by even more restrictive structures, but
instead by structures in which the liberation and fulfilment of
individuals overrides not only gender considerations but also class
and ethnicity too. And it is as well to remember that a solution
does not necessarily lie in the transition from a capitalist to a
socialist mode of production, unless the elimination of patriarchal structures and the sexual division of labour are political
and social objectives of the same order as the removal of the
private ownership of the means of production and class relationships.

The task of this book has been to highlight the existing processes by which women are schooled for their work and to expose
the disadvantageous position which that schooling places them in
when compared with men, as well as beginning to suggest ways in
which the processes of sexual discrimination in education may be
eliminated. The job of actually altering the schooling of women
lies outside the scope of any book, but it is in the profound
belief that uninformed action often produces undesirable and ill-
conceived changes, whilst theoretically and empirically informed
action stands at least a better chance of success, that this
collection of views is offered.

NOTES

1 See Tolson (1977).
2 For example, Kelsall and Kelsall (1969) detail much research
   of this kind; and the approach is also exemplified in Pollard
   (1974).
3 Some preliminary progress towards this kind of research may be
   found in the work of Bennett (1976) and in Hannam et al. (1976).
4 Stott and King (1978) give an excellent account of the images
   of women portrayed by the media.
5 Research on the socialization practices of parents may be found
   in the work of Newson and Newson (1968 and 1976).
6 See Chesler (1978).
7 Tolson (1977).
8 For a more elaborated discussion of how the hidden curriculum
   affects the schooling of girls, see Byrne (1978) and Deem (1978).
9 Discussions of the biases found in school subjects frequently
   assumed to be neutral may be found in the work of Overfield
   (1978), Hine (1977) and Wynn (1977).
10 See Deem (1978).
11 It is important not to forget that the notion of most pupils
   making any meaningful and considered choice between school
   subjects is probably illusory; see Woods (1976).
12 Maccoby (1966).
13 'School Examinations' (1978) sets out the arguments for and
   against a common 16-plus examination.
14 See Byrne (1978) for a more detailed consideration of the
   situation in further education.
15 Smith (1978) suggests that a similar situation may also exist
   in journalism.
16 See Hall and Jefferson (1976) and Mungham and Pearson (1976)
   for detailed analyses of male youth cultures.

Bibliography

ACKER, J. and VAN HOUTEN, D.R. (1974), Differential recruitment and control: the sex structuring of organization, 'Administrative Science Quarterly', vol.19, pp.152-63.

ALDERSON, C. (1968), 'Magazines Teenagers Read', Pergamon, Oxford.

ALTHUSSER, L. (1971), Ideology and ideological state apparatuses, in 'Lenin and Philosophy and Other Essays', New Left Books, London.

ANGRIST, S.S. and ALMQUIST, E.M. (1975), 'Careers and Contingencies: How College Women Juggle with Gender', Dunellen, New York.

BABCHUK, N. and BATES, A. (1963), The prinary relations of middle class couples: a study in male dominance, 'American Sociological Review', vol.23, 1.

BAILYN, L. (1964), Notes on the role of choice in the psychology of professional women, in Lifton, R.J., 'The Woman in America', Beacon, Boston.

BANKS, O. (1976), 'The Sociology of Education', Batsford, London.

BARKER, D.L. and ALLEN, S. (1976), 'Dependence and Exploitation in Work and Marriage', Longmans, London.

BARRON, R.D. and NORRIS, G.M. (1976), Sexual divisions and the dual labour market, in Barker and Allen, op. cit.

BARRON, T. and CURNOW, I. (1979), 'The Future with Microprocessors', Frances Pinter, London.

BARUCH, G.K. (1972), Maternal influences upon college women's attitudes towards women and work, 'Developmental Psychology', vol.6, no.1, pp.32-7.

BEECHEY, V. (1978), A critical analysis of some sociological theories of women's work, in Kuhn and Wolpe, op. cit.

BELL, C. (1968), 'Middle Class Families', Routledge & Kegan Paul, London.

BELL, J.B. and BODDEN, B.F. (1971), The myth of the feminist revolution: future orientation, career revocability and role reciprocity among female graduate students, 'Sociological Focus', vol.5, 1, pp.55-70.

BELOTTI, E. (1975), 'Little Girls', Writers and Readers Publishing Co-operative, London.

BENNETT, N. (1976), 'Teaching Style and Pupil Progress', Open Books, London.

BERNARD, J. (1964), 'Academic Women', Pennsylvania State University Press.

184

BERNSTEIN, B. (1977), 'Class, Codes and Control', vol.3, 2nd edition, Routledge & Kegan Paul, London.
BERNSTEIN, B. (1977a), Open schools - open society?, in Bernstein (1977), op. cit.
BERNSTEIN, B. (1977b), On the classification and framing of know-ledge, in Bernstein (1977), op. cit.
BERNSTEIN, B. (1977c), Class and pedagogies: visible and invisible, in Bernstein (1977), op. cit.
BERNSTEIN, B. (1977d), Aspects of the relation between education and production, in Bernstein (1977), op. cit.
BEYNON, H. and BLACKBURN, R.M. (1972), 'Perceptions of Work', Cambridge University Press.
BHATNAGAR, J. (1970), 'Immigrants at School', Cornmarket Press, London.
BLACKSTONE, T. (1976), The education of girls today, in Mitchell, J. and Oakley, A., 'The Rights and Wrongs of Women', Penguin, Harmondsworth.
BLACKSTONE, T. and FULTON, O. (1975), Sex discrimination among university teachers: a British-American comparison, 'British Journal of Sociology', vol.26, September, pp.261-75.
BLACKSTONE, T. and FULTON, O. (1976), Discrimination is the villain, 'Times Higher Educational Supplement', 9 July.
BOSANQUET, N. and DOERINGER, P.D. (1973), Is there a dual labour market in Great Britain?, 'The Economic Journal', vol.83, June, pp.421-35.
BOURDIEU, P. (1973), Cultural reproduction and social reproduction, in Brown, R.K., 'Knowledge, Education and Cultural Change', Tavistock, London.
BOWLES, S. and GINTIS, H. (1976), 'Schooling in Capitalist America', Routledge & Kegan Paul, London.
BRAVERMAN, H. (1975), 'Labor and Monopoly Capital', Monthly Review Press, New York.
BRIERLY, J. (1975), Sex differences in education, 'Trends in Educa-tion', February, pp.17-24.
British Sociological Association (1975), 'Report of the Working Party on Status of Women in the Profession', London.
British Sociological Association (1977), 'Sociology without Sexism: a Sourcebook', London.
BROWN, R.K. (1976), Women as employees: some comments on research in industrial sociology, in Barker and Allen, op. cit.
BROYELLE, C. (1977), 'Women's Liberation in China', Harvester Press, London.
BYRNE, E. (1973), Education, training and equal opportunity, unpublished paper quoted in 'Educational Review', vol.27, June 1975.
BYRNE, E. (1975), Inequality in education: discriminal resource allocation in schools, 'Educational Review', no.27, vol.3, pp.397-404.
BYRNE, E. (1975), The place of women in the changing pattern of further education, London University Teaching Methods Unit, pro-ceedings of conference on 'Women in Higher Education', London.
BYRNE, E. (1978), 'Women and Education', Tavistock, London.
BYRNE, E. (1979), review of Deem, R. (1978), 'Women and Schooling', in 'Education', 16 February, pp.187-8.
CARNOY, M. and LEVIN, H.M. (1976), 'The Limits of Educational Reform', McKay, New York.

CARTER, M. (1976), Contradiction and correspondence: analysis of the relation of schooling to work, in Carnoy and Levin, op. cit.

Central Advisory Council for Education (1963), 'Half Our Future' (The Newsom Report), HMSO, London.

CENTRAL STATISTICAL OFFICE, 'Social Trends', HMSO, London, annually.

CHAMBOREDOM, J.C. and PRÉVOT, J. (1975), Changes in the social definition of early childhood and the new forms of symbolic violence, 'Theory and Society', vol.2, no.3, pp.351-50.

CHESTER, P. (1978), 'About Men', Women's Press, London.

CHETWYND, J. and HARTNETT, O. (1978), 'The Sex-Role System', Routledge & Kegan Paul, London.

CHIPLIN, B. and SLOANE, B.J. (1976), Personal characteristics and sex differentials in professional employment, 'Economic Journal', vol.86, December, pp.729-45.

CHISHOLM, L. (1978), The comparative career development of graduate women and men, 'Women's Studies International Quarterly', vol.1, no.4, pp.327-40.

CHISHOLM, L.A., HEATH, A. and WOODWARD, D. (1977), Methodological problems of quantitative and qualitative research: the national study of graduates, 'Angewandte Sozialforschung', vol.5, pp.195-208.

CLARRICOATES, K. (1978), Dinosaurs in the classroom: a re-examination of some aspects of the 'hidden curriculum' in primary schools, 'Women's Studies International Quarterly', vol.1, no.4, pp.353-64.

CLAUDE-MATHIEU, N. (1977), 'Ignored by Some, Denied by Others: the social sex category in sociology', Women's Research and Resources Centre, London.

CLIFT, P.S. (1978), 'And All Things Nice', unpublished paper.

COARD, B. (1971), 'How the West Indian Child is made Educationally Sub-normal in the British School System', New Beacon Books, London.

COMMITTEE ON HIGHER EDUCATION (1963), 'The Robbins Report', Cmnd 2154, HMSO, London.

'Commonwealth Universities Yearbook' (1914, 1922, 1931, 1952), Association of Commonwealth Universities, London.

COULSON, M., MAGOS, B. and WAINWRIGHT, H. (1975), The housewife and her labour under capitalism: a critique, 'New Left Review', no.89, January-February, pp.59-71.

COUNCIL ON INTERRACIAL BOOKS (1974), 'Ten Quick Ways to analyse children's books for racism and sexism', New York.

CURRICULUM DEVELOPMENT CENTRE (1975), 'Non-sexist Curriculum', Woden, Australia.

DALE, R. (1974), 'Mixed or Single Sex school? Attainment, attitudes and overview', vol.3, Routledge & Kegan Paul, London.

DALTON, M. (1950), Conflicts between staff and line managerial officers, 'American Sociological Review', vol.15, pp.342-51.

DAVID, M. (1978), The family-education couple: towards an analysis of the William Tyndale dispute, in Littlejohn, G. et al., 'Power and the State', Croom Helm, London.

DAVIES, L. and MEIGHAN, R. (1975), A review of schooling sex-roles with particular reference to the experiences of girls in secondary school, 'Education Review', vol.27, no.3, pp.165-78.

DAVIES, R. (1975), 'Women and Work', Arrow Books, London.

DAVIN, D. (1976), 'Woman-Work', Clarendon Press, Oxford.

DEAUX, K. (1977), Sex: a perspective on the attribution process, in Harvey, J.H. et al., 'New Directions in Attribution Research', vol.1, Wiley, Chichester.

DEEM, R. (1978), 'Women and Schooling', Routledge & Kegan Paul, London.

DEPARTMENT OF EDUCATION AND SCIENCE (1975), 'Curricular Differences for Boys and Girls in Mixed and Single-sex Schools', Education Survey 21, HMSO, London.

DEPARTMENT OF EDUCATION AND SCIENCE (1976), 'Statistics of Education 1975', HMSO, London.

DELAMONT, S. (1976), 'Interaction in the Classroom', Methuen, London.

DELAMONT, S. (1978), The double-conformity trap, paper given to BERA Seminar, 'Women, Education and Research', University of Loughborough, 14-16 April.

DOERINGER, P. and PIORE, M. (1971), 'Internal Labour Markets and Manpower', D.C. Heath, Massachusetts.

DONAY, F. (1974), The black explosion in schools, 'Race Today', February.

DORNBUSCH, S. (1974), To try or not to try, 'Stanford Magazine', vol.2, no.2, pp.50-4.

DOUVAN, E. and ADELSON, J. (1966), 'The Adolescent Experience', John Wiley, Chichester.

DREIJMANIS, J. (1978), Higher education and the labour market: a review, 'Sociology of Work and Occupations', vol.5, May, pp.251-4.

DRIVER, G. (1977), Cultural competence, social power and school achievement: a case study of West Indian pupils attending a secondary school in the West Midlands, 'New Community', 5, pp.353-9.

DUROJAIYE, M. (1970), Race relations among junior school children, 'Educational Research', 11, pp.226-8.

EBBUTT, D. (1978), Girls, science and options, paper given to BERA Seminar, 'Women, Education and Research', University of Loughborough, 14-16 April.

EISENSTEIN, Z.R. (1979), 'Capitalist Patriarchy and the Case for Socialist Feminism', Monthly Review Press, London.

ELDRIDGE, J.A., KELLY, J. and KEIL, E.T. (1976), 'Becoming a Worker', Loughborough University.

EPSTEIN, C.F. (1970), 'Woman's Place', University of California Press, Berkeley.

EPSTEIN, C.F. (1973), Positive effects of the double-negative: explaining the success of black professional women, 'American Journal of Sociology', vol.78, no.4, pp.912-35.

EPSTEIN, C.F. (1976), Separate and unequal: notes on women's achievement, 'Social Policy', vol.6, March, pp.17-23.

EQUAL OPPORTUNITIES COMMISSION (1977), 'Second Annual Report', HMSO, London.

ERNEST, J. (1976), 'Mathematics and Sex', Maths. Department, University of California, Santa Barbara.

FEE, F. (1976), Domestic labour: an analysis of housework and its relation to the production process, 'Review of Radical Political Economics', vol.8, no.1, Spring, pp.1-8.

FELDMAN, S. (1974), 'Escape from the Doll's House', Carnegie Commission, McGraw-Hill, New York.

FENNEMA, E. (1974), Sex differences in mathematics learning - why?,
'Elementary School Journal', 75, no.3, pp.183-90.
FERGUSON, C. (1977), Unpublished internal report, University of
London Schools Examination Department.
FERGUSON, C. and WOOD, R. (1974), The unproven case for co-education',
'Times Educational Supplement', 9 October.
FLUDE, M. and AHIER, J. (1976), 'Educability, Schools and Ideology',
Croom Helm, London.
FOGARTY, M. et al. (1971), 'Sex, Career and Family', Allen & Unwin,
London.
FONER, N. (1976), Women, work and migration: Jamaicans in London,
'New Community', 5, pp.85-98.
FRANKENBERG, R. (1979), Methodology: social or individual?, paper
given to BSA Methodology Conference, 5 January, University of
Lancaster.
FRANSELLA, F. and FROST, K. (1977), 'On Being a Woman', Tavistock,
London.
FRAZIER, N. and SADKER, M. (1973), 'Sexism in School and Society',
Harper & Row, New York, 1973.
FREUD, S. (1960), 'Jokes and their Relation to the Unconscious',
Routledge & Kegan Paul, London.
FULLER, M. (1976), Experience of Adolescents from Ethnic Minorities
in the British State Education System, in P.J. Bernard (ed.), 'Les
Travailleurs étrangers en europe occidentale', Mouton, Paris/The
Hague.
FULLER, M. (1978a), Sex Role stereotyping and social science, in
Chetwynd and Hartnett, op. cit.
FULLER, M. (1978b), Dimensions of Gender in a School, PhD thesis,
University of Bristol.
FURLONG, V. (1976), Interaction sets in the classroom, in Woods, P.
and Hammersley, M., 'The Process of Schooling', Open University
Press, and Routledge & Kegan Paul, London.
GARNSEY, E. (1975), Occupational structure in industrialized
societies, 'Sociology', vol.9, no.3.
GARNSEY, E. (1978), Women's work and theories of class stratifica-
tion, 'Sociology', vol.12, no.2, pp.223-44.
GAVRON, H. (1966), 'The Captive Wife', Routledge & Kegan Paul,
London.
GEE, M. (1978), The capitalist labour process and women workers,
paper given at Conference of Socialist Economists, Bradford,
Yorkshire.
GINZBERG, E. et al. (1966), 'Lifestyles of Educated Women',
Columbia University Press, New York.
GLASTONBURY, M. (1978), Holding the pens, in Elbert, S. and Glaston-
bury, M., 'Inspiration and Drudgery: notes on literature and
domestic labour in the Nineteenth Century', Women's Research and
Resources Centre, London.
GREENS, D., SOMMERS, M. and KENNAN, O. (1973), Personality and
implicit behaviour patterns, 'Journal of Marketing Research', 10.
GROSS, E. (1971), Plus ça change? the sexual structure of occupations over time, in Theodore, A., 'The Professional Woman', Schenk-
man, Cambridge, Massachusetts.
HAGAN, R.L. and KAHN, A. (1975), Discrimination against competent
women, 'Journal of Applied Social Psychology', vol.5, no.4, pp.362-76.

HALL, S. and JEFFERSON, T. (1976), 'Resistance Through Rituals',
Hutchinson, London.
HALSEY, A.H. (1972), 'Trends in British Society since 1900',
Macmillan, London.
HALSEY, A.H. and TROW, M. (1971), 'The British Academics', Faber &
Faber, London.
HANNAM, C., SMITH, P. and STEPHENSON, N. (1976), 'The First Year of
Teaching', Penguin, Harmondsworth.
HARDING, J. (1975), What has Nuffield done for girls?, 'Times
Educational Supplement', 30 November.
HARGREAVES, D.H. (1967), 'Social Relations in a Secondary School',
Routledge & Kegan Paul, London.
HARTMANN, H. (1979), Capitalism, patriarchy and job segregation by
sex, in Eisenstein, op. cit.
HARTNETT, O. (1978), Sex role stereotyping at work, in Chetwynd and
Hartnett, op. cit.
HER MAJESTY'S INSPECTORATE (1977), Maths, science and modern
languages in maintained schools in England, 'The Times', 22 January.
HILSUM, S. and START, K. (1974), 'Promotion and Careers in
Teaching', National Foundation for Educational Research, Slough.
HIMMELWEIT, S. and MOHUN, S. (1977), Domestic labour and capital,
'Cambridge Journal of Economics', vol.1, pp.15-31.
HINE, J. (1977), Political bias in school physics, in Whitty, G.,
'School Knowledge and Social Control, E202, Open University Press,
Milton Keynes.
HOCHSCHILD, A.R. (1975), Inside the clockwork of male careers, in
Howe, F., 'Women and the Power to Change', McGraw-Hill, New York.
HOLT, J. (1964), 'How Children Fail', Penguin, Harmondsworth.
HORNER, M.S. (1970), Femininity and successful achievement: a basic
inconsistency, in Bardwick, J., 'Feminine Personality and Conflict',
Brooks Cole, California.
HUDIS, M.P. (1976), Commitment to work and family: marital status
differences in women's earnings, 'Journal of Marriage and the
Family', vol.38, no.2, pp.267-72.
HUNT, A. (1968), 'A Survey of Women's Employment', 2 vols, HMSO,
London.
HUNT, A. (1975), 'Management Attitudes and Practices towards Women
at Work', HMSO, London.
HUTT, C. (1972), 'Males and Females', Penguin, Harmondsworth.
JACKSON, P. (1966), The student's world, 'The Elementary School
Journal', 66, pp.343-57.
JEGHELIAN, A. (1976), Surviving sexism: strategies and consequences,
'Personnel and Guidance Journal', vol.54, no.6, pp.307-11.
Jex-Blake v. Senatus Academicus of the University of Edinburgh
(1873), XI Machp. 784, Court of Sessions.
KAMM, J. (1965), 'Hope Deferred', Methuen, London.
KEDDIE, N. (1971), Classroom knowledge, in Young, M.F.D., 'Know-
ledge and Control', Macmillan, London.
KELLY, A. (1976), Women in science: a bibliographic review, 'Durham
Research Review', no.7, Spring.
KELLY, A. (1978), Feminism and research, paper given to BERA
Seminar, 'Women, Education and Research', University of Loughborough,
14-16 April.

KELSALL, R.K. and H.M. (1969), 'The School Teacher in England and the United States', Pergamon, Oxford.

KELSALL, R.K., POOLE, A. and KUHN, A. (1970), 'Six Years After', University of Sheffield.

KELSALL, R.K., POOLE, A. and KUHN, A. (1972), 'Graduates: the Sociology of an Elite', Methuen, London.

KEPNER, H. and KOEHN, L. (1977), Sex roles in mathematics: a study of the status of sex stereotypes in elementary mathematics texts, 'Arithmetic Teacher', 24 May, pp.379-85.

KEYS, W. and ORMEROD, M. (1977), Some sex-related differences in the correlates of subject preferences in the middle years of secondary education, 'Educational Studies', vol.3, no.2, June.

KING, J.S. (1974), 'Women and Work: sex differences in society', HMSO, London.

KING, M. (1978), The religious retreat of Isotta Nogarola (1418-66): Sexism and its consequences in the fifteenth century, 'Signs', vol.3, Summer, pp.807-22.

KOMISAR, L. (1971), The image of women in advertising, in Cormick, V. and Movan, B., 'Women in Sexist Society', Basic Books, New York.

KUHN, A. and WOLPE, A-M. (1978), 'Feminism and Materialism', Routledge & Kegan Paul, London.

LACEY, C. (1970), 'Hightown Grammar', Manchester University Press.

LAMBART, A. (1976), The Sisterhood, in Hammersley, M. and Woods, P. 'The Process of Schooling', Open University Press and Routledge & Kegan Paul, London.

LAVIGEUR, J. (1976), Educational opportunities for girls with special reference to co-educational and single-sex schools, MEd dissertation, University of Sheffield.

LEVY, B. (1972), The school's role in the sex-role stereotyping of girls: a feminist review of the literature, 'Feminist Studies', vol.1, pt.1, pp.5-23.

LEWIS, T.M. (1976), 'Social Anthropology in Perspective', Penguin, Harmondsworth.

LIGHTFOOT, S. (1975), Sociology of education: perspectives on women, in Millman, M. and Kanter, R.M., 'Another Voice', Anchor Books, New York.

LITTLE, A. (1978), Schools and race, Commission for Racial Equality and BBC, 'Five Views of Multi-Racial Britain', London.

LADNER, J. (1971), 'Tomorrow's Tomorrow - The Black Woman', Doubleday, New York.

LITTLEJOHN, G. et al. (1978), 'Power and the State'. Croom Helm, London.

LOBBAN, G. (1974), Presentation of sex roles in British reading schemes, 'Trends in Education', 16, Spring, pp.57-60.

LOBBAN, G. (1975), Sexism in Primary Schools, 'Women Speaking', 4 July.

LOBBAN, G. (1978), The influence of the school on sex-role stereotyping, in Chetwynd and Hartnett, op. cit.

LOCKWOOD, D. (1958), 'The Black-Coated Worker', Allen & Unwin, London.

LOMAX, P. (1977), The self-concepts of girls in the context of a disadvantaging environment, 'Educational Review', vol.29, no.2, February.

MACCOBY, E. (1966), 'The Development of Sex Differences', University of Stanford Press, California.
MACCOBY, E. and JACKLIN, C. (1974), 'The Psychology of Sex Differences', Stanford University Press, California.
MacDONALD, M. (1977), 'Curriculum and Cultural Reproduction', E202, Open University Press, Milton Keynes.
MACKIE, L. and PATULLO, P. (1977), 'Women at Work', Tavistock, London.
MARINI, M. and GREENBERGER, E. (1978), Sex differences in occupational aspirations and expectations, 'Sociology of Work and Occupations', vol.5, no.2, May, pp.147-78.
MARKS, P. (1976), Femininity in the classroom, in Mitchell, J. and Oakley, A., 'The Rights and Wrongs of Women', Penguin, Harmondsworth.
MATTFIELD, J.A. and VAN AKEN, C.G. (1965), 'Women and the Scientific Professions', MIT Press, Cambridge, Massachusetts.
MATTHEWS, E. and TIEDEMAN, D.V. (1964), Attitudes towards career and marriage and the development of lifestyle in young women, 'Journal of Counselling Psychology', vol.2, pp.375-84.
MAYNARD, M. (1979), The response of social workers to domestic violence, paper given to Patriarchy Study Group, 27 January, University of Warwick.
MacDONOUGH, R. and HARRISON, R. (1978), 'Patriarchy and relations of production', in Kuhn and Wolpe, op. cit.
McINTOSH, N. (1978), Women in distance education: the Open University experience, paper given to the World Conference of the International Council for Correspondence Education, 8-15 November, New Delhi, India.
McINTOSH, N., CALDER, J. and SWIFT, B. (1976), 'A Degree of Difference', Praeger, New York.
McKEEFERY-REYNOLDS, V.L. (1977), Career patterns and career choice of the young adult woman, paper given to the annual meeting of the Mid-West Sociological Society.
McROBBIE, A. (1978), Working class girls and the culture of femininity, in Women's Studies Group, CCCS, op. cit.
McROBBIE, A. and GARBER, J. (1976), Girls and sub-cultures, in Hall and Jefferson, op. cit.
McWILLIAMS-TULLBERG, R. (1975), 'Women at Cambridgep, Gollancz, London.
MEAD, M. (1935), 'Sex and Temperament in Three Primitive Societies', William Morrow, New York.
MILES, R. and PHIZACKLEA, A. (1977), Class, race, ethnicity and political action, 'Political Studies', 27, pp.491-507.
MILLER, J., LABOVITZ, S. and FRY, L. (1975), Inequalities in the organizational experiences of women and men, 'Social Forces', vol.54, December, pp.365-81.
MITCHELL, J. (1971), 'Women's Estate', Penguin, Harmondsworth.
MOODIE, G. and EUSTACE, R. (1974), 'Power and Authority in British Universities', Allen & Unwin, London.
MOON, C. (1974), Individualized reading: comparative list of selected books for young people, 'Reading for the Teaching of Reading', University of Reading.
MORRELL, J. (1976), 'Power and Authority in Higher Education', Society for Research into Higher Education, Guildford, Surrey.

MUNGHAM, G. and PEARSON, G. (1976), 'Working Class Youth Culture', Routledge & Kegan Paul, London.

MYRDAL, A. and KLEIN, V. (1968), 'Women's Two Roles', Routledge & Kegan Paul, London.

NASH, R. (1973), 'Classrooms Observed', Routledge & Kegan Paul, London.

NEWSON, J. and E. (1968), 'Four Years Old in an Urban Community', Allen & Unwin, London.

NEWSON, J. and E. (1976), 'Seven Years Old in the Home Environment', Allen & Unwin, London.

OAKLEY, A. (1976), 'The Sociology of Housework', Martin Robertson, London.

OAKLEY, A. (1976), 'Housewife', Penguin, Harmondsworth.

OKELY, J. (1978), Privileged, schooled and finished: boarding school education for girls, in Ardener, S., 'Defining Females', Croom Helm, London, 1978.

O'NEILL, N.J. (1973), Class and social consciousness: variations in the social perspectives of industrial workers, unpublished PhD thesis, University of Hull.

OPEN UNIVERSITY, 'Digest of Statistics, 1971-7', (1978), Open University Press, Milton Keynes.

ORMEROD, M.B. (1975), Subject preferences and choice in co-educational and single-sex secondary schools, 'British Journal of Educational Psychology', vol.45, pp.257-67.

ORMEROD, M.B. and KEYS, W. (1977), Some factors affecting pupils' subject preferences, 'Oxford Review of Education', vol.3, no.1.

OVERFIELD, K. (1978), Science and patriarchal ideology, paper given to Patriarchy Study Group, 28 October, University of Bradford.

Oxford University Department of Educational Studies (1971), 'The academic motivation and career aspirations of girls of high ability', report for Political and Economic Planning.

PAHL, R.E. (1963), Education and social class in commuter villages, in 'Sociological Review', New Series, 2, pp.241-6.

PAHL, R.E. (1965), Class and community in English commuter villages, 'Sociologia Ruralis', vol.2, pp.5-21.

PAYNE, G. (1977), Occupational transition in advanced industrial societies, 'Sociological Review', vol.15, no.1.

PERUCCI, C.C. and TARG, D.B. (1978), Early work orientations and later situational factors as elements of work commitment among married women college graduates, 'Sociological Quarterly', vol.19, Spring, pp.266-80.

PETTMAN, B.O. (1977), Womanpower: an under-utilized resource, MCB Monograph, MCB Books, Bradford.

PETTMAN, B.O. (1979), Women in Work, 'Employee Relations', vol.1, no.1.

PETTUS, I.M. (1900), The legal education of women, 'Albany Law Journal', 61, p.375.

PHILLIPS, C. (1969), 'Changes in Subject Choice at School and University', Widenfeld & Nicolson, London.

POLLARD, M. (1974), 'The Teachers', Eastland Press, Suffolk.

Proceedings of the International Colloquium (1977), 'Women in Management', INSEAD, Fontainebleau.

PRATHER, J. (1971), Why can't women be more like men: a summary of the socio-psychological factors hindering women's advancement in the professions, 'American Behavioural Scientist', vol.15, December, pp.172-82.
QUINE, W. (1974), Polarized cultures in comprehensive schools, 'Research in Education', 12, pp.9-15.
RAUTA, I. and HUNT, A. (1975), 'Fifth-form Girls; their Hopes for the Future', HMSO, London.
REYNOLDS, D. (1976), When teachers and pupils refuse a truce: the secondary school and the creation of delinquency, in Mungham and Pearson, op. cit.
RICKS and PYKE (1973), quoted by Lobban (1978), op. cit.
ROBINSON, O. (1978), 'Report on Low Pay', Department of Manpower Services, HMSO, London
ROSEN, B.C. and ANESHENSEL, C.S. (1978), Sex differences in the educational-occupational expectation process, 'Social Forces', vol.57, September, pp.164-86.
ROSENBERG, M. and SIMMONS, R. (1972), 'Black and White Self-esteem: the Urban School Child', American Sociological Association, Washington.
ROSENTHAL, R. and JACOBSON, L. (1968), 'Pygmalion in the Class-room', Holt, Rhinehart & Winston, New York.
RUDD, E. and HATCH, S. (1968), 'Graduate Study and After', Weidenfeld & Nicolson, London.
RUDD, E. and SIMPSON, R. (1975), 'The Highest Education', Routledge & Kegan Paul, London.
'School Examinations' (1978), Report of a Steering Committee, parts 1 and 2, Cmnd 7281, 7282, HMSO, London.
SCOTT, H. (1976), 'Women and Socialism', Alison and Busby, London.
SCRIBBENS, K. (1977), Women in education: some points for discussion, 'Journal of Further and Higher Education', vol.1, no.3, Winter.
SEARS, D.O. and FREEMAN, J.L. (1968), 'Social Psychology', Prentice-Hall, Englewood Cliffs, New Jersey.
SEARS, J. (1965), Development of gender role, in Beach, F., 'Sex and Behaviour', John Wiley, Chichester.
SHARP, R. and GREEN, A. (1976), 'Education and Social Control', Routledge & Kegan Paul, London.
SHARPE, S. (1976), 'Just Like a Girl', Penguin, Harmondsworth.
SHAW, J. (1976), Finishing school: some implications of sex-segregated education, in Barker, D.L. and Allen, S., 'Sexual Divisions and Society: Process and Change', Tavistock, London.
SLAUGHTER, D. (1972), Becoming an Afro-American Woman, 'School Review', 80, pp.299-318.
SMITH, D.E. (1978), A peculiar eclipsing: woman's exclusion from man's culture, 'Women's Studies International Quarterly', 1 (4), pp.281-95.
SMITH, R. (1978), Images and equality: women and the national press, in Christian, H., 'Journalism and the Press', Sociological Review Monograph, Keele, Staffordshire.
SOMMERKORN, I. (1967), On the position of women in the university teaching profession in England, unpublished PhD thesis, University of London.

SOPHIA, A Person of Quality (1739), 'Woman not Inferior to Man',
republished 1975, Brentham Press, London.
SPENDER, D. (1978), Educational research and the feminist perspec-
tive, paper given to BERA Seminar, 'Women, Education and Research',
14-16 April, University of Loughborough.
STACEY, M. and PRICE, M. (1979a), 'Women and Power', paper given to
Political Studies Association Conference, Sheffield.
STACEY, M. and PRICE, M. (1979b), The law is not enough: the con-
tinued oppression of women, paper presented at BSA Conference,
'Law and Society', 10 April, University of Warwick.
STENTON, D. (1957), 'The English Woman in History', Allen & Unwin,
London.
STOTT, M. and KING, J. (1978), 'Is this your life?', Virago, London.
SUTER, L.E. and MILLER, H.P. (1973), Income differences between men
and career women, 'American Journal of Sociology', vol.78, January,
no.4, pp.200-12.
SWIFT, B. (1979), 'The Value of Open University Studies and Qualifi-
cations: its graduates' views', Open University, Walton Hall,
Buckinghamshire.
TAYLOR, J. (1978), Girls' science education and possible text-book
bias, unpublished MEd thesis, Chelsea College, London.
TOLSON, A. (1977), 'The Limits of Masculinity', Tavistock, London.
TOURAINE, A. (1974), 'The Academic System in American Society',
McGraw-Hill, New York.
TRESEMER, D.E. (1977), Assumptions about gender role, in Glazer, N.
and Youngelson Waehrer, H., 'Woman in a Man-made World', Rand
McNally, Chicago.
TROYNA, B. (1978), Race and streaming, 'Educational Review', 30,
pp.59-65.
University Grants Committee (annually), 'Reports', HMSO, London.
VALENTICH, M. and GRIPTON, J. (1978), Sexism and sex differences in
career management of social workers, 'Social Science Journal',
vol.15, no.2, April, pp.101-12.
WAIT, R.F. and DYE, S.E. (1977), Sex-role stereotyping in the career
planning of high school women, paper given to the annual meeting of
the North Central Sociological Association.
WALLACH, A. (1975), A view from the law school, in Howe, F.,
'Women and the Power to Change', McGraw-Hill, New York.
WALUM, L.R. (1977), 'The Dynamics of Sex and Gender', Rand McNally,
Chicago.
WARD, J.P. (1976), 'Social Reality for the Adolescent Girl',
Faculty of Education, University College, Swansea.
WEINREICH, H. (1978), Sex role socialization, in Chetwynd and
Hartnett, op. cit.
WELLENS, J. (1977), Girl technicians for engineering, 'Industrial
and Commercial Training', vol.9, no.3.
WERTHMAN, C. (1963), Delinquents in school, 'Berkeley Journal of
Sociology', 8, pp.39-60.
WHITE, R. and BROCKINGTON, D. (1978), 'In and Out of School',
Routledge & Kegan Paul, London.
WHITEHEAD, A. (1976), Sexual antagonism in rural Herefordshire, in
Barker and Allen, op. cit.
WILKINSON, D. (1975), Black youth, in Havighurst, R. and Dreyer, P.,
'Youth', University of Chicago Press.

WILLIAMS, G. BLACKSTONE and METCALF (1973), 'The Academic Labour Market', Elsevier Scientific Publishing, The Hague.
WILLIS, P. (1977), 'Learning to Labour', Saxon House, Farnborough.
WOLFF, J. (1976), Women in organizations, in Dunkerley, D., 'Critical Issues in Organizations', Routledge & Kegan Paul, London.
WOLFSON, K.P. (1976), Career development patterns of college women, 'Journal of Counselling Psychology, vol.23, no.2, pp.119-25.
WOLPE, A.M. (1974), The official ideology of education for girls, in Flude and Ahier, op. cit.
WOLPE, A.M. (1977), 'Some Processes in Sexist Education', Women's Research and Resources Centre, London.
WOLPE, A.M. (1978a), Education and the sexual division of labour, in Kuhn and Wolpe, op. cit.
WOLPE, A.M. (1978b), Girls and economic survival, 'British Journal of Educational Studies', vol.26, no.2, June, pp.150-62.
Women's Studies Group, Centre for Contemporary Cultural Studies (1978), 'Women Take Issue', Hutchinson, London.
WOODHALL, M. (1973), The economic return to investment in women's education, 'Higher Education', vol.2, pp.275-300.
WOODS, P. (1976), The myth of subject choice, 'British Journal of Sociology', vol.37, no.2, June.
WOODS, P. and HAMMERSLEY, M. (1977), 'School Experience', Croom Helm, London.
Working Party on Equal Opportunites for Women (1974), 'Report', Standing Conference of University Appointments Services, Careers Centre, University of East Anglia.
WYNN, B. (1977), Domestic subjects and the sexual division of labour, in Whitty, G., 'School Knowledge and Social Control', E202, Open University Press, Milton Keynes.
YOUNG, M.F.D. (1971), 'Knowledge and Control', Macmillan, London.

Index